About Pearson

Pearson is the world's learning company, with presence across 70 countries worldwide. Our unique insights and world-class expertise comes from a long history of working closely with renowned teachers, authors and thought leaders, as a result of which, we have emerged as the preferred choice for millions of teachers and learners across the world.

We believe learning opens up opportunities, creates fulfilling careers and hence better lives. We hence collaborate with the best of minds to deliver you class-leading products, spread across the Higher Education and K12 spectrum.

Superior learning experience and improved outcomes are at the heart of everything we do. This product is the result of one such effort.

Your feedback plays a critical role in the evolution of our products and you can contact us - reachus@pearson.com. *We look forward to it.*

Marketing Management: Indian Cases

MARKETING MANAGEMENT: INDIAN CASES

Pearson

Editors—Acquisitions: Varun Goenka and Pradeep Kumar Bhattacharjee
Senior Editor—Production: C. Purushothaman

ISBN 978-93-325-8710-6

First Impression

Published by Pearson India Education Services Pvt. Ltd, CIN: U72200TN2005PTC057128,

Head Office: 15th Floor, Tower-B, World Trade Tower, Plot No. 1, Block-C, Sector 16, Noida 201 301, Uttar Pradesh, India.
Registered office: 4th Floor, Software Block, Elnet Software City, TS-140, Block 2 & 9, Rajiv Gandhi Salai, Taramani, Chennai 600 113, Tamil Nadu, India.
Fax: 080-30461003, Phone: 080-30461060
in.pearson.com, Email: companysecretary.india@pearson.com

Compositor: CEPL, Puducherry
Printed in India by Saurabh printers Pvt. Ltd.

Contents

About the Contributors

Prachi Gupta serves as the Head of Department of Marketing at the ITM Business School, Kharghar, Navi Mumbai. She has more than 16 years of work experience in academics and corporate. She is a brand enthusiast and involves herself in continuous development & sharing of knowledge in this field by engaging in research, live projects, lectures and workshops. Continuous development of innovative teaching pedagogies which are relevant, contemporary & engaging, make her unique and highly successful as a faculty. She is leading various initiatives in her current role, which have led to strong brand building of the organization. She is currently pursuing her Ph.D. in the stream of Branding.
(Contributed: Case 2, Case 3, Case 6, and Case 12)

Dr Ashita Aggarwal serves as an Associate Professor and Head of the Department of Marketing at SPJIMR, Mumbai. She has more than 17 years of corporate and academic experience. Her research interests focus on the study of consumer–brand relationships. She is an organizational consultant in various sectors including retail, education, hospitality, consumer products and automobiles. She has specialized knowledge on branding, consumer behavior and marketing communications.
(Contributed: Case 9, Case 10, and Case 11)

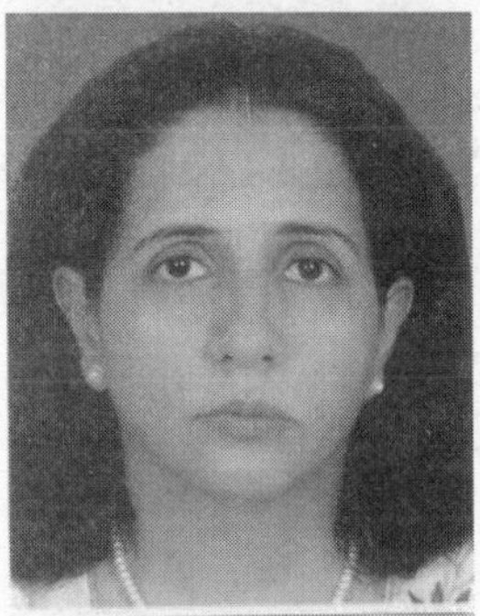

Dr Hufrish Majra serves as an Assistant Professor of Marketing at the School of Business Management, Narsee Monjee Institute of Management Studies (NMIMS), Mumbai, India, where she received her doctor of science degree in Management. She teaches Marketing Management, Market Planning, Integrated Marketing Communication and International Marketing at the post-graduate and executive MBA level. She has received widespread recognition, publications in the area of customer experience and technology adoption in services. She has 17 years of corporate and academic work experience.
(Contributed: Case 13)

Isaac Jacob is Professor and Area Chairperson – Marketing and International Business at K. J. Somaiya Institute of Management Studies and Research (SIMSR), Mumbai. Additionally, he heads the PGDM Communications (Integrated Marketing Communications), PGDM International Business and PGDM Executive programmes. He began his career with M.A. in Economics from Mumbai University. He earned an MBA from Jamnalal Bajaj Institute of Management Studies (JBIMS), University of Mumbai.

In his industry career spanning over 30 years, Professor Jacob has held posts from a salesperson to a CEO ranging across responsibilities in sales, brand management, marketing and general management. He has worked on brands such as Barbie Dolls, Hotwheels, Mercedes-Benz, Tata Safari, Hexit Force (winner of India's First Cannes Gold medal in print advertising, 1995), Parachute coconut oil, Hindustan Unilever's Nihar coconut oil, Puma shoes, Smirnoff, Lux , Citibank, Tata Mutual Fund, Strepsils, Burnol, Tata Housing etc.

A passionate teacher, Professor Jacob has over 27 years of management teaching experience at the post graduate level. He is a visiting faculty in marketing at JBIMS and has also taken marketing courses at IIT SOM (Mumbai), IIM Trichy and SIMSR where he is Full Time Faculty in Marketing since 2007. He is a visiting faculty at the DHBW University, Stuttgart, Germany on Global Marketing. His article "Building a Higher Education Brand" has appeared in the *Journal of Marketing for Higher Education*. He is on the Editorial Review Board of the *Journal of Marketing Communications*, UK; *International Journal of Emerging Markets*, Hong Kong, and reviews research papers for the European Marketing Academy (EMAC). He is the co-author of Strategic Brand Management (4th Edition, Pearson Education) with Kevin Lane Keller.
Link - Google Scholar Profile
https://www.somaiya.edu/simsr/academic/faculty/0001 70044/prof__isaac_cherian_jacob/0
(Contributed: Case 7, Case 14, Case 17, and Case 18)

Dr Varsha Jain is an Associate Professor of Integrated Marketing Communications and the Chair, Dissertation, Co-chair, Research at the MICA (India). Dr Jain has authored 85 publications in international, national and trade journals, book chapters and case study collections, including the Journal of Product and Brand Management, the *Journal of Marketing Communication, Healthy Marketing Quarterly, Ivey and the Emerald Emerging Markets Case Studies Collection*. She has also won gold medals in the categories of not only, "Outstanding Management Researcher Award - 2016", "Young Outstanding Management Researcher – 2013", but also "Outstanding Woman Management Researcher–2012", awarded by AIMS (The Association of Indian Management Scholars) International. In her research and teaching career, she was visiting guest and scholar at Goizueta Business School Emory University in April 2017, The Medill School, Northwestern University, USA in May 2013 and April 2015, and visiting professor at the Indian Institute of Management (IIM), Indore in July 2013 and IIM, Trichy in December 2014. Her research specialties lie in mobile and digital marketing, luxury branding, and digital natives. Dr Jain's current work entails writing books on Indian Consumer Behaviour in an Interactive Market Place and Customer Relationship Management with Prof. Don Schultz (Northwestern University, USA) with Prof. Jagdish Sheth (Emory University, USA) and Prof. G. Shainesh (IIM, Bangalore, India).
(Contributed: Case 4, Case 5, and Case 8)

Dr Gajulapally Radha Krishna is a PhD in Management. He has 27 years of rich work experience in Marketing with a focus on Advertising and Consumer behavior, and 22 years in Teaching & Research with 5 years in Industry as Marketing Manager. He served for various nationally and internationally reputed institutions such as, BITS, Pilani and T.A. Pai Management Institute as Faculty Member. Before joining – NMIMS, Hyderabad in 2013, he rendered his experience as Area Coordinator in Marketing Strategy Department and Associate Professor at IBS Hyderabad for 12 years.
(Contributed: Case 1 and Case 22)

Dr (Mrs) Ritu Narang was the former Director MBA (Retail Management) and Co-OSD Institute of Management Sciences. She is a distinguished academician with more than two decades of meritorious teaching experience in the Department of Business Administration, University of Lucknow. She is well known for her contribution in the field of Marketing, Advertising Management, Retail Management and Organizational Behaviour. She has received D.Lit. degree in Business Administration focussing on *Developing and Managing Rural Health Care Systems* and her Ph.D. thesis is based on *The Indian Rural Market*. Twice, she has been serving as a Senior Distinguished Fellow at the Hanken School of Economics, Finland and at the Tianjin Normal University, Republic of China.
(Contributed: Case 21)

Dr Shanthi is the Chairperson of the Centre for Ethics and Governance at LIBA. She is a gold medalist in Economics from the University of Madras with over 7 years of corporate experience as a marketing professional and over 12 years of experience in teaching students at the post-graduate level. She is known for her immaculate organizational skills for several major events held at LIBA. She has specialized knowledge in the areas of marketing analytics, digital marketing, destination branding and impulse buying behaviour.
(Contributed: Case 15, Case 19, and Case 20)

Dr Suresh Paul Antony is a Fellow of the Indian Institute of Management, Lucknow. He took up his appointment as an Associate Professor of IIM, Trichy in April 2012 in the field of Marketing. He previously held various academic and administrative positions at the XLRI School of Business & Human Resources (Jamshedpur), Indian Institute of Management (Kozhikode) and Thiagarajar School of Management (Madurai) in addition to visiting academic appointments at the Asian Institute of Management (Manila) and the Indian Institute of Management (Lucknow). Besides, he has about 14 years of hands-on customer interface experience in the automotive, financial services, direct selling, and music retailing industries, and across both business and consumer markets.
(Contributed: Case 16)

Prof (Dr) Susobhan Goswami is a distinguished academician with more than three decades of experience in teaching and 3 years in corporate sector . In his academic stint, he has taught in reputed institutes in India like IMT, Ghaziabad, Amity University, Noida. He graduated in Economics from Calcutta University, Master's in Marketing from Pondicherry University and has received Ph.D. from Allahabad. He is well known for his contribution in the field of Strategy and Marketing.
(Contributed: Case 23)

CASE 1

MTR Foods-A Marketing Marvel

► INTRODUCTION

MTR foods is a successful company due to continuous marketing activities by focusing on the customer's requirements and creating products satisfying the customer's needs wants and demands.[i] In past MTR foods (erstwhile MTR Tiffins) was doing marketing activity in emergency situations by introducing new and different products as MTR masala powders. It shows that the legacy of the MTR company as Marketing Orientation by catering to needs of customers and providing products matching with their needs.

Its a reality that any company or business entity doesn't operate in isolation but driven by environment parameters Known as PESTEL or SLEPT factors. S-Social L-Legal, E-Economical, P-Political T-technological.

MTR foods operated in the food industry environment with quality as a product or USP to attract and retain customer.[ii] Any company or business unit is successful in strategy when it is able to map its internal resources with external environment and create value for customers in the process revenue to the company. In this context, MTR company has legacy of "Marketing strategy thinking" in the food industry for seven and a half decades.

Here is an illustration of the MTR company's ability to identify opportunity from the dynamic external environment (SLEPT) and providing a gamut of successful business reorientations by evolutions from MTR Tiffin's MTR foods by creating products like Ready-To-Make (RTM) Masala ingredients, Ready to cook (RTC) like upma, idli, dosa, etc.

We can say that MTR is a marketing marvel because of its ability to understand the industry environment demand drivers that dominates food industry i.e food habits and food consumption of consumer, and based on that, was able to create appropriate the marketing mix (Annxeure-II) elements -4Ps Product, Price place, and promotion.[iii] We explore and understand the MTR as a marketing marvel case in the above context.

► THE INDIAN FOOD INDUSTRY ENVIRONMENT: A SNAPSHOT

The Indian food industry growth is increasing every year (Data provided in Annexure–III) An opportunity for immense potential for value addition, particularly within the food processing industry, the food sector has emerged as a high-growth and high-profit sector. The food industry, which is currently valued at US$ 39.71 billion!, is expected to grow at a Compounded Annual Growth Rate (CAGR) of 11 % to US$ 65.4 billion by 2018. Food and grocery account for around 31 % of India's consumption basket. Accounting for about 32 % of the country's total food market, The Government of India has been instrumental in the growth and development of the food processing industry. The government through the Ministry of Food Processing Industries (MoFPI) is making all efforts to encourage investments in the business. It has approved proposals for joint ventures (JV), foreign collaborations, and industrial. The Indian food processing industry accounts for 32% of the country's total food market, one of the largest industries in India and is ranked fifth in terms of production, consumption, export, and expected growth. It contributes around 14% of manufacturing Gross Domestic Product (GDP), 13% of India's exports and 6% of total industrial investment. Indian food service industry is expected to reach US$ 78 billion by 2018. The Indian gourmet food market is currently valued at US$ 1.3 billion and is growing at a Compound Annual Growth Rate (CAGR) of 20%. India's organic food market is expected to increase by three times by 2020.[iv]

Food Industry & Trends

The online food ordering business in India is in its nascent stage, but witnessing exponential growth. The organized food business in India is worth US$ 48 billion, of which food delivery is valued at US$ 15 billion. With online food delivery players like FoodPanda, Zomato, TinyOwl, and Swiggy building scale through partnerships, the organised food business has a huge potential and a promising future. The online food delivery industry grew at 150% year-on-year with an estimated Gross Merchandise Value (GMV) of US$ 300 million in 2016. According to the data provided by the Department of Industrial Policies and Promotion (DIPP), the food processing sector in India has received around US$ 7.47 billion worth of Foreign Direct Investment (FDI) during the period April 2000-December 2016. The Confederation of Indian Industry (CII) estimates that the food processing sectors have the potential to attract as much as US$ 33 billion of investment over the next 10 years and also to generate employment of nine million person-days. Mr Tomasz Lukaszuk, the Ambassador of the Republic of Poland, had also highlighted the keen interest shown by Polish companies looking for opportunities in India to expand collaboration and invest food processing.[v] (Annexure 1)

Government Initiatives Food sector

There are various government initiatives taken to support Indian food industry in recent budgets so that an economic fillip given to this industry. The gamut of operations areas covered are from quality control, regulations to promotional board of investment from FDI, and encouraging entrepreneurs in this industry. This government initative gives a direction to industry to sustain in long term with particulars quality standards. (Refer Annexure IV for details)

▶ Company Evolution MTR Foods - Mavalli Tiffin Rooms[vi] to MTR Foods

The Mavalli Tiffin Rooms (commonly known as MTR) is the brand name of a food- related enterprise located in India. Having its origin in the city of Bangalore, it has a restaurant located on the Lal Bagh Road in Bangalore and 6 other branches in the city, as well as one each in Singapore, Dubai, and Muscat. MTR also claims to be the inventor of the popular South-Indian breakfast item, Rava idli. MTR was founded as a restaurant by Yagnanarayana Maiya and his brothers in 1924. In the mid-1970s when India was under emergency, a Food Control Act was introduced which mandated that food was to be sold at very low prices. This move made it difficult for MTR to maintain high standards in its restaurant business and forced it to diversify into the instant food business, selling ready-to-eat snacks such chutneys and rasams. Since the 1970s, MTR has expanded and diversified, with MTR Department Stores opened next to the restaurant, and an outlet opened in Chennai. Currently the MTR brand represents two separate entities; the *MTR restaurant* business and *MTR Foods*, the pre-packaged food business. MTR Restaurant is a vegetarian restaurant located in Bangalore, India. It was founded in 1924. It has also been featured on television in the global travel-related series, *Globe Trekker*. The food served at the MTR is a regular, wholesome Karnataka Brahmin fare and has its origins in the Udupi Brahmin cuisine of the coastal region of Karnataka. The decor is outdated, as more attention is paid to cleanliness and food quality than ambiance. For many years, the customers entered the restaurant through the kitchen so that they would be able to satisfy themselves about the restaurant's cleanliness before they ate there. During World War II, MTR found it difficult to make idlis since rice was in short supply. According to MTR, they experimented with semolina instead of rice and thus invented the very popular breakfast item of Rava idli. MTR also holds a record of being the first fast food restaurant in the world to serve 21,000 customers in seven hours. MTR restaurant is currently headed by Hemamalini Maiya, Vikram Maiya, and Arvind Maiya (grand children of Yajnanarayana Maiya). One uniqueness of this restaurant is that silver tumblers are used to serve beverages.

This restaurant was closed in the period of Indian emergency (mid 1970s) when the Food Control Act made it non-profitable to serve food items until it was reopened in 1984. To save the jobs during the time it was closed, MTR started selling spices and roasted flour mixes. That was the beginning of its entry into the convenience and instant food business, and in a sense, a turning point. MTR Foods was headed by Sadanand Maiya (son of Yajnanarayana Maiya) until it was sold to Orkla, a Norwegian company for $80 Million in March 2007. It produces packaged foods in different ranges—spices, instant mixes, ready-to-eat foods, vermicelli, ready-to-cook gravies, range of frozen products, papads, pickles, chips, snacks, and ice creams. It bought the packaging technology from the Defence Food Research Laboratory in Mysore and there are no preservatives added to the food while packaging. MTR is also the first Indian processed foods company to be certified with the Hazard Analysis Critical Control Point (HACCP) certification which is a rigorous standard of food safety and hygiene. It has also been sponsoring magic shows and theatre performances a means of giving live demonstrations of their products and to hand out free samples to the audience. MTR Foods is also the first company in the world to have created a frozen dosa, which can be heated and eaten right away. MTR Food products are exported to the countries in the Persian Gulf, United States, and United Kingdom. It is believed that MTR is the one who brought the first ice cream vending machine to India.

► Marketing Mix Perspective[vii] of MTR Foods

MTR foods a Product Dominant Company

MTR Foods is a food product company offering a diversified range of packaged food products. It uses authentic recipes, high-quality oil, and best ingredients to retain and ensure homemade aroma, taste, and flavor. Products are prepared in the strict hygienic atmosphere so that packs retain crispiness and freshness. It includes items for breakfast, meals, and in-between meals like-Frozen Foods. The above company backdrop shows MTR as a company that continuously innovates and produces product with match of consumer needs wants and demands. Product efforts are Quality as strength to attract and retain customers. The frame work of "Customer Vs Product" matching of this company can be understood as marketing marvel Company. (Refer Annexure V for frame work) To enable has Product Company MTR focussed on "Product & Quality certifications" by different Food quality Regulators. FSSAI This company has concentrated on single product line.[viii] Products based on different features, benefits, quality, variety items, and assortments. In this process of product assortment of the company, it is able to create value to the customer. This is done with a strong quality assurance system and certification. Product mix of the company is able to generate sufficient revenues for the business of the product. Product Profile[ix]

Place in the Marketing Mix of MTR Foods

Place in marketing mix means distribution or channel for selling the products. Here for MTR foods they used its own MTR tiffin centers to sell the products then started selling through other retail shops. MTR is spread it business in different parts of the worlds starting from Benguluru as its headquarters in Karnataka. Its products are exported to several countries in world market like Singapore, Malaysia, Mauritius, Japan, Middle-East, New Zealand, Australia, Germany, United Kingdom, Canada, and the United States. MTR has also opened its fast-food restaurants on franchisee concept called MTR Super Shops and these are located in most cities and towns of India. It has seven facilities to conduct manufacturing process. It has a strong and extensive distribution network that includes services of distributors and retailers. Its products are easily available to consumers through its own stores and in super markets, hyper markets, discount stores, convenience stores, and grocery stores. MTR Foods has launched its e-commerce platform from Bangalore as a venture to move with changing times. Online selling is e-commerce platform for company and its comes under place in marketing mix elements.

Promotion in the Marketing Mix of MTR Foods

Promotion is the tool in marketing to make customer aware inform and create a positive ATTITUDE towards company and products. The tools of promotion that includes advertising, personal-selling sales promotions and publicity are given in (Annexure II). MTR Foods is pursuing an aggressive and intensive marketing strategy at regional, national and international levels. It has organized sampling activities at popular places and launched several ad campaigns via television, magazines, newspapers, and social media platforms to garner maximum coverage. It has collaborated with Jiggs Kalra, celebrity chef, to increase its brand visibility. MTR Foods in the year 2002 was awarded ISO 9002 certification as it successfully met the food hygiene and safety standards in the international arena. It was the first company in India to receive an award for Technology Absorption by P[x]

Price in the Marketing Mix Of MTR Foods

Price is the last one marketer discusses but its critical one when compared all other marketing mix elements. As all other elements are cost-inculcating factors but price is the revenue generators. Price with together product creates value for customer. MTR follows the differential pricing for each benefits, features it adds. (Refer Annexure II for various Price methods). MTR Foods is estimated as rupees 700-crore company with a growth rate at 18% CAGR. Its exports account for nearly 20% and sales in Southern states to 60% of its total revenues. MTR Foods has adopted a market penetration pricing policy and has implemented reasonable rates for its products. Pocket-friendly and affordable rates will help the company in reaching further markets. MTR Foods has launched its web portal as a much-needed initiative to garner larger profits as it will be able to cut down on its distribution costs. It has also implemented promotional policies and offers incentives like 20% extra product with the original.[xi] The fifth P of marketing mix is packaging is dominant by this MTR company as its product-based firm and food-based industry.

► Road Ahead

Going forward, the adoption of food safety and quality assurance mechanisms such as Total Quality Management (TQM) including ISO 9000, ISO 22000, Hazard Analysis and Critical Control Points (HACCP), Good Manufacturing Practices (GMP) and Good Hygienic Practices (GHP) by the food processing industry offers several benefits. It would enable adherence to stringent quality and hygiene norms and thereby protect consumer health, prepare the industry to face global competition, enhance product acceptance by overseas buyers and keep the industry technologically abreast of international best practices. As Peter Drucker, The Father of Management, says that The main aim of marketing is to make selling redundant. MTR is able to provide products matching over shooting the expectations needs wants and demands of customers as per frame work and able to create the Customer delight and customer loyalty Through its philosophy of Quality as USP. We hope MTR sustains its marketing marvel even in new regime of globalization in digital world.

ANNEXURE–I*

- Industry trends & Investments.
- US-based food company Cargill Inc, aims to double its branded consumer business in India by 2020, by doubling its retail reach to about 800,000 outlets and increase market share to become national leader in the sunflower oil category which will help the company be among the top three leading brands in India.
- Mad Over Donuts (MoD), outlined plans of expanding its operations in India by opening nine new MOD stores by March 2017.
- Danone SA plans to focus on nutrition business in India, its fastest growing market in South Asia, by launching 10 new products in 2017, and aiming to double its revenue in India by 2020.
- Uber Technologies Inc plans to launch UberEATS, its food delivery service to India, with investments made across multiple cities and regions.

- Di Bella, the Australia-based coffee chain, plans to invest Rs 67 crore (US$ 10 million) for setting up around 20 new outlets in Mumbai, besides entering Delhi and Bangalore by 2017.
- KKR & Co LP, the US-based private equity firm, plans to invest about Rs 520 crore (US$ 77.38 million) in dairy company Kwality Ltd, which will be used to strengthen its milk procurement infrastructure and increase processing capacity.
- Henry Ford Health Systems (HFHS), a US-based health and wellness group, plans to enter India by signing a franchise partnership with Chandigarh-based hospitality and food services firm KWalls Hospitality, and set up "Culinary Wellness" branded stores across the country.
- Mondelez International, the US-based confectionery, food, and beverage major, inaugurated its new manufacturing plant in Andhra Pradesh set up for Rs 1,265 crore (US$ 190 million), with an annual production capacity of 250,000 tonnes.
- PureCircle, a Malaysia-based natural sweetener producer, plans to invest around Rs 1,300 crore (US$ 200 million) in India to set up a manufacturing plant and make the country its regional production and export hub in the next five years.
- Swiggy, a food delivery start-up owned by Bundl Technologies Private Limited, has raised Rs 230.34 crore (US$ 33.80 million) in a Series C funding round, with its existing investors SAIF Partners, Accel Partners, Norwest Venture Partners, and Apoletto Asia Ltd contributing 79% of the new funds raised.
- Gujarat Cooperative Milk Marketing Federation (GCMMF), popularly known as Amul, plans to invest Rs 5,000 crore (US$ 733.6 million) to establish ten new processing plants as well as expand the current capacity to touch 32 million litres per day (MLPD) capacity by 2020.
- Private Equity (PE) firm India Value Fund Advisors (IVFA) plans to invest around US$ 100–150 million in the food business in India over the next two years.
- Zomato, a restaurant search and discovery platform, has raised US$ 60 million from Singapore government-owned investment company Temasek, along with existing investor Vy Capital, in order to explore new business verticals.
- ITC Limited plans to invest Rs 800 crore (US$ 117.4 million) to set up a world-class food processing facility in Medak, a district located in Telangana. The company has also formulated plans to enter the dairy market.

*__Source:__ https://www.ibef.org/industry/indian-food-industry.aspx

ANNEXURE–II

Fig 1.5 page 23
Of chapter 1 Kotler 15 e. add here
The Four p components of the marketing

ANNEXURE–III

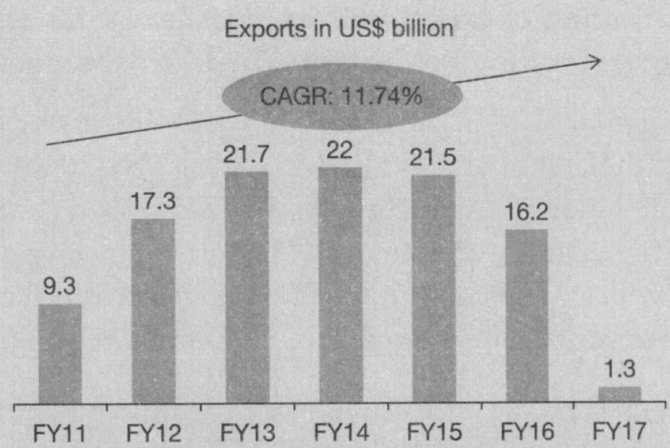

Source: Agricultural & Processed Food Products Export Development Authority (APEDA), DGCIS, TechSci Research.
Notes: FY–Indian Financial Year (April–March), FY17*–Data for April 2016.

ANNEXURE–IV

GOVERNMENT INITIATIVES-FOOD INDUSTRY*

Some of the major initiatives taken by the Government of India to improve the food processing sector in India are as follows. In Union Budget 2017–18, the Government of India has set up a dairy processing infra fund worth Rs 8,000 crore (US$ 1.2 billion).

Union Budget 2016–17 proposed 100% FDI through FIPB (Foreign Investment Promotion Board) route in marketing of food products produced and manufactured in India.

- The Government of India has relaxed foreign direct investment (FDI) norms for the sector, allowing up to 100% FDI in food product e-commerce through automatic route.
- The Food Safety and Standards Authority of India (FSSAI) plans to invest around Rs 482 crore (US$ 72.3 million) to strengthen the food testing infrastructure in India, by upgrading 59 existing food testing laboratories and setting up 62 new mobile testing labs across the country.

- The Indian Council for Fertilizer and Nutrient Research (ICFNR) will adopt international best practices for research in fertiliser sector, which will enable farmers to get good quality fertilisers at affordable rates and thereby achieve food security for the common man.
- The Government of India allocated Rs 1,500 crore (US$ 225.7 million) and announced various measures under the Merchandise Exports from India Scheme (MEIS), including setting up of agencies for aquaculture and fisheries in coastal states and export incentives for marine products.
- Government of India plans to allow two Indian dairy companies, Parag Milk Foods and Schreiber Dynamix Dairies, to export milk products to Russia for six months, after these companies got approval for their products by Russian inspection authorities.
- Ms Harsimrat Kaur Badal, Union Minister for Food Processing Industries, Government of India inaugurated the first of its kind Rs 136 crore (US$ 20 million) mega international food park at Dabwala Kalan, Punjab. She has also expressed confidence that the decision to allow 100% Foreign Direct Investment (FDI) in multi-brand retail with 100% local sourcing condition, will act as a catalyst for the food processing sector, thereby controlling inflation, uplifting the condition of farmers, and creating more jobs in the country.
- FSSAI has issued new rules for importing products, to address concerns over the entry of sub-standard items and simplify the process by setting shelf-life norms and relaxing labelling guidelines.
- The Ministry of Food Processing Industries announced a scheme for Human Resource Development (HRD) in the food processing sector. The HRD scheme is being implemented through State Governments under the National Mission on Food Processing. The scheme has the following four components:
    - Creation of infrastructure facilities for degree/diploma courses in food processing sector
    - Entrepreneurship Development Programme (EDP)
    - Food Processing Training Centres (FPTC)
    - Training at recognised institutions at State/National level
- FSSAI under the Ministry of Health and Family Welfare has issued the Food Safety and Standards (Food Product Standards and Food Additives) Regulations, 2011 and the Food Safety and Standards (Contaminants, Toxins and Residues) Regulations, 2011 which prescribe the quality and safety standards, respectively for food products.
- Spices Board, set up by the Ministry of Commerce to develop and promote Indian spices worldwide, aims spice exports of US$ 3 billion by 2017.
- The Government of India has approved the setting up of five numbers of Mega Food Parks in the states of Bihar, Maharashtra, Himachal Pradesh and Chhattisgarh. The

Government plans to set up 42 such mega food parks across the country in next three to four years.

Source of Information: Ministry of Food Processing Industries (MoFPI), Agricultural and Processed Food Products Export Development Authority (APEDA), Media reports and Press Releases, Department of Industrial Policy and Promotion (DIPP), Press Information Bureau (PIB), Confederation of Indian Industries (CII),Union Budget 2016–17, Union Budget 2017–18.

ANNEXURE–V

CUSTOMER EXPECTATIONS REMARKS

Customer C	C Company Name	Brand Name
U	U Utility	
S	S Satisfaction	
T	T Technology	
O	O Options	
M	M-Monetary aspect	
E	E-Evaluation	
R	Responds by buying or not buying	

PRODUCT MEANS OR ENABLES

PRODUCT P	P-Performance	Catering to the needs
R	R-Reliability	
O	O-Options	
D	D-Durable	
U	U-utility	
C	C-Communicable	
T	T-Technology	

ANNEXURE–VI

Vada with Sambhar and Chutney

- Idli with Sambhar and Chutney
- Mysore Masala Dosa with Sambhar and Chutney

Pickles

- Lime Pickle
- Mango Sliced Pickle

Sweets

- Gulab Jamun
- Rasagolla

Masala Pastes

- Biryani Paste
- Lemon Rice Paste
- Pulliogare Paste

Meal Mixes

- Sambhar Mix
- Rasam Mix

Snack Mixes

- Muruku
- Bajji and Bonda
- Gobi Manchurian

Pure Spices

- Haldi Powder
- Chilli Powder
- Jeera Powder

Vermicelli

- Seviyan Vermicelli
- Beetroot Vermicelli
- Carrot Vermicelli

Ready-to-Cook

- Methi Matar

- Chana Masala
- Veg Kadhai

Drinks

- Chocolate Drink
- Badam Drink

Single Serves

- Rasogolla
- Basundi
- Rasamalai

Ready-to-Eat

- Sambhar Rice
- Dal Makhani
- Palak Paneer

Breakfast Mixes

- Khaman Dhokla
- Spinach Idli
- Poha

Sweet Mixes

- Mango Kulfi
- Gulab Jamun
- Basundi/Rabri

Masala Powders

- Curry Powder
- Rasam Powder
- Sambhar Powder

MTR SnackUp

- Pepper Banana Chips
- Spicy Banana Chips
- Huli Thengols

Beverages

- Badam Drink Mix

CASE 2

Customer Value – Explored, Created, Communicated & Delivered

Related to India's e-commerce Market

"Innovation is whatever brings value to the consumer—it takes many forms, sometimes it's a breakthrough in technology and sometimes it's just about thinking different in the way we approach problems" says Andrew Garrihy, chief marketing officer for Western Europe at Huawei.

► INDIA'S E-COMMERCE SPACE

India's e-commerce space today is mainly dominated and defined by 2 players—Flipkart and Amazon. Flipkart is the fashion leader. After acquisition of Myntra and Jabong, Flipkart commands more than two-thirds of India's fast growing online fashion retail market. Amazon is the tech power. Over 20 years of learnings in technology and online retail business has resulted in faster execution and fewer mistakes. Amazon excels in providing powerful search and recommendation engines to users.

India's apparel and lifestyle market is worth $70-billion, and currently only 2% of that is online. According to a recent Google report, the sector is expected to scale up to $35 billion by 2020, growing at four times in the coming years. The report also states that fashion will outstrip consumer electronics as the largest online retail category, accounting for about 35% of consumers' total online spending by 2020.

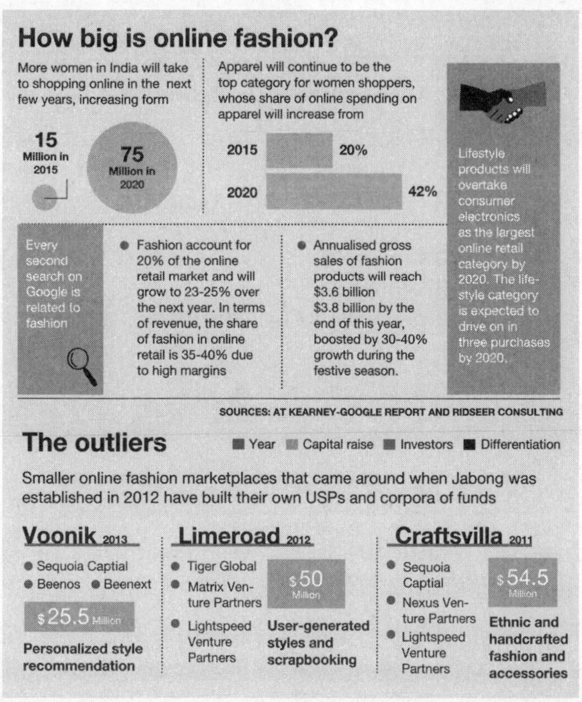

▶ The Growth Story of Flipkart and e-commerce in India

For a vast multilingual nation like India, building an e-commerce company was indeed a tough task for Flipkart. Some of the factors like weak infrastructure, myopic bureaucracy, and above all, an ingrained distrust of the merchant class made the task even more challenging.

The Bansals, the founders of Flipkart were confident on one thing, that India was ready for e-commerce. The country's highly fragmented retail sector, mostly ruled by mom-and-pop stores with poor services were the major problems identified by Bansals which had the potential to get converted into opportunities for building up a new business in 2007.

Flipkart found the right gaps in the market and offered relevant products and services that fitted those areas perfectly. Finding that few Indians use credit cards, Flipkart pioneered cash on delivery. In Mumbai, it deployed *dabbawallas*, the famed lunch delivery network, to get packages to customers. Its pledge to take back unwanted goods for a full refund was a big propeller. Two of its strongest ethos of customer-friendliness and genuineness of its products connected very well with the Indian consumers.

The company added third-party sellers to its platform and set up its own logistics company, Ekart in 2009, with warehouses and an army of delivery personnel. By 2011, sales had reached $100 million, and very soon Flipkart was seen in different categories—sports equipment, electronics, baby goods and more.

In 2012, sales in the Indian e-commerce market were estimated at $1.6 billion. Flipkart, Jabong & Myntra, all home-grown players were leading the Indian e-commerce market at that time. Some of the major tactics which helped these players to gain market share in the Indian market were cash-on-delivery payments, liberal return policies, free or subsidised shipping and in-house logistics. Since its founding nine years, Flipkart has become the nation's most valuable start-up which introduced online shopping to the Indian masses.

Amazon launched its Indian website on June 5th, 2013 with the third-party marketplace model instead of selling directly. This forced consolidation in Indian market and Flipkart acquired the on-line clothing retailer Myntra in 2014 followed by Jabong in 2016. This deal further strengthened its' number one position in the fashion and lifestyle e-commerce category with an estimated market share of 60-70%.

In this hyper competitive market, consumer is having last laugh and is being pampered with choice, service and experience. Each player is continuously forced to innovate and take steps steps that add value to its consumers in a "real and meaningful way". Stuart Eames, Operational Improvement Manager at Waitrose put it very well "If you don't evolve, if you don't do something better or different to the competition you end up not being around."

▶ Changing Models of Business Enhancing Value

The online stores from the inventory model moved to third-party marketplace model where independent merchants in their network sell products directly to shoppers. It turned out to be a viable way to work in order to overcome the problems posed due to poor logistics and high costs of inventory. Further movement has come in when many online commerce companies have now started venturing into the hybrid model of running online stores with selective physical presence.

Global e-commerce giant Amazon in 2016 opened a brick-and-mortar store in New York. In India, players like furniture e-tailer Pepperfry and eyewear seller Lenskart have explored the offline route as well.

E-tailers are under pressure to grow profitably and hence, Fashion e-tailer Myntra has created "top-selling" outdoor lifestyle brand, 'Roadster', which has a current sales of ₹600 crore, contributing 8% to the overall revenue and expected to reach sales of ₹1,000 crores by 2019. Seeing this kind of growth potential of this brand, Myntra. in association with one of its franchise partners, has in March 2017, launched the first retail store for its private label Roadster in Bangalore.

► Cost Efficiencies on Value Chain

New companies indulge in market expansion activity and have high spent in the initial period hoping for future gains resulting in negative cash flow (known as burn rate). In a bid to acquire maximum customers, Flipkart indulged in aggressive spent on marketing and discounts, biggest being in October 2016 "Big Sale", resulting in its burn rate at its highest two years ago. As of 2017, its burn rate is said to be $40-50 million per month, according to industry estimates. Flipkart successfully lowered its burn rate by 5-10% every quarter in 2016 and wants to sharply accelerate this process.

The board has asked Flipkart to bring down the burn rate to one-fourth by March 2017 and is forcing Flipkart management to think differently to grow and to streamline its operations. The company also decided to slash the budget of Myntra by about 10% and re-allocate these funds to itself to fight the ongoing war against Amazon. To ease its cash crunch situation, Flipkart plans to save $150-200m by Dec 2017 and is also in talks with Walmart stores for investment of $1b. At the same time, Amazon's Chief Executive Officer Jeff Bezos pledged in June 2016 to invest another $3 billion in his company's Indian operations, bringing the total to $5 billion, which definitely sounds a big threat to Flipkart, the home-grown e-tailer.

To bring in sharper focus on its core business model and make it nimbler, Flipkart is consolidating the operations of its logistics and supply chain arm. Delivery to customer's doorstep even in the remotest location popularly termed as last-mile connectivity plays a vital role in the online business and Ekart, the in-house logistics arm, has been able to provide this service efficiently and forms the backbone of its business. Flipkart has also started monetising EKart and offers warehousing solutions and end-to-end logistics and supply chain capabilities to other clients.

The two fashion verticals, Myntra and Jabong, owned by Flipkart, commands a 45% market share in this vertical. They are bringing together their back-end operations and supply chain for stronger integration.

They are also integrating their private brand portfolios in order to give a push to the trifling private label business at Jabong. Despite such integrations, the consumer-facing platforms continue to run independently as the consumer segments and geographies targeted by each of them differ widely. While Jabong's main revenue source is North and East, Myntra is big in South and West. Similarly, Jabong's consumer base mainly consists of women and first-time shoppers, while Myntra targets more towards men and affluent consumers.

► Market Share v/s Profits

In a country like India where affordability means value for the masses across various categories, Flipkart took different initiatives on this front as a big bet to revive sales. Initiatives like low-interest monthly payments clearly attended to affordability issue; under "Flipkart Assured" stringent quality checks were provided. There were exclusive partnerships, exchange programme on smartphones, and sales of its own brands or products.

The Seattle-based Amazon has also experienced success with private label offerings. Across categories as diversified as electronics, accessories and baby care, Amazon has built a robust private label unit. It launched AmazonBasics in September 2015 in the consumer electronics category, home and kitchen brand Solimo in early 2016, followed by fashion offerings Myx and Symbol in the latter half of the year. "Private brands play a role in providing great value to the customer by reducing costs from the value chain (optimised design for ecommerce)" says an Amazon India spokesperson. The private brands developed in-house help ecommerce firms squeeze out additional margins—15-20% more than competing-third party brands—from this business. Private brands offering reliable products at an attractive price point are backed by high intent to purchase.

At a time when discounting and deep discounting had become a norm in the highly competitive e-commerce space, it's then Myntra announced the launch of its biannual sale event, "Big Fashion Gig" from April 8 to 10, 2017. Unlike other previously run sale events, this one claimed to be different in terms of being a low-discount event with a sharp focus on exclusive brands. The event also saw the launch of a new line and style by celebrities on the platform. Unique propositions were built for the customers such as guaranteed `never-on-discount' brands and other features to gain competitive advantage. 35 new brands were launched including international names such as Dorothy Perkins, Next, Aeropostale, Forever 21 Men, Clinique, Bobbi Brown, Corelle, and Howards. Myntra's efforts to spice up its premium fashion brand positioning with an exclusive line-up of brands is definitely to strengthen its dominance in online fashion sales and boost profits through higher margins. Premiumisation of line is expected to bring in new users and also attract existing ones looking for new benefits and experience.

► Customer Experience and Engagement—A New Value Tapped

To differentiate itself and enhance the shopping experience of its customers, Flipkart has given a new, vibrant and glamorous look to its fashion section. Data derived from extensive research suggests that customers searching for fashion are mainly influenced by celebrities, Bollywood, Hollywood, friends, and other influential brands. Thus, Flipkart has tied up with such brands, celebrities, TV channels and Bollywood movies and has completely revamped its fashion section where selections will be seen presented in line with consumer liking. The country's ecommerce major has relaunched its core fashion category by putting in place a team of 100 style consultants, who will help curate outfits based on searches made by customers.

Myntra has started to open physical stores for its private brands like Roadster, All About You and HRX, is converting these stores into experience zones and the stores are loaded with technology at every step and promises a great brand experience. The Roadster store has highly engaging elements which include a video wall controlled by shoppers through a futuristic, multifunction touch-interface. This wall showcases to them the intricate details of Roadster products and provides an update on key international trends and communicates the brand story. Data on key looks and the Roadster catalogue can be accessed by the interested shoppers through multiple touch screen displays around the store. Then there is this unique 'Scan & Go' purchase mechanism which allows shoppers to add their favourites to their shopping cart on the Myntra App, doing away with shopping bags, check-out counters or billing queues.

Global loyalty marketing agency ICLP (A Collinson Group Company) released a research report recently whose findings on personalization and customer recognition by e-commerce top rivals say that 70% of Amazon and 67% of Flipkart customers felt that they were provided with relevant recommendations for products and services that were of interest to them. On customer recognition front, 63% of Amazon and 58% of Flipkart shoppers expressed that their chosen retailer had taken the time to really get to know them and understand what they want.

► Into the New Age of Artificial Intelligence

"Voice is a big part of the computer interface of the future," said Gene Munster, a veteran equity analyst and now head of research at Loup Ventures. "Whoever owns voice will be the gateway of commerce."

Amazon is all set to make a headway in developing voice assistants or "chatbots" to decode speech. In April 2017, technology powering voice assistant Alexa was rolled out to developers so that they can build chat features into their own apps. Alexa is said to compete with Apple Inc's Siri. Amazon will take the text and recordings people send to apps to train Alexa to understand more queries.

On the similar stand is Flipkart, working on project Mira, an artificial intelligence-focused effort. It will lead the search experience of the customers to be guided with relevant questions, conversational filters, shopping ideas, offers, and trending collections.

Not just quenching the customer's needs but Mira will also help streamline the back-end processes, including accurate classification of products, accurate product descriptions, and avoiding duplications. Once streamlined, this will later be used in issues such as product returns and quicker delivery.

Globally, Amazon and eBay have invested exhaustively in artificial intelligence to improve their marketplaces. In India, it is still in its infancy with a lot of ground to cover as Indian shoppers are still coming to grips with buying online.

► Sellers' Experience

Various measures are being taken by the e-commerce marketers to expand their network of sellers, to keep them satisfied and add to their experience. Amazon is doubling its investment in the year 2017 on seller infrastructure, spending on warehouses, fulfilment services, service provider network, in-person support, and other services like seller cafes and instant registration to attract the potential investments. All these initiatives have made Amazon a seller-friendly marketplace, offering a frictionless experience to the sellers.

"As of March, there has been 160% year-on-year growth in the seller network on Amazon India, with more than 1.75 lakh sellers. This has ensured that on an average, there are 1.8 lakh products for sale in the marketplace at any given time, compared with about 15,000-20,000 products in a brick-and-mortar supermarket," said Gopal Pillai, Amazon India director and general manager (seller services).

Flipkart in order to make itself the most low-cost marketplace for sellers has altered seller fees for certain categories and price ranges. "When we reduced rate cards, we reduced fixed fee, shipping fee and collection fee and also offered a 10-20% discount for gold and silver (tier I and II category) sellers," said Nishant Gupta, director of marketplace, Flipkart. The fee reductions and discounts so offered are passed on by 60-65% sellers across categories to consumers in the form of reduced prices resulting in at least a 25% jump in sales.

Both platforms are seen by the sellers as fairly even now on the cost front. Difference between the two is only while Amazon has brought global technology experience, Flipkart has compensated by giving localised features and inventory management.

▶ Relevance Factor Well Attended

To gain an edge over its rival, Amazon, certain value additions in its services were brought in by Flipkart such as introduction of 7am deliveries which reached customers in Mumbai and 43 other cities reliably. Smartphones being the biggest revenue generating category of Flipkart, was proactively attended to by adding a unique service primarily to reduce the number of returns on them. A team of technicians was created who were sent by Flipkart to fix minor glitches before customers returns them and hence, providing experience similar to nearby electronic store.

Amazon has rolled out its global Prime membership service in India which gives customers access to unlimited free one-day and two-day delivery on lakhs of products. Membership further extends to include Prime video service which gives its members access to movies and TV shows from Indian and global content providers.

With developments in the market taking panther pace, Flipkart in order to keep itself armed strongly, is setting sight on new businesses. With its biggest round of funding of ₹9,000 crore from Tencent, eBay Inc and Microsoft in this year 2017, it aims to grow its payments arm PhonePe, expand its portfolio of private labels, and relaunch categories with high potential such as furniture and grocery.

Competitive intensity is being seen at its peak, with new entrants in this space, newer benefits for all stakeholders, business models turning more efficient and flexible, and technology setting a revolution engulfing all.

Most recent development being the launch of Paytm Mall, a pure play marketplace, which does not stock any inventory. It has tied up extensively with brands, distributors, and multi-brand stores, thus offering same-day delivery and installation of large appliances across 20 cities to make the most of the high margins and prices that this segment offers. For fulfilment, Paytm Mall has also created a massive network of 40-plus service partners like Blue Dart, Delhivery, and Xpress Bees to handle logistics with specialised services on correct handling and shorter delivery time.

Sensing the looming threat, Flipkart and Amazon India are following suit. They have also announced their investments for installations of large appliances ordered on their platforms, creating a chain of specialised warehouses and distribution centres.

► Image Benefit as a Crucial Element to Value

After investing big in India, offering tailor-made features, and providing benefits filling the right gaps, one setback that Amazon faces time and again is of it being tagged as non-Indian. Especially in contrast to the home-grown leader, Flipkart who claims to understand the needs of its countrymen much better than any foreign player. Amazon in order to raise its brand equity further in the Indian market had to work on changing its perception in the minds of Indian consumers.

Amit Agarwal, head of Amazon India, once responding to the 'foreign' tag said his company was very much Indian. "I just want to reiterate that Amazon (India) is a company incorporated in India, domiciled here. It follows all mandated laws, such as two-factor authentication, and pays service tax as well."

Efforts made by Amazon to emotionally connect with Indians include the airing of TV spots that talk about Indians' love for *asli* (original) 100% original products and their desire to browse through innumerable options. Then there are series of ads where Amazon is referred by Indians as *apni dukaan*, or our own store. Amazon sponsors a Kabaddi league to connect with grassroot Indian consumers.

The company is shunning many of its global practices as well and is banking on a host of locally tried and tested methods. To further add the value of Indianness to its image, in December 2016, Amazon.in launched a programme called Amazon Launchpad, a dedicated web store that enabled Indian start-ups to launch, market and distribute their products to customers not just in India but globally. The company very aptly linked it with the Indian Government's "Start-Up India" initiative.

As Bezos of Amazon had done 13 years earlier, Binny and Sachin Bansal of Flipkart also started out with selling books. From then to now, these 2 behemoths of the e-commerce segment—along with so many others—have continually been developing unique plans and creating superior value for the consumer. May be time has arrived for the e-commerce giants to abandon their obsession with GMV (gross merchandise volume) and develop new barometers to measure their success.

► Questions

1. Customers always seek to maximize value from every purchase. They will buy from the firm that they perceive to offer the highest customer-delivered value (difference between total customer benefits and total customer cost). Explain with reference to the given case.
2. Explain the value delivery process which involves the exploration, creation, communication and delivery of superior value to the customer. (With the help of any example covered in the case)
3. Market oriented strategic planning by Flipkart enabled it in staying in sync and relevant to the changing market opportunities. Explain.
4. In the light of the case explain the Porter's value chain and its key activities and how it has helped Flipkart to bring cost efficiencies and create value in a specific business.
5. Continuous value enhancement for the customer is the new goal of every marketer to differentiate and stay ahead on the curve. Lay down in detail the various value enhancing initiatives being taken by different players in the e-commerce segment.

CASE 3

Customer Loyalty – The Ultimate Objective of Every Marketer

As we speak, consumers in India are going through a transformation. They have become empowered, quite experimental, highly quality conscious and are buying intelligently. It is reflecting in their buying behaviour, they are more vocal, expressing their views and demanding better experience. A huge change in consumer dynamics is being witnessed, with a large-scale shift from offline to online consumption of goods and services. Also, rapid movement is being witnessed in new and unconventional categories like furniture, health and beauty care, apparel and groceries, as opposed to traditional online categories of books and consumer electronics.

In today's world where loyalty is becoming a rare phenomenon, be it your friend or a job, brand loyalty also seems to be fading. Brands operating in mature markets face intense competition making it difficult to sustain. Therefore, it is important for companies to know how to retain their existing customers.

► Repurchases Most Commonly Linked to Loyalty

Brand has come to play a very important role in today's global and intensively competitive world. Brand loyalty is the consumer's conscious or unconscious decision—expressed through intention or behavior—to repurchase a brand continually. In common parlance, customer loyalty refers to the repeated behaviour of purchasing a specific product/brand over time. This behaviour can be self-induced by a satisfied customer and also many a times induced by the marketer to drive sales.

Amazon India launched its flagship membership programme, Amazon Prime, in 2016 to boost repeat transactions on its platform, and this effort is already paying off. Amazon Prime membership provides free and priority delivery, additional quality check for the consumer creating higher customer confidence for a small fee. As per latest declaration by Amazon, two out of three daily essentials transaction on Amazon Pantry, and one in every three orders in the second highest selling fashion category, is from a Prime member. Overall, Prime members already account for one-third of all the orders placed on Amazon India. This success can be attributed to typical behaviour of consumers who, after committing once, tend to first visit Amazon before exploring other options. Thus, Prime will make an impact in the long run in making people stick to a single online marketplace. Major impact will be seen in the FMCG category which offers a selection of about 1.9-million products from 9,000 sellers on the platform, and frequency of buying in this category is higher and will drive sales in other segments also. Amazon is also waiving off the box fee of ₹ 20 (for every 15 Kg box) for Prime customers. Very recently in May 2017, Amazon had a four day "Great Indian Sale" where Prime members accounted for 35 % of the orders and purchases made by them grew 100 % over a similar sale in January.

▶ Customer Acquisition and Loyalty

Innovation and brand consultant, Anisha Motwani, believes that free trials or sampling as a strategy is mostly prevalent and successful in categories that have deep-seated habits and have high frequency of consumption Brand switching in this category require attitude and behaviour changes and free sampling influences customer to try new brands and thus increasing the probability of purchase. Such categories could include newspapers, food products, etc. Free trials can also be found in case of expensive offerings where consumers prefer sampling before making a final commitment.

In March, 2017, a unique trial-driven marketing experiment in the unusual category of apparel was done by women's denim brand, Jealous 21. It offered free jeans to its customers in Delhi, Mumbai, Bengaluru, and Chennai. The process to avail the offer involved registration by interested women on the company's website, get a unique code to visit its store, uploading a selfie in a Jealous 21 garment at the store, and tagging @jealous21 and #freejeansday on Instagram or on Facebook to walk away with a free pair of jeans. The brand made sure that there were no hidden terms and conditions which made it a very enjoyable experience for its customers. Total 30,000 people registered for participation and 5,000 free jeans were claimed. Though jeans as a category does not quite fit into this kind of trial-driven marketing, but this brand achieved spread of positive word of mouth leading to referrals. "The real impact of this is the viralization of such an activity. The brand is earning this buzz—rather than paying for advertising—and is being talked about," says Motwani.

Trial-driven marketing is based on the assumption that once the prospective customers experience the product/service, they might get ready to make a lifetime commitment to the brand. "A consumer is more likely to buy a product after trying it. Typically, food products have tried sampling stations while cars invite you to go on a test drive," says Alpana Parida, managing director at brand strategy firm, DY Works.

Success of Reliance Jio in the intensely competitive Indian telecom market brings forth the strength of trial marketing strategy, even in the service industry. Reliance Jio Infocomm Ltd offered free sampling of Jio's voice calling, text messaging, and data services, and acquired stupendous 100 million subscribers, of which it continued to retain 72 million even after the free trial period ended.

Conventional wisdom suggests that brands that indulge in trials and discounts erode brand value. "Here's the reality though. People value brands. But people also seek value for money. They prefer to buy brands, especially when they are offered at the best price or that have been experienced first-hand and generated a positive word of mouth," Motwani says.

▶ Trust and Commitment – Requisites for Building True Loyalty

The concept of true brand loyalty is not just limited to consistent repurchase but is broader in including all kinds of positive attitudinal elements. Commitment is a necessary condition for true brand loyalty to occur. Working with Professor Rogge of the University of Rochester, ICLP (Global loyalty marketing agency) applied Sternberg's Triangular Theory of Love to the relationship between shoppers and brands, and defined the ideal, or "devoted" relationship, as one where shoppers feel passion, intimacy, and commitment towards the brand.

ICLP research on shoppers' relationship with particular brands and their associated loyalty programs throws light on lot of areas which can be used to build loyalties. Some of the findings are:

Indian shoppers easily feel attached to the brands they shop, but only 21% are currently in a devoted relationship, especially in respect to the retail brands which indicates that marketers need to find ways to raise the emotions of Indian customers to the highest level of bonding with brands.

Another finding revealed that just 44% of Indian shoppers feel sufficiently rewarded for making a personal recommendation to their friends and only 47% said that the rewards received are tailored to their individual needs, which gives direction to the kind of reward programmes which marketers need to develop.

In the current data-driven world, personal data of shoppers so collected through all different channels, is not capitalised to its maximum potential as only 56% of Indian shoppers said that their chosen brand made relevant recommendations for products and services that interest them.

Even as Online retailers like Amazon and Flipkart build loyalties through the tools of customer recognition and personalization, multi-brand physical retailers like Big Bazaar and Shoppers Stop are getting consumer trust through consistent quality, value for money and respect for customers. Thus, different retail sectors in India can learn from one another as they look to build loyalty and closer relationships with their customers.

► Customer Experience and Connect Sustains Relationship

Iglesias et all (2010) in their research studied that loyalty is achieved by brands capable of delivering a unique and distinctive experience by managing both functional and emotional elements. Experience adds memories and great value to the relationship. Giving customers unique experiences as rewards strengthen the emotional bond customers have with the brand, ensuring the relationship continues long after the experience itself.

OnePlus phones, which are sold only online, do carry offline plans as well. They are experimenting with different types of offline selling modes, like recently, they opened four exclusive service centres which also serve as experience centres for prospective buyers. They also came up with pop-up stores which remain for a short period. One such store in Mumbai drove in huge traffic. Pop-ups are a way to make users meet and experience OnePlus brand and meet some of their staff. Company also uses this as a way of feeling the pulse of the market. "Consumer loyalty is boosting our organic growth", says OnePlus co-founder Carl Pei.

Connect with the customers is the key to developing loyalty. A conversation-driven sale that is high on empathy and knowledge, low on price and discounts has long been a staple of loyalty. It focuses on understanding the needs of consumers and delivering an exceptional experience. We are living in the age of "conversational commerce", a term coined by Chris Messina, the inventor of the hashtag, which refers to the ability of a digital tool to interact and engage with a consumer using natural language. And multicultural millennials constituting nearly half of the demographic are the new set of consumers to interact with, who know what they like, and are not shy about sharing that information with their friends and contacts. According to Forbes magazine, "a good Word of Mouth marketing (WOMM) campaign generates thousands of conversations, recommendations and triple sales in just a year (even for the boring products)". "When it comes to loyalty, multicultural millennials give as much as they get," said Buzz Marketing Group CEO and founder Tina Wells.

In India, one kind of retail channel on which a large part of population, especially the lower rung of society depend upon is the ration shop. This traditional, government-controlled retail provides basic everyday consumed commodities like sugar, oil, etc., at subsidised rates. Due to lack of proper management and leakages, the network of ration shops has come under lot of criticism. However, their wide network and strong connection with daily lives has caught the attention of Kishore Biyani of Future Group. He took up a mammoth project of giving a complete makeover to 5,000 traditional ration shops in Rajasthan. This public-private experiment is not just to revive and rebrand this channel but Biyani plans to supply FMCG products to them, train the manpower, and computerize the outlets. Other states of Chattisgarh and Madhya Pradesh are also being explored for the similar initiative. This seems to be a great way for Future Group to make inroads into the remote areas of these states which are devoid of modern retail facilities. This is creating early customer familiarity with the brand which can get converted to loyal customer base as and when Future Group's modern retail stores make their entry in those areas.

Easyday, one of the store of Future Retail Limited, launched its very first loyalty program in September 2016 called "Har Mahine Bonus" which offers free bonuses and vouchers worth ₹ 300 to every shopper who buys goods worth ₹ 1,000. Easyday is a supermarket chain of 330 stores and has this loyalty program running across segments. On the importance of customer connect, Manish Sabnis - CEO Easyday - Future Retail Limited, puts in very beautifully, "Success of supermarkets lies in becoming the store of the community. At Easyday, we take multiple initiatives every month to become the preferred "Pados ki Dukaan". "Har Mahine Bonus" is a program launched to incentivise loyal shoppers and at the same time attract new customers to our stores."

In today's world where consumers have wide choices available in all categories, loyalties have weakened. India's retailing giant, the Future Group, is all set to pioneer into setting up "loyalty-driven convenience stores". There are 2 basic ideas which go behind these stores. One, to provide member-shoppers with higher discounts than those offered by brick-and-mortar chains such as D'Mart, or online rivals like Amazon and Flipkart, and two, to stock each store with merchandise suited for that locality and consumer base. The concept is a hybrid between the *kirana* (neighbourhood) store, connected commerce, and large supermarket. It targets to have five-lakh members in the fiscal 2017–18, and has plans of opening 10,000 of such stores in next 4 years.

A strong groundwork has already been done by Future Group to ensure success of this new format. The entire ecosystem such as logistics, partnership with FMCG companies, and customer database around the stores has been built.

Big competitive advantages have been created by Biyani. While rivals have been focusing on big-box formats, he took the acquisition route and in past 5 years acquired almost all convenience-store format brands that existed in India. As a result now, the new smaller stores (loyalty driven) planned by him will have three badges—Easy Day, Heritage Retail, and Nilgiri's. Also while rivals are pure-play retailers, Future Group itself owns FMCG and logistics company, thus, having advantage through integration in the chain. To make it more attractive it has tied up with mobile payments and commerce platform Paytm to enable the wide base of Paytm-users to shop Big Bazaar goods on the online marketplace.

► CONTINUOUS INNOVATIONS—A SURE WAY TO RETAIN CUSTOMERS

Innovations give life and new energy to the brands. In order to retain the best of the customers and to influence all of its stakeholders, brands have to innovate continuously. Technology and digital media has opened up innumerable opportunities for brands to innovate. Future Group which has many new initiatives to its credit has launched a digital wallet, FuturePay, to integrate its loyalty programmes across different Future Group outlets—Big Bazaar, Ezone and Hometown.

Best experience coupled with lowest prices is what FuturePay offers its customers. "Price Match" is its one important feature, which matches items from the customer's bill with the advertised prices of any competitor retail store. If it finds a lower price elsewhere, it credits the difference to the buyer's wallet. Another feature is its Oxygen Services, which enables customers to make transactions at any of its retail outlets, or through credit and debit cards, and net-banking.

These technology-based innovations are definitely creating impact on everyone, especially on the digital millennials. The company states that they already have 60,000 downloads for FuturePay so far (by Oct 2016) and are targeting one crore downloads in the next 18 months.

There is also a flip side to the use of technology. Customer loyalty can get completely jeopardized over an unsatisfied digital experience. Indian Digital Experience report by SAP, unveiled in April 2017, stated that only 8 % of customers unsatisfied with their digital experience would continue to remain loyal to the brand. In order that the brand remains relevant for its customers a strong digital infrastructure is imperative.

There are many brands in other sectors, too, which are experimenting with different ideas, and the success largely depends on the relevancy factor that those experiments attend to. Like McDonald's is planning to lure consumers through a new breakfast menu that will include culinary delights suiting Indian palates, ranging from *masala dosa* burgers with *molaga podi* sauce, to the familiar *anda bhurji*.

As part of a brand transformation, McDonald's is moving towards a healthier menu over the past few years offering lower sodium in fries and nuggets, lower calorie sauces, and preservative-free patties. The restaurant is also launching soups and salads. All initiatives going in line with the current consumer trend towards choosing healthy food options

McDonald's India is also launching a series of concept restaurants called "Experience of the Future" (EOTF), with features of self-ordering kiosks, table service, and healthy menu. The first one of this kind has already opened in Mumbai in March 2017, with enhanced digital capabilities to improve customer experience. It plans to open 5–10 more outlets in the city in the next 18 months.

Another big brand that is walking the health route is Nestle. This world's largest packaged food group has made a scientific breakthrough by discovering a completely new way to use the traditional, natural sugar so that it get reduced in its candy products by up to 40% with no difference to taste.

► CRITICAL FACTORS FOR THE SUCCESS OF LOYALTY PROGRAMS

Rijish Raghavan, Vice President, PAYBACK India, in one of his interviews has emphasized on factors like transparency, convenience, relevance, engagement and ease of use for the effectiveness and success of a loyalty program. A clear and transparent communication while providing offerings and benefits to the customers goes a long way in developing their loyalty.

In the online world, personalization of experiences is the key to purchasing consideration while segmentation with locational considerations is critical to offline retailers.

Consistent delivery on the promises is what turns customers into loyal ones. Brand advocates cannot be made overnight. Building an effective loyalty program and pool of brand advocates can stand brands in good stead in times of crisis.

► THE FUTURE

In the current environment, loyalty to the brand has become crucial from the marketing strategy perspective where the very survival and continuity of the organization relies on loyal customers, who may be willing to pay more for a brand.

Brand loyalty generates greater market share and brings in new customers with Word of Mouth publicity. Brand loyalty is not just a marketing instrument but its strength goes beyond and influences the goal and vision of the organization.

In India, loyalty transactions have been growing consistently over the past few years due to more real-time and personalised experience being delivered to the customers. Loyalty programs are omnipresent in business and have evolved and grown beyond the discounts and coupons game. The demographics are changing and big spends are being made in all different categories from fuel, apparels, entertainment, travel, financial services and daily needs. In such a dynamic scenario, coalition loyalty program would be game-changer as it offers a diverse portfolio of partner brands with options to earn and spend points, and avail rewards. Loyalty programs which consolidate the rewards across partner brands will go a long way in ensuring customer long term retention.

► QUESTIONS

1. 'Trust, commitment and customer satisfaction are the pillars to building customer loyalty.' Enumerate through different examples, keeping the case in context.
2. 'Delivering customer value has a strong linkage to generating long-term customer loyalty.' Provide arguments from diverse sectors supporting the statement.
3. Relevance, experience, engagement, personalisation are some terms gaining importance in the current age for customer acquisition and retention. Explain how these have added new dynamics to the game of building brand loyalties.
4. Customer relationship management (CRM) process aims at enhancing customer loyalty. What are the various initiatives on the establishment of customer connect, management of data, investment in technology, and people development being taken by organisations today for an effective CRM strategy?

CASE 4

Starbucks India: The Human Coffee Experience

A wonderful moment is created when the consumer is willing to grab a cup of coffee. This moment becomes more wonderful and enlarged when it is connected to Starbucks. Thus, the company ensures that this connection is strengthened and grows in strength at every touch point. In line with this, Starbucks enhances these connections with the consumers by offering world-class coffee and by increasing consumers' communities. To do so, Starbucks first buys the roasted coffee. Subsequently, the excellence in quality of the selected coffee beans is enhanced by systematic data collection and information systems. Though, superb coffee is the only core business, Starbucks does as it is a part of the story.

► About Starbucks

Starbucks Coffee houses are the favourite of coffee lovers. Consumers come to Starbucks as they are aware that the service will be superb. Further, they will also be assured of an enticing ambience, an excellent cup of highly roasted and amply brewed coffee. To enhance this experience, Starbucks also offers tea, exceptional pastries and other delightful treats to stimulate the taste buds of the consumers. Additionally, the music that is played at the Starbucks further enhances the coffee experience. This experience is magnificent. This appeals to all coffee lovers. Thus, consumers visit Starbucks for chatting, talking, discussing, meeting at personal and professional levels. Starbucks is a gathering place, which is part of the daily activity of the consumers, which can make them happy and blissful. Consumers become stress free in this pleasing environment. Thus, Starbucks is more than brewing a cup of coffee. This is due to the fact that the company focuses on enhancing the coffee house experience with all the possibilities.

The main mission of Starbucks India is to aspire and develop the human spirit with every individual, every cup, and every neighborhood simultaneously. Starbucks India is 50:50 joint venture of Tata Global beverages and Starbucks. They have 75 outlets in the seven cities in India. Their headquarters and first store are in Mumbai. Here, the coffee offered is always of top quality. Further, the exquisite coffee beans are roasted and brewed with the enhancement in the life of people who grow and develop with the company. Starbucks calls themselves as partners as these tasks are not restricted to their jobs. It comes from their passion. Thus, they embrace diversity as every individual is provided the space and freedom to be themselves. All the individuals are treated with respect and dignity at Starbucks while celebrating different cultures. The company offers services in the culturally relevant way. Consumers are always connected and involved with Starbucks as they laugh, crack jokes and celebrate their life with this memorable moment. These moments start with an excellent cup of coffee and goes until strong human connections are developed. Thus, consumers have a sense of belongingness at the stores, forget their worries as they meet their friends and embellish the life with some slow and fast moments with humanity ("Starbucks Coffee Company", 2017).

▶ Business Philosophy

Every store belongs to a part of the community and the connection among the company, consumers', and communities is tied strongly with Starbucks by strategic partnership. There is a high sense of responsibility and has high potential. To ensure the same, Starbucks has set up high standards for this task.

In line with the same, Starbucks also deals with environmental issues, creates creative and flexible solutions, environmentally friendly products, establishes environmentally friendly corporate values, and monitors all the projects with the mission. All of this are accomplished by doing business ethically. These ethics are reflected in their services and all communication channels. Further, the partners become employees who engage with different consumers and serve various communities. Additionally, the suppliers of Starbucks have programs that can enhance their business relationship. Thus, each partner at Starbucks integrates talent, expertise and knowledge and enhances the humanity and connections with the customers with these elements ("Starbucks", 2017).

These philosophies, approaches and practices are very close to Indian consumers as they aim for enhanced human connection. Thus, Starbucks is totally in sync with their mindset and thinking. Thus, coffee lovers in India adore Starbucks and can see and feel the connect. Starbucks also connects with the consumers with the different kinds of coffee they offer in India such as whole bean, roasted (blonde, medium, dark), flavoured, unflavoured and so on. They also have Indian tastes blend such as chocolate, herbal, Kenya which is juicy and complex, Italian roast, Sumatra which is earthy and herbal Colombia, which is balanced and nutty and so on. These flavours signify that there is a blend of Indian and international taste. This is because consumers prefer this kind of flavours as they like the glocal (combination of global and local) concept ("Business Ethics and Compliance | Starbucks Coffee Company", 2017).

▶ Starbucks and Information System

In line with the same, Starbucks uploads all the policy documents on the website and other online sources that are accessible in the public domain. This is because the company works ethically and likes to be transparent with all the partners (consumer, employees, suppliers and so on). Additionally, they also provide the information of Starbucks India Mobile app as consumers are extensively using these platforms. Consumers can access the information about the Starbucks through all the sources including stores ("Starbucks", 2014).

▶ Data Collection

To be updated with these policies and remain connected with the partners, Starbucks collects data from multiple sources.

(1) Customer or Consumer level data Collection

(a) Personal Information: The company gathers data from all the customers and consumers along with their personal information. This information include name, surname, email, mobile number, birthdays, demographics and any other data that the individual would like to share with the company.

(b) Financial Information: Data include details about the bank, account details, credit card detail and payment options

(c) Purchase Information: Data may include details on products bought from the company, timing, location and frequency.

(d) Digital Information: Data are extracted though the Starbucks India mobile app about the device id, location, stores that are close to the consumer and places that the consumer has visited.

(e) Other Information: Additional data that the consumers can provide about other areas that are of their interest.

Outcome: Starbucks Card and My Starbucks Reward Account (provides massive data to the company and helps in retention of the consumers, community analytics and development of the community which are the key aims of Starbucks).

(2) Digital Level Data Collections: Starbucks collects the data from the websites, online sites visited by the customers and consumer and through mobile app. Digital data provide information about the internet service provider, operating system, browser type, IP address, access time, web pages that have been browsed and so on. This information is used by the company to provide the appropriate cookies and web beacons that are on relevant time and would be acceptable and informative to the consumers.

(a) Cookies: These are small data files that are saved in the hard drive of the various websites. These cookies are used by the company to enhance the overall web experiences by providing relevant and contextual data and information to the consumers. These cookies help the company to understand areas, features and visits by the consumers on various websites.

(b) Web Beacons: These are electronic images and visuals used on the websites are visited by the consumers. These images are used for delivering cookies, making counts of the visit and the usage pattern of the consumers. These images are further supplemented by the flash cookies, which are known as local shared objects as they can easily get adjusted in the digital screens in accordance with the consumers' usage. Thus, data are gathered by the company about the consumer with the good web experience.

(3) Company level Data: The company also collects data about the consumers anonymously as the focus is not on a particular person or individual. The aim is to primarily understand the consumers' perspectives and insights about the company. Data are collected by the third party about the consumers of the company. Based on this, Starbucks understands what their consumers feel, think, and experience about the brand. They also like to understand the expectation and suggestions that the consumers would like to offer to the company.

This is very important for the company as they consider consumers to be their partners. Subsequently, they also aim for developing strong human connection, which embellishes the coffee house experience at Starbucks (Bamb, 2016).

► Information Usage by Starbucks

Starbucks uses the information in the various ways:

(1) Managing the Consumer Purchase: Starbucks uses the information to process and manage the purchases and products and services used by the consumers. This includes accounts and program participation of consumers who can aid them in getting personalized experience from Starbucks.

(a) Quick Response: This information provides the company with consumer inquiries and Starbucks responds quickly with the relevant data and information. This is essentially managed by the customer care services of the company. Additionally, comments and suggestions posted on the blog and other online websites are also considered by the company. Thus, they can quickly take appropriate actions.

(b) Customized Promotion: Starbucks uses the information and provides customized and personalized promotions to the consumers with personal and non-personal information. This information includes type of purchases, amount sent and the benefits that can be derived by the consumers through this personalized promotion.

(c) Strong Communications with Company: Starbucks strengthen their communication with this data as order, purchases, services and program data facilitates the company to link the consumers with the relevant contest and sweepstakes that could further help the consumers.

(d) Better Communication with Other Partners: Consumers' data help the company to connect its consumers with other co-branded programs and partners. This further facilitates consumer and the company strengthens their relationship (Boulton, 2016).

► Data Sharing

Starbucks also shares the consumers' data with credit card processes, mailing houses, HR, CRM departments, site managers (primarily for the online data) and data managers who are the partners of Starbucks. These departments help the company to market the product, add consumers to the appropriate mailing list and develop loyalty program systems. However, they use information by following the proper legal processes and comply all the laws and legal approaches. Based on the same line, Starbucks never shares any information based on the personal data without the prior permission of their consumers. Thus, they take the written permission from the consumers if they are publishing any of their information in the public domain.

▶ Data Safety and Security

Starbucks provides all the opportunities to consumers to update, modify and edit the data as the rights are with the consumers. Data are very safe as the company would never make the changes in their personal data. More specifically, the promotional messages will not be sent to the consumer if they would like to opt out of the process. Consumers can also remove and reject the cookies if they want. If the consumers withdraw the consent about any information, company would not take further processing. Based on the same, they can develop approaches based on the consumers. More importantly, the company can also take care of all the information pertaining to loss, misuse of the personal information. However, there is full guarantee by the company for 100% security of data as the data transmission is very quick and fast through the various online sources and websites which cannot be monitored or tracked by the company easily ("Privacy Statement |Starbucks Coffee Company", 2017).

Information Processing and Storing: The company processes and stores the information of only adults as minor details cannot be saved by the companies, according to the Indian law. However, if the parents and guardians share the minor's information, they become the care takers along with the company. Starbucks uses safeguards for the data such as firewalls, physical access, data encryption and other administrative and control systems. Further, highly sensitive information such as details about the credit cards is transmitted either through the company website or company's mobile apps that uses secure sockets layers (SSL) protocol. In addition, there are security technologies that safeguard the personal information about the consumers. In line with the same, if there are changes in the processing and storing of information or privacy policies, the company mentions it on the website and other digital platforms so that the consumer is aware about the change. Finally, the company also stores the consent form for the consumers where they provide the authority to the company to retrieve, store, process and share the personal information ("MIS-Starbucks", 2015).

Further, data are used for analytics. Thus, the big data so collected facilitates the company to manage their loyalty programs. Due to this, Starbucks is also able to track and monitor their customers very closely. This helps them to develop the human connection and strengthen their relationship with the consumers and to develop the rich coffee experience. This is done as Starbucks makes the segments of the consumers' based on the data and set up the rule which is in sync with their purchase behaviour. This is usually carried on their smart phones of the consumers. This monitoring of the consumer habits helps the companies personalize the offers as well. For example, with the data, which were collected and processed in India, Starbucks grabbed an opportunity to serve tea brand "Teavana" in the country. The company also developed the best class in social media, which was again derived from the data the company collects from the various sources (Adkins, 2015).

▶ Way Ahead

The chairman of the company also thinks that Starbucks is the research-driven organization and excellent in collecting and gathering consumer data. He strongly holds that the reputation of the company has to be earned.

Starbucks has successful in making significance presence in India by adhering to the retail model of the country. Starbucks has taken care of the local requirement, which is relevant to the local culture in India. This was achieved as Starbucks believes in employee-centric organization. Thus, they invest heavily on their employees, who are their "partners". With these policies, Starbucks opened 50 outlets in the first year of their operation and successfully increased their stores. One of the reasons for the same is the middle class which is increasing exponentially in India and increasing the business opportunities for Starbucks. Thus, India is the fastest potential market for Starbucks. The company wants to explore further opportunity to sell Starbucks coffee at Vistara, Tata's airlines in India. They are also focusing on the merchandizing which includes books and music (Anand, 2017).

CASE 5 The Techy Amazon Insight

Amazon India began its operation as a powerhouse of retailing in the US. They entered the Indian e-commerce market with their user-friendly website. They added many titles and widened their product portfolios. They also created the ecosystem that was related to wholesale purchase of the products. Further, they tactically fixed the centers and contracts so that these goods can be easily shipped into and across the country. Amazon realized that more than a billion people in this country have not been exposed to the e-commerce markets.

The Indian market bore good as well as bad news for the company. The good news was that more than 65% of the consumers were under the age of 35 years with a high percentage of disposable income, owned smart phones, and widely used the internet. The bad news was that 67% of Indian population still lived in the rural set up and had under-developed infrastructure. Further, only 35% of the Indian population had access to the internet. Customers preferred cash transactions to digital payments. FDI rules also restricted a foreign multibrand retailer to sell the products and goods directly to the consumers through the digital channels. Thus, Amazon would need a third party seller for the Indian market. To do all these tasks and deal with complexities, Amazon had to understand strategic market research (Youderian, 2016).

► Business Issues and Approaches

Amazon needed the innovative business model to finalize ways to sell the products and goods in India. There was no shortage of the products that were manufactured and produced in India, but the vendors were small in scale. In this situation, a few e-retailers tried to seek the products online in India, but a cash-based economy model could not succeed in their businesses. To address these issues, Amazon launched their Indian website in 2013, and recruited suppliers as their partners to conduct business in India. They launched "Amazon Chai Cart". These mobile tea carts navigated on the streets of the cities, served refreshments, and educated the small business owners about the way e-commerce is used. This cart travelled 9,400 miles across 31 cities and involved 10,000 sellers. Subsequently, they launched "Amazon Tatkal" which was the "studio on wheels" and provided various services such as registration, imaging, cataloging, and training.

They also used the centralized shipping platforms and developed around two dozens warehouses in India in Telangana. Amazon further introduced "easy ship" and "seller flex". Through these systems, Amazon couriers picked the products from the seller's place and delivered to the consumers. Subsequently, warehouses were designated for the courier and Amazon fully coordinated the delivery systems and logistics. This system was expedited by the "neighborhood" approaches where it was easy for the seller to expedite the product delivery. The major delivery systems were contacted such as India Post and Blue Dart. The company also developed the Amazon transportation services where bikes and bicycles were used to deliver products in the urban and rural areas of India. However, there were challenges with the rural areas due to lower literacy rate and limited infrastructure.

Interestingly, there were many Indians who were not ready to rely on online services and considered mom-and-pop stores to be more convenient. There were issues related to internet services and basic infrastructure. However, all these concerns were addressed, and Amazon India achieved business to the level of $3 billion. This was due to the fact that there is very high potential in India, and the company was even ahead of the competitors, including Flipkart and Snapdeal (Sen, 2014).

▶ Processes of Research

These wonderful results were achieved by using effective approaches such as usage of appropriate key words for their brand which was commonly used by the consumers. This approach helped the company to reach out to consumers who were actually looking for online retailer or products. There were many up selling and cross selling carried out by the company with the help of the cookies and web beacons. The cookies provided the company with the customized data about the purchase history and other behavior patterns. Amazon provided these users very personalized offers based on their past history. This relevant information was approved of by the users. Additionally, they also worked on the presentation and packaging of the products. When consumers sent the products as gifts to another person, it was amazingly packaged and personalized. Further, Amazon also tracked the computers using the software. They used Chrome extension to track the history and received product details which helped them develop the subsequent competitive advantage strategy.

More specifically, all the challenges and issues were addressed by the company by conducting proper research. This research had many problems as we have seen. Thus, data was collected from various sources, including offline and online platforms and analyses was carried and these approaches were developed. This research was in sync with the vision of a company which aims at providing customers with a satisfying experience. In line with this, they offered low prices and more alternatives and easy merchandizing. Thus, all the approaches of the company were customer centric. Subsequently, the marketing messages have to be offline and online channels with the aim of maximizing customer value proposition. Amazon provided easy to use functionality, quick and credible customer service with a variety of content and trust in every transaction (Chaffey, 2014; Ray et al., 2013).

▶ Data Collection Methods

The company's website has customer reviews and product information that were in sync with the customer requirements. There were buying guidelines and free shipping offers offered by the company to increase the customer spend. In line with these, the company offered the latest inventory records and estimates of delivery dates with fast track delivery options. Further, the company used many techniques such as business intelligence, machine object coaching, queueing systems, neural networks and so on to understand the consumers and make customer oriented strategies and approaches. The data from these methods were used at the boot camps that were organized for the top level management. In these camps, the focus was on understanding human behavior and its complexities.

Subsequently, with this robust research and findings, they worked on the revenue per review. Additionally, they tried to understand how the approaches affect their business.

This also meant that the "data" is king in the company. Amazon managed the details of all the transactions at various stages online and displayed the status to the consumers. These data also helped the company bid for paid search advertising. Amazon also worked on the review conversion power by ensuing that each review was paid. Further search optimization and review count were also undertaken by the company. They realized that high review is great, but if it is in proportion to the review count, it is outstanding. Amazon realized that clicks do not work in their business. Thus, they had to go deeper and work on untapped markets. They modified the search and used to reach the stage of completion. This meant that when the users typed something, it was filled by Amazon (Madden, 2012).

► Initial Benefits by Research

They also used research that helped the company to sell the products in the niche markets. Further, sellers can even work on the statured markets to earn high profits. Thus, Amazon worked on the in-depth reviews and more scientific market research that facilitated the company to track the products that were in demand. For this research, Amazon used "Jungle Scout". This software provided data about the revenue the company achieved on various products. Amazon essentially worked on data analytics and market research. In line with this, Jungle Scout was used as a research tool for the Amazon sellers, and it is a software product. This software collects data from different data points and facilitates the sellers. Additionally, the company educated them with regards to the purchasing decisions. Therefore, they could identify excellent products that could be sold via Amazon.

This software also worked on sales estimates as many users provided the data while making the purchase. It works on the "best sellers rank" for which the algorithm is developed to track and monitors at least a hundred thousand products. The best sellers rank also correlates the unit sales on a monthly basis. Additional algorithm is created to get this update every month, which provides the sales estimates to Amazon and how they are performing on their business metrics (Sen, 2016).

► Extended Techy Methods for Research

More importantly, Amazon used "Splitly and Review Kick", which acquired the reviews and manages them on the platforms. Thus, if the user would like to receive the reviews about the Amazon product, they could get this information from the review option. Here, several coupons are being provided to the real buyers for the review that they have carried out for Amazon. Thus, Amazon received reviews that were really effective and legitimate. This tool was initially a product research tool, which has moved to a suite tool for the Amazon sellers.

Subsequently, there is the Amazon selling machine that provided tremendous information about the products, which was the initial thought of the company. They have moved from offline products to products online on Amazon. It means that Amazon has changed the way data needs to be looked at and considered for the business decision. This new business perspective changed the entire plethora of the products that Amazon offers. They offered products from gloves, yoga mat and so on. The company also looked at those products that enjoyed heavy demands by the consumers. The products are not too competitive and have multiple reviews. If the products are statured, it is very challenging for the company to get into that market.

However, products, such as barbeque gloves or garlic paste, would be easier for the company to get into the market. These products are considered as cool and user-friendly by the consumers. They are less competitive and have more and better business opportunities.

To ensure this, there is keyword search on Google; this platform is connected to the revenue and Jungle Scout. As it monitors the demand and the sales. For example, if a user is searching for a water bottle, this software will provide the data which could state that three sellers are in the top 10 results category and have 50 reviews. More importantly, Amazon encapsulates the overall listing which may include private labels.

Amazon focuses a lot on keyword research as it is significantly connected to the number of units sold. To strengthen the search, Amazon uses Merchant words—the algorithm which relates the Google keywords to the sales. Conventionally, Amazon related the search with the products, but it was not making any sense in terms of the business decision. The integrated search, which is associated with Google of the search, is important for the company. This resulted in increasing the bottom line of the company.

However, the most challenging part for Amazon is to sell the non-differentiated products as white labelling (re-branding and marketing the products by the company to ensure that they are their own in spite of the fact that they manufactured and developed by the other company) do not work for the consumers anymore. Products have to be exclusive and of excellent quality (Bhasin, 2017).

► RACE Framework

In line with the same, Amazon works on the RACE framework which means:

(1) Reach: it is derived from the AdWords and key words
(2) Act: develop simple and transparent experiences by thorough testing
(3) Convert: customize and provide relevant recommendations
(4) Engage: involve and engage with the users

This approach leads to "customer obsession" and is always evaluated and monitored thoroughly by the company. To do so, Amazon conducts many experiments. They developed internal experimentation platforms, which are known as "weblab". This platform was used by the company to assess the improvements in the company's website and products. They also added a feature known as "ask an owner" where the user can ask the questions related to the products. And amazon can route these queries to the relevant sellers or owners. Further, real-time experiments were also conducted where page design, features, ranking, relevance of ranking and so on were studied. However, the research was conducted for a few days or a week. This was because the company wanted to understand the pulse of the business in terms of session time, length, and so on. The overall online experience was also assessed with the statistical methods.

In line with the same, Amazon uses the data derived from this research for:

(1) Enhancing the website traffic
(2) Increasing awareness about the products

(3) Creating incremental products and opportunities for increasing revenue for the services

(4) Strongly developing the "Amazon" brand

These approaches were used by the company because they believed that significant marketing campaigns and communication also enhanced the customer experience, which is the core objective for their business. These communications helped the company develop e-word of mouth and word of mouth promotions which help allure new customers and getting repeat purchases from the existing customers. Further, the company also connected with the customer based on their interest areas and helped them selecting the products that were in sync with their needs and requirements. More specifically, they conducted online advertising which included paid search marketing, search optimization-mails campaigns and interactive ads. The data also helped Amazon to create leaflets for the non-competing websites such as Expedia, Makemytrip and so on.

Interestingly, Amazon found that a significant number of customers who have downloaded their app and visited their site did so mainly through their smart phones in India. This change in the user behavior encouraged the company to develop mobile-oriented user experience, as the screen was small. They made their interface more user oriented. Thus, this orientation could be easily used on their phones. Consumers were easily able to track their products via these apps. This resulted in a fivefold increase in the sales as compared to their competitor i.e. Flipkart. They also launched the grocery service with a delivery time of 2 hours. This further enhanced the shopping experience of the consumers in India (Chaffey, 2016).

▶ Data and Findings Usage

This consumer-oriented data were used by the company in three different ways:

(1) Relationship marketing driven by Data: This was undertaken by Amazon with the big data and web search for all the customer transactions. The data were shared with the call center. Based on this, they understood the customer relevance and context. Thus, they interacted specifically based on what the customer was interested in. Additionally, there is the facility of opt in and out for the customer for the promotional messages from Amazon. These approaches helped Amazon enhance the relationship with the customers.

(2) High ease of Shopping: The comprehensive data helped the company increase the ease and convenience of the online shopping for the customers. There were many technological platforms by which customer were able to access the information very quickly. There were "one-click ordering" dash buttons were installed at home where the push of button can result in shopping. Further, the Amazon Prime facility was provided to the customers to receive the coupon based on their location and time of the day or event.

(3) Exquisite Experience: The data helped the company to enhance the social and online experience of the customers. The social element was taken care of by the relationship marketing team of Amazon as they were free to share their opinions and experience with their family and friends easily. Amazon also encouraged a continuous feedback process to improve their performance.

More specifically, the research data also facilitated the company in increasing their B2B business, apaert from enhancing the B2C category. They signed up with Aditya Birla Group's online retail fashion store. This collaboration helped the company to enhance their offerings in the fashion category and wider options were provided to the customers. There was more margin for the business in this category (Warrillow, 2015; "Relationship Marketing for amazon.com - O2I", 2017).

► WAY AHEAD

India is very nascent in e-commerce, video streaming, and cloud computing. Yet, there are multiple opportunities in this country. This is because there are 1.3 billion people, which is four times the US population. The country is growing at an annual rate of 5%–10%. Indians are conversant in English. Further, there is a high penetration of smart phones in the country and shipping is cheaper in India as compared to the US. There is a prediction that by 2020, there will be 175 million shoppers in the online retailing space. This means the business would be extended by US$ 100 billion. Mobile wallet and credit cards would increase further business. However, India needs more investment not only in currency abut also in patience and perseverance in dealing with the infrastructure coupled with a long-term perspective. The complexities of culture, preference, liking, and consumer behavior are really complex and dynamic. Thus, this country needs constant and continuous research to understand and provide excellent customer experience to all its consumers across the country. (Shah, 2016).

CASE 6

Consumer Behaviour — Its Wide Facets and Deep Implications

Customer connect, Customer loyalty, consumer relationships, changing society, transforming buying behaviours, etc., are the buzz words today around which strategies are being framed by the marketers.

We see lot of acceptance and also a lot of intolerance co-existing in the present society. Numerous structural and social barriers that have long existed are breaking down leading to a major cultural shift. The younger generation is openly expressing its voice. The attitude of people to different issues is changing. Hence, brands are continually trying to cope with all these changes. Brand strategist Harish Bijoor very well says that, "There will come a time when habits and attitude will count more."

Consumer attitudes are a combination of beliefs, feelings, and intentions related to a particular object. or concept. Like in the present milieu, issues related to environment, society, finances, health, and well-being are gaining importance, and attitudes—both positive and negative—are being developed towards them. It is becoming imperative for the marketers to understand consumer attitudes in order to understand the customers better and also to know how they can influence or respond to those attitudes.

► New Parameters in the Consumer Purchase Decision Journey

The internet is evolving and so the consumers are changing and engaging differently with brands. The evolution of consumer buying decision process is bringing in new marketing mantra. Below is the conventional consumer purchase decision journey.

EXHIBIT 1

CONVENTIONAL CONSUMER PURCHASE DECISION JOURNEY

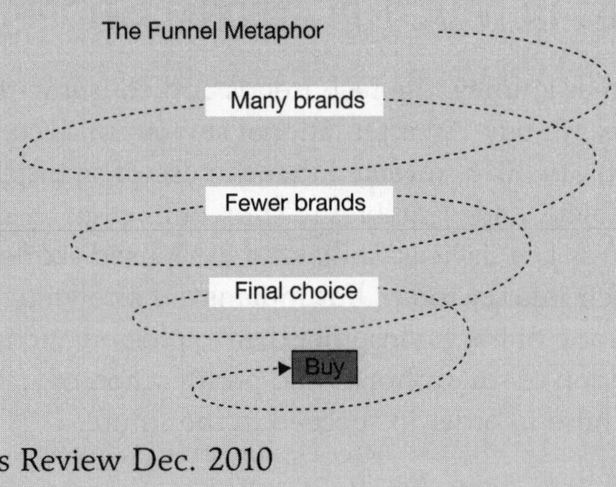

Source: Harvard Business Review Dec. 2010

In the conventional process, after the purchase the relationship with the brand is focused mainly on the use of the product. Since the time of internet evolution, this process has changed radically. Now consumers want to share their experience online after buying the product, and it has created new parameters of brand advocacy and brand bonding. Below is the consumer purchase decision journey process post-internet evolution.

EXHIBIT 2

NEW CONSUMER PURCHASE DECISION JOURNEY PROCESS POST-INTERNET EVOLUTION

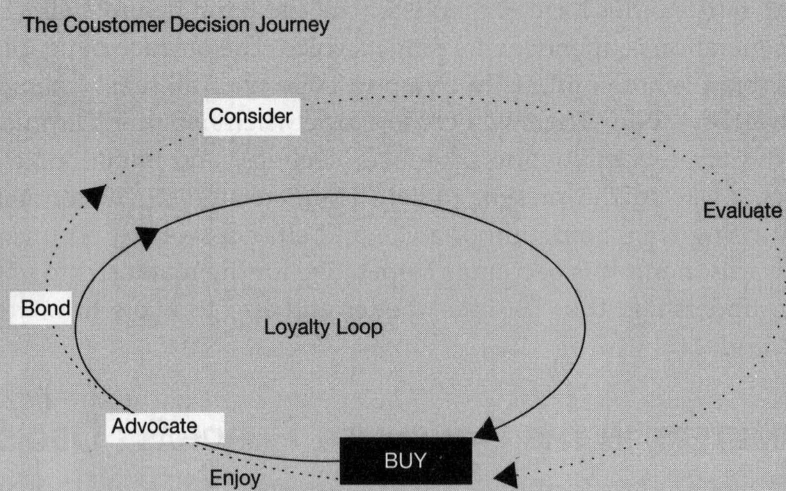

Source: Harvard Business Review Dec. 2010

Thus, it is clear that brand advocacy and brand bonding play a vital role in today's consumer purchase decision process.

▶ Emerging Trends in Multi-platform Shopping

In the new connected customer journey, the tech trends and consumer habits are completely transforming how, where, and why we buy. An international survey conducted by a global marketing and technology agency, DigitasLBi, in 2016, revealed that the use of smartphones and other connecting devices, including laptops, tablets, and wearables to shop online has increased. The study found that whereas the global average was five devices, India and UAE used six devices on an average.

These trends may be in their infancy today, but Indians are known to leap frog in the adoption of technology. A new phenomenon of huge consumer data explosion and immense content generation has arisen due to the penetration of smartphones and proliferation of screens. Brands definitely need to understand and leverage these in order to succeed in the future.

Personalised and special offers by retailers recorded greater sales as admitted by 87% of online shoppers in the survey by DigitasLBi. Mobile payment is another phenomenon that is gaining traction though data security and privacy has emerged as a major concern.

Customer service is becoming an increasingly important factor for consumers to choose a brand. According to the findings of the American Express 2017 Global Customer Service Barometer, 30% of the consumers in India are ready to use messaging tools such as live chats and SMS for interaction with companies. This percentage is higher when compared with countries like Hong Kong and Italy, with 26% each and Mexico at 25%. Hence, companies in India are also increasingly using social media as a way of conveying the company's intent on service. But definitely a need to balance digital channels with physical ones is the key to success.

Traditionally festivals were strongly connected to shopping intent. But now with e-commerce penetration and frequent discount sales, purchases have become affordable enough to make shopping a regular activity. Diwali, India's biggest festival is no longer the sole occasion to get consumers to shop. People are fashion savvy today, and shopping for fashion is turning out to be a high involvement activity. These days, for many customers, every weekend is a buying day, apart from the festivals. Convergence of categories and channels and easy accessibility of fashion are bringing in such changes in consumer behaviour.

IPG Media Lab, NY has launched Outlook 2017, highlighting 3 defining tech trends of consumer behaviour—Advanced interfaces, Global culture and Augmented Intelligence that all brands should be cognizant of. Touch and Voice are some of the interfaces already being experimented by brands to create engaging experiences for the customers. On the global front, the appeal of sports, music, and entertainment is transcending boundaries and finding wide target base amongst the Indian consumers. Sharp-edged differentiators in the form of "chatbots" are being created by e-commerce players which will enable powerful and personalised interactions with the customers. Artificial Intelligence, truly augmented!

► New Influencers in Town

Micro influencers are the new breed of influencers swelling on social media today. Neither movie stars nor sports celebrities, these are just regular consumers who after being active on different social media platforms could see the potential of these and get experimental on harnessing content to influence other fellow consumers. Thus, they have assumed the role of campaign managers, especially active on product categories as diverse as fashion, food, fitness, beauty, and music.

One such big time social media influencer with more than one lakh followers on Instagram is former fashion stylist, Shereen Sikka Bharwani, who has to her credential brands like Maybelline, Dove, Jet Airways, who have signed her on for the London Fashion Week. Giants like Audi, Jaguar and Burberry have also solicited her presence.

Another global brand L'Oreal works with about 200 key Instagram influencers. Its make-up artistry brand, NYX, was the first in the category to be launched online in India in 2016, and the company relied heavily on influencers for its promotion.

It's the wide reach and cost efficiency of micro influencers which is making more and more brands turn to it in order to capitalise on this medium. "Micro influencers are now being used by about 50% of the brands for their new product launches through Facebook Live, Instagram stories and Youtube videos", as stated by Aditya Gupta, cofounder of iGenero.

On one hand, brands are benefitting from the digitally literate and active denizens of the social media world. On the other, realizing the wide-scale impact that influencers can create, brands like Google and Tata trust are running "Internet Saathi" program, spreading digital literacy among rural women who in turn are roping other womenfolk to this new world of internet, thus gaining power and influence.

Currently, over 2.5 million women in 60,000 villages across 10 states have been trained by 18,000 *Saathis* travelling the countryside on their branded bicycles. A sense of identity and status is instilled along with mobility through newly acquired skill of internet usage and additional knowledge. Social impact beyond measure can be seen through various instances like *Saathis* using and helping other women use the Internet to find information about health, government programs, and agriculture. In one instance, a *Saathi* used pictures of formed foetus to raise awareness and empathy which has helped reduce the number of female foeticide in her village.

► Role and Status of Women

Michael Silverstein, senior partner and managing director, Boston Consulting Group, once said in an interview that the female economy will have a global economic impact greater than Brazil, Russia, India. and China.

In India a new power consumer group, that of rural women is getting highlighted and tapped extensively by brands. Accenture's survey, "Masters of Rural Market series — Women consumers in rural India" brings forth some very subtle and apparent changes taking place in small towns and villages of India. With literacy levels rising and increasing number of women getting employed in rural India, the family income is seeing a surge. This coupled with greater exposure and usage of mobile devices and internet is bringing transformation in rural consumer behaviour and landscape.

Data presented by Accenture survey unearths some very startling facts and shuns many myths on the consumer purchase process related to rural India.

Need recognition is triggered by the practical concern over currently used products getting obsolete. 46% of the respondents surveyed cited this as the prime reason for indulging in new purchases. Also, the basic necessity and influence of family and friends work as additional triggers. This gives a clear-cut direction to the marketers to design their marketing campaigns which can tap into the opportunity to replace consumers' existing goods.

While gathering information about products, 53% of rural women depend on word-of-mouth, while 32% depend on local mom-and-pop stores. This kind of survey finding can be a guiding factor for marketers in identifying right influencers in the local community and in developing an effective media strategy. Nature of influence is changing in many parts of rural India, moving from traditional (such as Sarpanch) to newer ones, such as educated youth, friends, and individuals with specific expertise (like electricians who can advise women on consumer durables).

While evaluating various parameters of a product before making a purchase, as against popular notion, price does not account to be a primary evaluative criterion for rural women. Survey found that just 34 percent of the working women and 35 percent of the non-working women cited price. This is indicative of the big change where the requirements and aspirations of rural women are evolving fast and marketers in order to cope have to come up with new differentiations to appeal to this segment. They have to go beyond pricing and talk a different language communicating emotional and functional benefits like value for money, quality, social status, increased convenience, comfort, and freedom.

While making the final purchase, branded products are being increasingly preferred by the rural female consumers. Survey states that of the total respondents, 60 percent of the working women and 67 percent of the nonworking women cited trustworthiness and reliability as the main reasons for their being conscious about brands.

Many of the rural females indulge in impulse buying as well. They even go to nearby villages and cities to make such purchases. Survey reports that they have started ordering such products over the internet also but the trend is slow to pick up due to less awareness and confidence towards online purchasing.

Post-purchase, major reason for dissatisfaction which came forth from 84% of the women consumers was poor performance and low quality of the products. As rural women are not educated enough to go through the process of logging formal complaints, they tend to remain dissatisfied, and hence, lose trust on the companies. One repercussion which immediately stems out of this situation is the spread of negative word-of-mouth, highly prevalent in closely knitted rural society. So, companies have to strategize accordingly to train customers, to streamline a swift feedback and complaints handling mechanism which may build trust and ease anxiety amongst rural consumers. Highly proactive and powerful strategy to reach out to customers can help differentiate and win.

Through the survey, more of the myth busters got revealed which throw different light on rural consumers and need to be attended carefully by marketers. 35% of rural women as against 21% of the urban hold paying jobs. Women in rural India take greater advantage of social security schemes. As far as the rural women's role in the household purchase decisions is concerned, out of those interviewed, 37% of the non-working and 40% of the working women said that they make purchases on their own. Majority of rural female consumers buy high value products as against the popular belief of rural consumers attached to low value goods.

The key elements of the purchase journey of rural consumers have undergone a vast change and marketers need to master the critical imperatives associated with each stage of that journey.

Not just in rural, but changes of different kind and magnitude are being observed in urban setting too. A major shift in the conservative Indian mindset can be highlighted through the example of Tinder which recently launched its India operations, but within no time has become highly popular dating app. In a country like India where dating as a concept is not only perceived as a male prerogative but is also seen as taboo, a huge change is being witnessed as women are seen to be more active and engaged on Tinder than men as revealed by India head of Tinder, Taru Kapoor. Today women in India are more mobile, independent, self-confident, and keen to develop their own self-identity than ever before. According to a survey, one in every four scooter-buyers is a woman, and an overwhelming majority of these women customers are young. Yet another survey states that, when it comes to buying high-end bags, most of the women shoppers go for luxury products because of their social circle. All these changes should appear as gateway of opportunities for marketers of different brands.

► Roots of Culture and its Influence

Brand's place of origin plays an important role in consumers' choices. A 2016 Nielsen study shows different global and local brand preferences in a consumer's shopping journey. Indian respondents ranked personal/beauty care as the top category where consumers look for global brands. As this category is considered to be modern and trendy, so culturally they are considered to belong to the Western world, and accordingly lies the preferences for brands. While in other category such as food items, local giants take the lead. As equity to the food brands come from they being rooted to one's own culture.

Now seeing the profits emerging from the growing personal/beauty segment, marketers are trying to attach the element of culture to it in order to hook in more customers. Research firm Euromonitor in its survey reported that it is words such as "natural", "organic", "botanical", "free from chemicals", and even "religious compliance" drives purchases of personal care products like shampoo, hair colour, skin creams, and lotions.

71 per cent of consumers surveyed said that they would pick up a face cream or lotion if it claimed to be "natural", 38% said they would buy a shampoo or hair oil if it was made with "botanical" ingredients.

"In a market like India where herbal and ayurvedic hair and skin care has a legacy of usage (for example, *henna, bhringraj or brahmi* oil, or herbal face packs), awareness and benefits of herbal or botanical ingredients is high," Euromonitor International survey analyst Priyanka Bagde remarked.

Data received both from supermarkets and online stores have recorded 20–25 per cent year-on-year growth in "natural" products versus 10 per cent for regular ones. "Millennial consumers are leading the trend as they are becoming savvier about "green" choices. Hence, a marked shift is happening in favour of natural products", said Praveen Jaipuriar, marketing head-personal care of Dabur, maker of Vatika shampoo and Fem bleach. Now international brands are also speaking the "organic" and "natural" language. French cosmetics giant L'Oreal has rolled out ayurvedic shampoo, conditioner, oil, and cream under its Garnier Ultra Blends brand; Hindustan Unilever relaunched, Ayush and acquired hair oil brand, Indulekha.

► Advertising Reflects Society for a Better Connect

Brands communicate with its customers through plethora of activities and channels. Advertising is one of the most potent of them all. Advertising is changing now from the clichéd and conformist approach to becoming socially inclusive, more realistic, human, and all encompassing. Marketers are realising that with the buying experience moving online, emotional touch points are reducing; hence, if brands have to talk to millennials and build affinity with them, then they have to touch upon the issues that are important to them. In today's world of digital media, customers are bombarded with different stories with a continuous hunger for more. "Brands have realised that only the most unusual and best stories will survive. So, they have to excite or completely touch somebody deeply or nudge the society in a particular direction," says Swati Bhattacharya, chief creative officer, FCB Ulka India. Today in society there are more conversations around subjects like gender equality, transgender rights, differently abled people and other relevant social concerns which are getting portrayed through advertising to build the right connect with the target audience.

Tea brand Brooke Bond Red Label from Hindustan Unilever Ltd recently came out with an advertisement featuring an elderly woman who suffers from Alzheimer's. Then came another ad from cough and cold brand Vicks (from Procter and Gamble) which touched upon the sensitive subject of transgender rights in India, as it focused on a transgender mother and her young daughter within the theme of "Touch of Care". Another one raising a pertinent issue comes from Tata Tea's Jaago Re series which says "Alarm Bajne se Pehle Jaago Re". This campaign identifies with the growing issue of student depression and suicide, and urges parents to do their bit to avoid any tragedies, even if is just saying #ItsOk.

"The idea behind more inclusive advertising is to be top of mind, be a better story teller and get the best recall," says Santosh Padhi, chief creative officer and co-founder at Taproot Dentsu. India struggles with a lot of issues, "And brands taking up these issues is not a bad thing. Advertising influences people. It can help change behaviour, even if it has a subtle impact," says Padhi.

► Certain Unusual Insights and Stories

Big online retailers like Amazon, Flipkart depend extensively on data collected from multiple sources, such as behaviour tracking and demographic profiling, to help them identify potential customers and approach them in the best way possible. This wealth of information thus collected is deciphered to enable retailers to strategize on all fronts for optimum results while dealing with customers.

Their data-mining efforts have revealed that young working mothers in their 30s are looking for products across categories such as toys, diapers, kids wear, beauty and are more likely to purchase high-end lingerie from online marketplace. This becomes a fine touch point for the retailers to detail out their communication in the way that would reach out the best to them.

Similarly brick and-mortar retailer, Walmart found out through data mining that beer sales would go up on a Friday afternoon. This data pattern surfaced the fact that it was young males coming to store to pick up diapers for their new-borns who were responsible for the surge. And behind the data and the fact was the insight that the fathers, who had to stay home to take care of the baby, could not go out to meet friends, and hence, bought beer to drink at home. Strategy that followed was, Walmart moved beers next to the diapers section resulting in rise in sales.

A unique start-up, attending to a social and behavioural issue facing young generation was launched recently known as iitiimshaadi.com by its founder Taksh Gupta. It is a matchmaking site which is on an unusual idea as it matches degrees not *kundalis* (horoscopes) of the prospective couples. Increasing rate of divorces among young couples led to this venture as its founder believes that major cause of marital break-ups is differences in opinions and behaviors, which arise among people, who have dissimilar educational backgrounds and are thus not able to understand each other's work and living styles. "Mental compatibility is equally or even more significant than the ones based on caste, religion. or any other factor," says Taksh Gupta. "Education to an extent is a new caste system in place," says brand strategist Harish Bijoor. The more educated you are, with premier pedigree institutions as your alma mater, the more of Brahmana you become, he adds.

► FUTURE TRENDS

With over 460 million internet users, India is the second largest online market, ranked only behind China. By 2021, there will be about 635.8 million internet users in India. Internet penetration rate in India stood at about 10 percent in 2011 which reached to 26 percent in 2015. Furthermore, men dominated internet usage in India with 71 percent as compared to women at 29 percent.

According to the Com Score study, 75% of the internet audience in India is aged 35 years and below, which signifies that in the coming years there will be a huge young population over the internet. With the proliferation of the Internet, it has become relatively easy for customers to gain more up-to-date information about the products and/or services before they make their purchase decision. Customers can now validate the claims of the companies related to the products/services beforehand (Ind and Riondino, 2001). The issue of consumer empowerment is increasingly becoming a popular area of inquiry in recent times and trust-based advocacy marketing is emerging as an effective means to empower customers (Yamaoka, 2004)

As per the report released in March 2017, by The Boston Consulting Group's (BCG) Center for Customer Insight (CCI), "The New Indian: The Many Facets of a Changing Consumer", consumption in India is set to triple to $4 trillion by 2025. It is the rising affluence levels which is driving changes in consumer behaviors and spending patterns leading to big implications for companies.

The report states following factors shaping growth in future:

- The elite and affluent income segments for the first time will represent the largest consumption segment constituting 40% of all spending by 2025
- Next big growth will be coming from the new emerging cities (those with populations of less than 1 million) which will constitute one-third of total consumer spending by 2025
- Three-fourths of all households will be nuclear families
- 30% to 35% of all retail sales will be influenced by Digital channels and 8% to 10% of retail spending will be online by 2025

India's consumer market is poised for fundamental change," said Nimisha Jain, a BCG partner and report co-author. "As the consumer market continues to grow and evolve, companies will need to shed conventional wisdom, try multiple business models simultaneously, and be prepared for rapid change internally to adapt to changing consumer needs and behaviors."

► QUESTIONS

1. In the present digital world, new tech trends are emerging and consumer habits are completely transforming how, where, and why we buy. Explain in context with the case.
2. Analyse critical stages in the purchase-decision process and how changes in them is making marketers develop different strategies which can lead to success.
3. On the consumer characteristics front, three factors mainly cultural, social and personal are said to influence consumer buying behaviour. Keeping the case in context, illustrate in detail the role of these factors and the changing influence being observed today. Also highlight how habits and attitudes will come to play an important influencing role.

CASE 7

ZICOM – Leveraging Corporate Trust and Technical Strengths in the B2B Market

"If you know the enemy and know yourself, you need not fear the results of a hundred battles"
– Sun Tzu, Art of War

► Introduction and Background

Efficiency, effectiveness, and experience are the three Es that have been instrumental in helping Zicom to carve a niche for itself in the field of electronic security surveillance in India. With more than 20 years of operation, Zicom has achieved several milestones in its journey of securing lives. Moving from a company slogan "Feel Safe" to "Awake Always", Zicom is on its path to reach the pinnacle. Started in 1994, Zicom has expanded its reach to 4 countries, 1023 cities, and over a million happy customers with an annual turnover of Rs. 1122 crores. What makes Zicom's products and service offerings so unique is that it is in the business of satisfying the most basic human need i.e. security. The intellect and expertise of Zicom together make it possible for businesses to maintain safety.

► Company Profile

"To be the Company you Trust the most, To Protect what you Value the most"

With such compelling vision, Zicom has been successful in becoming the most reliable, competent, and comprehensive provider for delivering security solutions. It has been able to transcend from mere transactional relationship to a more holistic and engaging relationship with its various stakeholders. The customer is at the heart of its business model. The value proposition of Zicom is safety and security, business intelligence, loss prevention, comfort, and convenience.

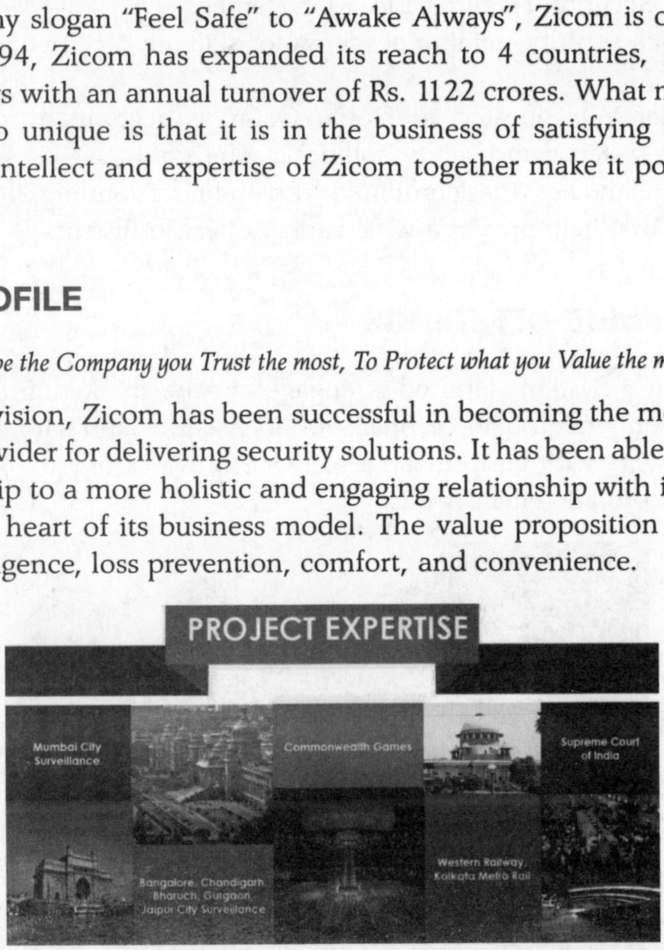

The entity has been credited with project expertise of Mumbai, Bangalore, Chandigarh, Bharuch, Gurgaon, and Jaipur city surveillance, Supreme Court of India, Commonwealth Games, Western Railway, and Kolkata Metro Rail. Zicom serves rich clientele like Punjab National Bank, Indiabulls, Ultratech Cement Ltd, HDFC Bank, Pizza Hut, Videocon, Tata Housing, McDonald's, Federal Bank, Lodha Housing, Shriram Transport Finance to name a few. Zicom has helped meet its security needs at reasonable fraction of costs.

► Zicom Group of Companies

Zicom has unfolded its range of services under e-SaaS (Electronic Security as a Service), offering affordable security services to housing societies. It adds value to the efforts of maintaining a safe and secure environment by acting as the virtual security guard aimed at protecting the property at all times. It also serves retail and banking and financial institutions without customers having to own or manage the system. It offers remotely managed electronic security services supported by the Command Centre Service.

UNISAFE fire protection specialists LLC, a subsidiary of Zicom Electronic Security Systems, provides steadfast fire protection services all over the seven Emirates, Qatar, and in India. The Institute of Advanced Security Training and Management Pvt. Ltd (ASTM), another group of companies of Zicom, is a security-training academy for skill advancement of security professionals and vocational training.

Phoenix International WLL located in Doha, Qatar, is a company committed to providing customized firefighting systems and safety solutions. The company uses its deep and extensive knowledge of fire science and activities combined with an understanding of codes and regulations to develop safety systems that help protect a wide variety of environments.

► Product/Service offerings

Zicom Electronic Security Systems Limited is engaged in the marketing and selling of electronic security systems and equipment. The company offers security and safety products and services. The standardized hardware with customizable software provides unique analytical and diagnostic information to meet end-to-end client needs.

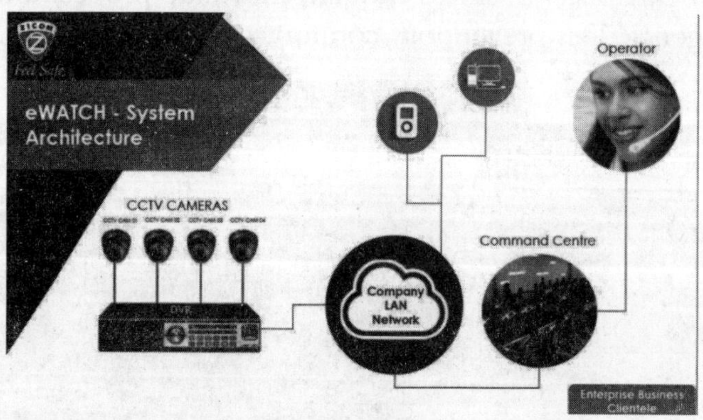

The company's solutions that use cloud technology include closed-circuit television (CCTV), surveillance system, access control system, fire alarm system, multi-apartment video door phones, intruder alarm system, fingerprint locks, and remote managed services (RAM). The Company offers biometric access control system, and proximity access control system. It offers home surveillance solutions as well. Its CCTV Surveillance systems include Box Cameras, Digital Video Recorders, Dome Cameras, Internet protocol (IP) Box Cameras, IP Infrared (IR) Bullet Cameras, High Definition Transport Video Interface (HD TVI), IR Bullet Cameras, IR Dome Cameras, Network Video Recorders, and Speed Dome Cameras. Its fire alarm systems include main panels, smoke detectors, heat detectors, and other accessories

► Awards/Recognition

Zicom has won several awards over the years like the Lions CSR Precious Award for Education and Skill Development in 2016, "Best Security Application in Retail" from Indian Retail Congress 2014, "Inc. India Innovative Award" in products category in 2013, Best Electronic Security award under Channel leadership in the 12th Annual VARINDIA Star Nite Awards 2013, Most Innovative Brand in Electronic Security Award 2013, Brand of Excellence Award in the segment of Electronic Security at the 11th VAR India IT forum 2013, Most Preferred Security Equipment Brand for innovation in Home Security Systems in 2012, Strategy Award for Zicom SaaS by Michael Porters' Institute of Competitiveness, among other accolades.

A typical consumer decision making process in Zicom goes as follows:

STAGE 1

PROBLEM DEFINITION OF MNK INSURANCE

MNK General Insurance Company Ltd, based in Guwahati, Assam, has invited tenders for supply, installation, and commissioning of CCTV surveillance system in 4000 different projects/units across India with four years post-warranty. The estimated value of the tender is Rs. 1.2 crores with a 90 days delivery period. Request for Proposal (RFP) was floated on 10th November, 2016 and the last day for submission of bids was 23rd December, 2016. The bidder must supply as per the standard terms and conditions, eligibility criteria, delivery norms, installation, commissioning, inspection, tests, security deposit, taxes, and duties, liquidated damages, risk purchase, force majeure, packaging for transit, etc. The bidder must also submit the point-wise compliance against each point of the technical requirement/specifications. If the bidder fails to submit the compliance statement against any of the above specification, then the offer may be bypassed. For all the details on technical and commercial specifications, bidders can visit the company website and download the necessary information.

MNK solicited the proposals from prospective contractors on how they intend to carry out that request, and at what price. Proposals in response to an RFP can be subject to negotiation after they have been submitted.

STAGE 2

SCOPING THE WORK – TENDER SPECIFICATIONS

Technical Bid for MNK Insurance contained the following mandatories:

A demand draft of Rs 1 lakh is to accompany the bid as Bid Processing fee and also Earnest Money Deposit of Rs 5 lakhs in the form of FDR/TDR or Bank Guarantee. A Bidder Information form duly completed in all respects, a proof of Similar Experience, and proof of Zicom's presence in Guwahati had to be a part of the tender-filling process. These had to be supported by other specified documents, such as audited balance sheet for past 3 years/certificate from Auditor; Original Equipment Manufacturer Authorization certificate; a list of technical staff, their qualifications, expertise and years of experience; letter of reference from past customers; bid documents and its annexures, including addenda/corrigenda with each page duly stamped and signed by authorized signatory; certificate of incorporation; copy of the PAN card and a written undertaking that Zicom is not blacklisted by State/Central Govt or by any Urban Local body.

STAGE 3

EVALUATION OF BIDS

- In stage I of technical bid evaluation, only those bids that are found to be responsive to the requirements of the RFP as specified above would be considered for evaluation and for selecting the selected bidder to undertake the project. The technical bid evaluation will be qualifying in nature.
- The capability of the bidders would be assessed based on the evaluation process and minimum threshold requirements. Any bidder meeting the threshold requirements and meeting the pre-qualification criteria set out by MNK Insurance Ltd., shall qualify for the financial round.
- Financial bid of only those bidders who meet the minimum requirements as set out in the bid document would be opened and evaluated.
- MNK shall use the factors, methods, criteria, and requirements defined in the bid document for evaluation of the bids.
- The result of evaluation of technical bid will be communicated to qualified bidders by MNK's technical consultant.
- The bidder ranking first in the technical bid and sufficiently low price will be declared the successful bidder and will be issued the purchase order.

Having received this brief from the industry networks, the key account manager-Sales at Zicom, Mr. Abhishek Bharadwaj discusses it with the Procurement head, Mr. Manoj Khadkikar. Following are the snapshots of the various stages of the tendering process, including final negotiations with MNK Ltd.

STAGE 4

PLANNING FOR QUOTING FOR THE BID

Vignette 1 – 15th November, 2016

(Key account manager Mr. Abhishek Bharadwaj calls for a meeting to discuss the RFP with the Procurement Head – Mr. Manoj Khadkikar. Mr. Manoj seeks the quotation from the vendor – OEM)

Abhishek: Good morning, Manoj. I hope you have checked the email that I sent you yesterday about the brief of MNK Insurance Co. Ltd.

Manoj: Yes, I went through your email.

Abhishek: Great, Manoj! This can be a breakthrough deal for us. In fact, this can open several avenues for Zicom.

Manoj: Certainly, Abhishek; don't worry. We will crack this one. Our excellent track record, robust system integration, and deployment capabilities set us apart from the rest.

Abhishek: You are right. The other day I was speaking to our client, SSK Ltd, and they seem to be highly satisfied with our deliverables. In fact, they told me that our easy upgrades, leap-through technology, service reach, competent technical manpower, customizable analytics, and diagnostics are the key factors for having sustainable relationship with them.

Manoj: You're right. Let us go through the timelines for the project. The last day for the submission of bid is 23rd December, 2016, 13.00 Hrs. One of the most significant changes in MNK's acquisition is the increased importance of "best value" i.e. instead of making awards to the lowest bidder as it generally did in the past, it can now make awards for the item that best satisfies its technical requirements at an acceptable price.

Abhishek: Yes, let's get going and try to wrap up our proposal by 1st December 2016. Meanwhile, I will work on the competitive assessment and the sales pitch for this project

Vignette 2 – 17th November, 2016 Zicom office

(The Technical Head – Mr. Steven Selvaraj and the Procurement head – Mr. Manoj Khadkikar discuss internally about the RFP)

Manoj: Hi, I have called for this meeting to discuss the tender response strategy for MNK Ltd.

Steven: Okay, Manoj. What additional information do we need to gather for the offer?

Manoj: We need to gather hardware requirements, product drawings, software functionality, deliverables, timelines and a breakdown of costs component at each stage of the project, etc.

Steven: Yes. I am going through the RFP and it specifically mentions that the application of the CCTV surveillance should cover the three main areas of each of their offices, namely the entrance, cash counter, and the store vault. They have not specifically mentioned the features, except the motion-based recording, private-zone masking and remote viewing.

Manoj: Besides this, I think we can easily propose additional features of alarm integration with smoke and intrusion system. The new technology demo that we saw a couple of weeks back of the integrated panel of CCTV, intrusion, and fire would be a great solution to offer here instead of the different solutions that they have asked for.

Steven: Yes, and because all this is on IP platform, we can offer more features and deliver solutions based on this at a later stage also to the customer.

Manoj: Fantastic! The services we can offer for remotely managed electronic security services supported by Zicom Command Centre is a deal clincher. Our customizable analytics can help us get that leverage and differentiate our products as compared to the competition. (Refer Command Center Annexure I)

[Steven and Manoj discuss point by point the entire tender offer to determine the resources required to fulfill the contract.]

Manoj: Okay so let me take this ahead with my team and get the quotes from our OEMs. We are working on a tight schedule for this as they have asked for deployment, installation, and commissioning of the project within 90 days from the date of release of the purchase order. As this needs a customized product, the delivery needs to be done on an urgent basis.

Steven: I would like to go for a site visit at MNK Insurance office in Guwahati with my team to get sufficient information relating to risk, contingencies, and other circumstances which might influence or affect the price and the installation.

Manoj: Steven, do you think we have that much time to spare? It is not mandatory like the CDE company project.

Steven: Yes, I am aware. The CDE company project specifically had mentioned that "failure to attend and register will lead to the non-acceptance of the tender by the owner" whereas there is no such clause here. I want to ensure that all the nuances related to the execution of this specific project are taken care of before the bid is send.

Manoj: Fine. Keep me posted about your site visit.

Steven: Sure

(Steven visits the site on 20th November, 2016. He shares the insights of this visit with Manoj and Abhishek)

Command Center Annexure I

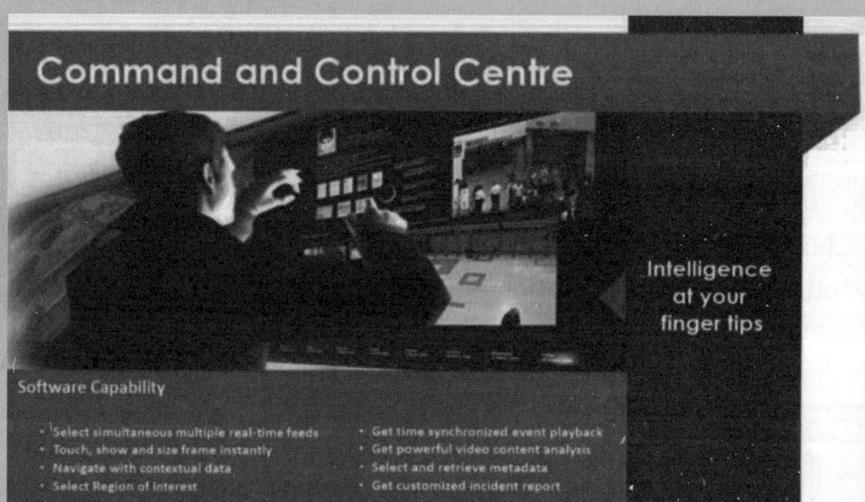

STAGE 5

BUILDING THE STAGE FOR NEGOTIATING FOR THE BID ON TECHNICAL AND COST PARAMETERS

Vignette 3 – 1st December, 2016 Zicom office

(On receipt of vendor quotes by the procurement team, the technical team scrutinizes and gets the best feasible products/services along with the most optimum pricing.)

Manoj (over the intercom) to Steven: I have received 3 quotes as per the specification discussed for the MNK project. I have mailed you the comparative chart depicting the quotations of these 3 vendors. As per our purchase policy and vendor analysis, vendor A fits the bill. I want you to look at it and discuss with your team.

Steven: Yes, certainly I will.

Manoj: I personally liked the quote sent by vendor A. Our experience in the past has always been positive with this vendor. But before we jump to conclusions, I want you to vet all the quotes. Tomorrow, the regional manager of Vendor A wants is to meet us at 3 pm. I hope you will be free at the time.

Steven: Yes, should not be a problem. Let's see what he's got to tell.

Manoj: Okay great. I will schedule the meeting tomorrow at 3 pm.

Vignette 4 – 2nd December, 2016 Conference room, Zicom's office, Mumbai

(Vendor A meets Manoj and Steven)

Vendor A: Thank you sir for sparing time for this meeting and giving me an opportunity to discuss this quotation further.

Manoj: Thank you for your quote and proposal. We sincerely appreciate the effort that you have put in submitting such a comprehensive proposal for our company.

Vendor A: It's my pleasure to serve such an esteemed client like Zicom.

Manoj: My team has considered the quote, and overall, we are happy with it. At the same time, we are going through an issue which has been outlined by our MD. The rates which you have quoted seem to be on the higher side, keeping in view of the prevailing rates in the international market

Vendor A: Sir, I have ensured that I offer the most competitive and affordable quote.

Steven: I sincerely appreciate the effort you put into determining the price of each unit and composing such a comprehensive proposal. Your thoroughness and professionalism is evident from the sheer effort at your end. But, times are changing fast and we analyzed all the quotations and they are giving us similar offerings.

Manoj: At my end, I had to research quotes from other vendors and was provided with two very reasonable quotations. While personally I would not like to work with any other supplier than you, I will have no say in the decision to choose one if the company is provided with a lower price quotation than yours. You realize that the first 4 products of your proposal are standard products in the market and we have been seeing the prices of these going down every few months. Technically, also your product features are same as the products from other competitors.

Vendor A: I value our continuing long-term association. But, I am assuring you that I have tried my best to give you these rates.

Manoj: Will it be possible to decrease the quote for this particular project so that we can continue working as we have in the past? I believe that if we sit down and discuss this, you can make suggestions as to what material costs can be excluded to bring the overall cost down. You can also work out the commercial terms of supply as you know that this project will require staggered delivery. The deployment time and the time for payment will also take a while.

[Vendor A, Manoj, and Steven negotiate point by point on the quotation to come at final consensus and at an agreed price of Rs. 35 lakhs]

STAGE 6

VENDOR SELECTION

Zicom selects its Original Equipment Manufacturer (OEM) based on the tender specifications and the following criteria: List of products manufactured, ownership status of the company, years of establishment, employee strength, plant location, production capacity, ISO certification, product certifications, financial status, order fulfilment capability, efficiency in delivery, and flexibility in payment. Keeping this in mind, vendor A is finalized.

Based on quotes given by Vendor A, there are 2 rounds of negotiation at Zicom's end.

1. Technical round: Key account manager plus technical and procurement team, to discuss and agree mutually on the technicalities, cite constraints of the offering.
2. Commercial round: key account manager plus MD, Mr. Pramoud Rao, to discuss on the financial, legal, payment terms, and milestones aspect of the offering. The bid offer is finalized for Rs 1.25 crores, keeping in mind the buffers for negotiating with the buyer. The lower bound limit for the project is set at 1.13 crores. (Annexure II)

Additionally, a final techno-commercial offer is sent to the customer, based on technical and commercial rounds. Based on the evaluating grounds, which usually qualifies to be a technically superior quote (T1) first and then the commercially competitive quote (L1), MNK meets each of the vendor for a negotiating round. Here are the excerpts from the meeting of Zicom team with MNK Ltd.

STAGE 7

NEGOTIATING FOR THE BID

Vignette 5 – 10th January 2017 at MNK's Office

(Mr. Pramoud Rao and *Mr. Abhishek from Zicom meet Mr. Ramesh Singh, the purchase head of MNK Ltd. along with Mr. Suhas Desai, consultant for security and surveillance at MNK Ltd.*)

Pramoud: Good Morning, Mr. Ramesh. We appreciate you giving us time from your hectic schedule. Please meet our key account manager, Mr. Abhishek.

Ramesh: We are thankful to you for your bid. Please meet our consultant, Mr. Suhas Desai who has been with us for the last 2 years. Well, I have one concern, Mr. Abhishek. We have never engaged ourselves in a business deal with you, how do we trust you with such a big order?

Pramoud: You are right. We have never transacted together. Our goal is to serve our clients to the best of our abilities and fulfill their security needs. We look for long-term association. In fact, I would like to place on record that our after-sales service is considered as best in the industry. Our policies and standards for technical product specifications, installation, and maintenance is diligently planned and methodically executed. These are as per your specified requirements.

Ramesh: Okay.Let's talk about the pricing. You have quoted Rs. 1.25 crores whereas your arch rival is ready to offer us at Rs. 1.12 crores.

Pramoud: Ramesh, the price differential is because of the superior quality hardware and dynamic software systems with easy upgrades. The Zicom Command Center is a terrific back-up service that we provide for remote sensing and diagnostics. Our service quality is unmatched with a very high percentage of repeat orders. We offer top of the line surveillance without hurting your bottom line.

Ramesh: That's fine, Pramoud, but you also need to understand that the bids by your rivals are very competitive and cost effective.

Pramoud: I think we can look at alternate CCTV camera brand with same technological qualities which should make us reduce the price by around 7 lakhs.

Ramesh: Pramoud, that's a good idea. As we are not compromising technological parameters, we can think of taking this ahead. Therefore, your bid price for us would be Rs. 1.18 crores.

Pramoud: That's right.

Suhas: But I have one concern. What happens if the CCTV system crashes?

Abhishek: I am glad you brought up this scenario. Since we are talking about a 24*7 security solution to safeguard your assets, you might have come across so many reports in the media where the customers come to know about their security system not functioning only after an untoward incident has occurred. Therefore, besides investing in the products, it is very important to have the system running all the time and any issue needs to be identified and addressed immediately. Hence, we always encourage our customers to look at Security as a Service (SaaS) like remotely managed services, besides products, whenever they compare us with competition.

Ramesh: We haven't heard about remotely managed electronic security services controlled by Command Centero how can we be sure of its benefits?

Abhsihek: This is a technology that many people are unaware of. However, it is not new by any means. Our robust Zicom Command Center is first in the country to give real-time analytics. Our research team has been working on fine tuning it, to create the most efficient and effective technology that we can offer.

Suhas: The rival bids that we received have quoted less than your bids.

Pramoud: Hmm. But our products are more reliable and upgradable as per your future requirements than any other in the industry. Our track record, our past clients and the number of awards received by us are testimony for our robust and dynamic service offering.

Ramesh: Your product looks great. But, we at MNK Ltd., are not very technologically inclined.

Suhas: See this is the first time MNK is entering a contract for electronic surveillance. So, I am sure you can understand our pressure and anxiety.

Abhishek: I understand your anxiety, but let me reassure you that we have been in the security and surveillance industry for the last two decades and have been working with a lot of key clients to advise them and build their surveillance infrastructure. In fact, a lot of them are first-time users of electronic surveillance systems and are highly satisfied with our services. Although the product has many features, they all are very easy to use and the integrated eSystem is very easy to navigate through. I can show you the testimonies of few customers who had similar concerns.

Ramesh: Okay, fair enough. Let me discuss this with our MD and will get back to you in this matter about our decision.

Pramoud: Thank you, Ramesh. We are glad that we could resolve all your doubts and concerns. Hoping for a positive reply from your end.

STAGE 8

POST NEGOTIATION EVALUATION AND PLANNING

Vignette 6 – 10th January 2017 outside MNK's Office

(The door closes. Pramoud and Abhishek take the elevator)

Pramoud: So, how did the meeting go?

Abhishek: I think the meeting went off very well. Ramesh and Suhas seem to be convinced with our company strengths and technical abilities. We should immediately contact Vendor A and discuss the concrete timelines for the project implementation.

(Pramoud gives a broad smile)

▶ QUESTIONS

1. Analyze and discuss a typical B2B buying process for a high-tech product in a tender contract format? Specify the pros and cons of the tender contract system.
2. Elaborate the common objections that have been raised in the final negotiation meet between Zicom and MNK Insurance Ltd.? Are they tenable?
3. Discuss the various avenues the Zicom followed to ensure that the company had covered all areas from a technical and cost perspective to ensure success on the negotiating table.
4. According to you, did Zicom bag this order? Why?
5. Explain the roles of various decision-making units in the B2B above case?

Note: Vignette 5 and 6 should be enacted in the class with participants representing Pramoud Rao, Ramesh Singh, Abhishek Bharadwaj, and Suhas Desai.

Annexure II

Particulars	Amount Rs.
Cost negotiated with Vendor A	35 lakhs
Cost of installation	20 lakhs
Cost of command center services	12 lakhs
Post warranty	05 lakhs
Zicom Profit – mandatory	40 lakhs
Scope for negotiation	13 lakhs
Quoted Price	**1.25 crores**

► ACKNOWLEDGEMENTS

- Ms Jinal Shah – Coordinator & Assistant Professor-Bachelor of Management Studies, SIES College of Commerce and Economics, Mumbai for content building and drafting the case study.
- Mr Pramoud Rao – MD-Zicom
- Mr Manoj Khadkikar – Head Channel Solutions Group-Zicom
- Ms Cynthia Gokhale – DGM Marketing and PR-Zicom

CASE 8

Facebook: Business Connections in India and China

Facebook dominates the global market due to its creativity and adaptability. It used approaches that are relevant and useful in different countries. In this case study, we will see how Facebook adapted itself to become one of the most creative and innovative organizations and gained massive success not only in developed nations but also in emerging markets such as India and China. One of its pioneering efforts in emerging nations was enabling videos to work on a low bandwidth as these nations always have had issues with the internet connectivity. Additionally, their campaigns were very consumer centric. For one such video, Facebook stated its mission in the following manner: "Connect with the next billion". This message denotes the connection with the population of India. Facebook also has a mobile app which is extensively used in India. There are around 1.5 billion active users on this apps on a monthly basis. While connecting with Instagram which is a photo sharing app, there are 300 million users (Thomas, 2016).

► Business Approaches for India

In India, three billion individuals can access the internet currently. With this extensive usage, Facebook has US $ 3.8 billion ad revenue on a quarterly basis. These in-depth penetrations and bottom lines are achieved by Facebook by using three approaches:

1. Facebook works everywhere: This is an excellent strategy of Facebook as it works with 4G LTE, 4G, 3G, and 2G connections. In most of the places in India, there are persistent connectivity issues. Here, 2G helps in the usage of Facebook. It is so effective that it works with all manners of connections and phones. The product team of the company was successful in creating various formats of this social media platform to match different phones and connections. Another important aspect was the nature of news feed stories and how people loaded them on their phones. For example, when the network is slow, a user would get those stories that they were looking for and load low resolution pictures. More importantly, the users never saw the buffering symbol as it was considered to be very irritating On the same line, users could see the previously loaded pictures and content even when the internet connection was not available. To facilitate this service, Facebook had a new initiative known as 2G Tuesday. It means that on every Tuesday, every employee has to sign up for 2G for an hour to experience slow internet connectivity. This practice helped the company understand what could be done when the internet is slow.

2. All users lead to making money: Facebook had to make money. Thus, it aimed to offer new features pertaining to ads even during slow connections. This is specially seen in the emerging nations such as India.

   To compensate this loss, they focused more on making money from the developed nations such as US and Europe as they have better connectivity. Additionally, in emerging countries, there are creative ways by which the ads are managed. For example, approaches that connect with the regional individuals and use local infrastructure were developed. They used an approach which was really effective known as "missed call" for the Indian market. Users were not using their data plan to make these missed calls. Advertisers were paying the data costs for sending the pictures, content of the celebrity via Facebook. More specifically, they also made adjustments with the ads. They developed slideshows ads that created videos in the low bandwidth. All these approaches enhanced the product experience, thus helping advertisers reach their audiences in a creative manner and Facebook earn their revenue.
3. Enhancing the reach and use of the internet: This approach basically worked for countries like India as the company had to motivate people to use the internet. To do this, Facebook does not focus on the government, local companies, and so on. The company developed ways in which people could easily get online via non-profit organization such as internet.org. Additionally, Facebook had collaborated with the local partners such as free basics which allowed the users to be online without paying so that they could use Facebook and other apps easily (Chu, 2014). This free basic have connection to solar energy sources connected with their network. Thus, it can also work also in those areas where fiber optics cables do not function. This practice helped the company allure new sets of users to come online and join Facebook and increase their ad revenue. Similarly, Google is also floating internet balloons in most of the remote areas ("Forbes", 2016).

► Customized Services for Indian Market

Facebook would like to reach out to everyone and connect with the all the users by letting them know how and when to connect. To do so, Facebook provided hyper-local services website for India. It provided all the relevant information about the local services and the businesses. This information is based on the selection of the user in terms of their location. There are around 80 services that are provided by Facebook. These services include plumbing, hair care, home care, events and so on. These services have user ratings and reviews. This segment is highly competitive in India as there are other players such as Urban Clap, house joy, Quickr services, and so on. These players operate in this space. These players charge a 10–30% commission on each transaction. However, Facebook has the cutting edge over these players as it has more than 2 million registered users who have small and medium businesses in India. These services also helped the company increase the ad revenue and leverage its growth. This resulted in an increase in the average revenue per user increment as there were 4000–6000 orders regularly on a daily basis. Further, this sector is very unorganized and has the potential to grow at US$ 100 to US$ 400 million (Nair, & Kashyap, 2016; Joishy, 2012).

► Marketers' Challenges and Approaches for India

However, Facebook realized that in India, the advertising revenues are comparatively less than in developed nations such as US and UK. This is because of the low per capita income in this country. Facebook would like to capitalize all the ways in which it could increase the ad revenue with a high and strong user base. Facebook helped the small and medium-sized businesses possess their own web pages so that they could connect easily, and hence, generating ad revenues from them.

Another strategy of Facebook was to connect with the start-ups as they cumulatively raised the funding of US$ 180 million. With all these strategies and approaches that Facebook India has used, the profit after tax increased to 33% and to 16 crores within a year. However, there are 138 million users in India. But the revenues for the company is still lower. The average earning is less than ₹ 9 per user in India as compared to ₹ 630 in the US. These numbers are less in India as many companies in this country started investing in digital and social media platforms but 70% of their budget is provided to Google. Thus, Google has a revenue of ₹ 4000 crores in India after having spent a decade in this country. However, Facebook has forecasted that companies would spread out their budget and invest more in Facebook for their ads in the coming years in India (IANS, 2016). More specifically, Reliance, a telecom company in India, has provided much subsidized rate for internet tariff to all the users in the country and this approach is the game changer for many organizations, including Facebook. Now, the problem in India is about net neutrality. The telecom regulator, TRAI have kept the deployment of commercial services on hold.

Marketers in India think that Facebook is the best platform to disseminate information, especially when they have to target micro-level consumers in terms of their locality. To leverage this opportunity, Facebook is alluring more advertisers and marketers by initiating the services such as Facebook Lite. This service is provided for a large number of users in India who use 2G connections. This service provided them the facility to quickly download their videos with this connection.

Interestingly, a market research company from New York has estimated that by 2019, the digital spend in India would be greater than that of France, Spain, Italy, and Brazil in terms of metrics. For example, companies related to mobile phones, telecom operators, automobile, FMCG organizations, while targeting young consumers, use these platforms extensively. This opportunity is significantly related to the economics of Facebook in India ("Challenges to Facebook International Strategy - The India Case", 2017).

► Complexities and Business Approaches for China

Similarly, the same opportunity is observed in China for Facebook as there are multiple users. However, China has blocked Facebook since 2009. This is because Mark Zuckerberg, CEO, Facebook posted his picture on this social media while he was jogging in smoggy Beijing. This post showed China and its capital in a disparaging light. This portrayal would create a negative image of China and its environmental policies. Further, because it was a Westerner who was seen jogging in the smog-filled environment, it created a complicit negative comparison between China's and the

Western world's living conditions. Finally, Zuckerberg was seen as an outsider with no moral authority to comment on another sovereign nation. Thus, China has further tightened their restrictions on internet freedom in terms of rules and regulations for foreign technology-oriented companies. After understanding these restrictions in China, the CEO of Facebook proposed providing a localized version of Facebook in China. This proposal was approved by the government. But, the company will have to follow some rules:

1. Overlaps: There should be very limited overlaps of this local Facebook version with the international version as the content would be censored. Facebook also has to follow the norms dictated by China Cybersecurity law, and the state administration of press, publication, radio, and film and television. They have clearly dictated the norms that the foreign internet company has to follow to operate in China.
2. User data has to be saved in China: The users' data is owned by the company. Further, there is an ongoing debate in the US and EU about this issue. However, the Chinese government made it very clear to Facebook that they could use and extract data from Facebook in China whenever they wanted. The China Cybersecurity law has provided the norms to Facebook regarding data storage as well. Companies like Uber, LinkedIn and so on save their data with the local telecom companies in China. Facebook preserves their data essentially in states and countries such as North Carolina, Oregon, Texas, and Sweden. However, in China they might have to share the data when there is a legal injunction by the Government.
3. Develop partnership with local companies: Facebook had to develop partnerships with the local companies in China. This is because China wanted that Facebook to share the experiences and enhance the mutual understanding about people and businesses among common individuals who are from China. They specifically mentioned that Facebook had to find a buddy and share with them the means of running businesses effectively.
4. Develop "great Firewall of Facebook": China censors the social media and internet data in different ways which are connected with the "great fire walls". They ensure that the users do not get access to certain webpages and blocked sites related to Google or The New York Times. Further, certain apps and fake IP addresses can be blocked very easily and quickly. China uses different kinds of algorithms to track the post that have used sensitive words and prevent them from becoming viral.

Specifically, they have human censors who manually remove the posts that the authorities have dictated. For example, they may remove the posts that are politically sensitive. Thus, if and when Facebook enters China and starts its operation, it will have to create the largest and complex censorship systems.

In China, users and organizations are screened thoroughly by the Chinese official accounts. Data from the overseas accounts are also saved at the overseas servers. This means that users in China may not see all the posts of their friends who are from outside China. Further, the posts from Zuckerberg were also removed and government-friendly version of Facebook works in China now (Isaac, 2016). However, Facebook has to share data about any users who could be activists, journalists and scientist with the government. If they do not share the data, Facebook would be held responsible for all the activities that users might have undertaken and be punished for the same.

Therefore, Zuckerberg stated that while "connecting everybody" Facebook had to investment heavily and underwent severe scrutiny based on different tests (Horwitz, 2015).

▶ Way Forward

India is poised to have a growing and massive middle class in its economy. Further, the spending power of the affluent class will have increased two-fold by 2025. A McKinsey report stated that the average household income would be three times more in India and would become fifth largest consumer economy by 2025. Their global consumption would be around 5.8% by 2020. More specifically, 600 million people would have access to the internet in India by 2020. This connectivity would change the consumer behavior of the users in the country. These global citizens would demand more design, performance, and technology. They would, in turn, become key drivers for Facebook in the Indian market. However, Facebook will have to understand the bureaucracy and regulatory issues in India along with the heterogeneous consumer behavior which originates from various cultures (Mathur, 2016).

Facebook has had a tough time conducting business in China. But, India provides ample freedom to undertake business operations. The language, cost, and workforce is also better in India as compared to China. This is because India has a liberal economy and China prefers Chinese companies exclusively. The issue with Facebook was that it entered very late in India as compared to Google. India is also gearing up for increasing efficiency in business operations and human resources aided by new governmental policies. This would be very beneficial for Facebook. This government is open to listening to the challenges of Facebook such as electricity, education systems, and slow internet speed. Subsequently, Prime Minister Narendra Modi started the new initiative in the country known as "Digital India"—an initiative to connect the length and breadth of India and put villages on the digital map. He also visited the Facebook office in Seattle as a part of his initiative to improve the technology and infrastructure set-up in India.

Facebook will continue to connect people of different countries and deal with their complexities creatively to derive a solution which would be win-win for both the stakeholders. It would thus enable the users to share their opinions, ideas, pictures, and videos within the ambit of norms and regulation of the specific countries. It will also connect users with other social media platforms effectively such as Instagram, WhatsApp, and so on. Facebook would also help the advertisers and marketers by providing them the relevant data so that revenue can be increased and user experience can be enhanced (Abutaleb, 2015).

CASE 9

Who will buy Xylo – Mahindra and Mahindra Automotive Sector*

Rajesh Jejurikar was instrumental in the Scorpio success story and worked on a robust marketing plan which took Mahindra & Mahindra (M&M) to leadership position in Utility Vehicle (UV) space. He had had set high standards for the marketing team at M&M. After experiencing many good years and fortunes with Scorpio, the business was now stagnating. As a leader in UV space, they had a choice to defend their shares or snatch from competition, but Rajesh with his team wanted to grow the category as they saw the potential for utility vehicles in India. On a hot and humid afternoon in 2006, he along with Vivek Nayer, the senior Vice President (marketing) at M&M, and other team members were looking at consumer and market data to decide on the marketing strategy for Xylo. And the first question was - *"Who will buy Xylo"? Who should be the target audience for Xylo?*

► Mahindra and Mahindra: Background

The USD 16.7 billion[1] Mahindra Group was an Indian multinational headquartered at Mumbai, India, with operations in over 100 countries. It was one of the most reputed Indian businesses with market leadership in utility vehicles and tractors, and was the largest tractor manufacturer (by volume) in the world. They had presence in almost every segment of the automobile industry, ranging from two-wheelers to UVs (utility vehicles), SUVs (sports utility vehicles), and CVs (commercial vehicles). Mahindra & Mahindra was one of the 20 largest companies in India in 2009 and Forbes ranked Mahindra among the top 200 most reputable companies in the world. M&M was the flagship company of the Rs.55 billion (US$ 1.2 billion) Mahindra Group. Mahindra & Mahindra started manufacturing utility vehicles in 1954 in collaboration with Willys Overland Corporation and light commercial vehicles in 1965. In 1982, the International Harvester brand was discontinued and the "Mahindra" brand was born as leaders in tractors market.

The market was changing and consumers were evolving to seek lifestyle and better-quality products. M&M was hence looking to be a market leader in the automotive sector, especially in the premium utility vehicle sector. They had already made a foray into this space with few offerings in utility vehicle space.

► Automobile Industry in India: History and Evolution

The automobiles industry in India was at 0.7 million vehicles per annum in year 2003, and had been growing at CAGR of 8% in the period of 1999 to 2003. In 2004, cars had a growth rate of 26% and a market share of 80%. Utility vehicles had a growth rate of 37% and a market share of 20%.[2]

This case was presented by Mahindra team at SPJIMR Marketing Impact Awards 2010. The company authorized SPJIMR to use the case content and material for academic dissemination.

With volumes of 275,556 units in FY10, the Utility Vehicles (UVs) accounted for little over 13% of the total market with growth averaging at 9% over 2006–09. The UV segment was primarily dominated by SUVs priced in the Rs. 7–11 lacs range. In line with the passenger car segment, top three players in the UV segment accounted for over 85% of the market, of which two were domestic players. A sizeable part of the UV market also catered to the people mover segment, which had been one of the key growth drivers striving on demand from the growing IT/ITES sector.[3] Mahindra and Mahindra dominated this segment and enjoyed a leadership position (exhibit 1)

► Mahindra Mission

M&M had a vision to continue the domination of utility vehicle (UV) market in India and be a global niche player. The founders of Mahindra passionately believed that Indians were second to none. They had a dream to make M&M known worldwide for the quality, durability, and reliability of its products and services, and at the same time, play an active role in the development of the nation. They wanted to retain their domestic market leadership with over 50% market share in the Indian utility vehicle segment by catering to all segments and also create their name in the global market.

► Utility Vehicle Segment

A utility vehicle is designed to carry out a specific task with more efficacy than a general-purpose vehicle. Sports utility vehicles (SUV) were like a station wagon but built on a light-truck chassis and equipped with four-wheel drive or all-wheel drive amongst other off-road hardware. Their primary purpose was to display superior off-road and towing capabilities, teamed with higher seating capacity. MUVs were larger vehicles which could tackle a wide range of applications. They typically allowed easy conversion between multiple combinations of passenger and luggage capacity.[4]

Utility vehicle segment was further divided into "pick ups", "soft tops" and "hard tops" (exhibit 2). The buyers of pick-ups used it for goods transport. Soft-top buyers generally used the vehicle for commercial purpose. Soft tops were rarely bought for the personal usage. Hard tops could be further divided into "low-end hard tops" and "high-end hard tops". Low-end hard tops were used for commercial purposes. High-end hard tops or sports utility vehicles could be compared to cars with respect to luxury and driving comfort. The buyers of these vehicles were typically luxury car buyers and a SUV was his second vehicle that they used as personal transport vehicle and for weekend leisure activities.

In India, M&M was the specialist in utility vehicles. They manufactured and marketed all kinds of utility vehicles i.e. soft-tops, hard-tops, and sports utility vehicles. In 2003, Mahindra & Mahindra commanded a market share of 36% in the utility vehicle market, and had significant presence in the individual as well as institutional segments, like the police force, armed forces, Government and large public and private sector companies. Market share rose to 40% in 2005–06. Scorpio launch and marketing push given to it led to this increase in M&M market share in the utility space.

▶ Mahindra Context

Mahindra, hitherto a leader in the UV segment, was fast witnessing stagnating market share. There was an increase in share in 2005 but it was stagnant at 40% all through 2007. Global players were entering the auto market and aggressively launching various products. There were more than 40 automobile brands and more than 14,38,000 cars and utility vehicles on road which led to brand proliferation and loss of differentiating brand proposition. Mahindra had a wide product portfolio but lacked products that catered to the modern urban consumer needs. The markets where Mahindra was strong were stagnating. The urban markets were seeing all the growth and action but the Mahindra range did not offer a product for those markets.

With stagnant market shares for Mahindra and overall UV sector seeing the decline, there was a need to grow the category. M&M were leaders, and hence, onus of growing the category primarily rested with them. This involved the need to expand the portfolio with differentiated brand proposition. However, the challenge of cannibalization, ROI (return on investment) erosion, and profitability could further affect the business. Rajesh, Vivek, and other team members prepared the proposal to look at new consumer segments and build a synergetic yet differentiated portfolio with an offering for every segment. This, when presented to the management body, was accepted without much qualms as it promised a growth trajectory for the company in utility vehicle space.

▶ Portfolio and Market Relationship

From the time it produced the Willy's Jeep, M&M was very clear in terms of its portfolio and market relationship. Willy's Jeep was meant for rough terrain and interiors of rural India where the approach roads were not available, and for the armed forces who needed a vehicle that was sturdy and could handle difficult terrain. The deep understanding of market needs was reflected in their entire portfolio. Exhibit 3 gives the competitor framework and USP of its other four offerings (2006–7) in both hard tops and soft tops.

The portfolio, though well balanced, was not addressing the changing consumer needs. It was not diverse enough and did not have offerings for high-end growing segments. Therefore, the company not only had the challenge of growing the market share from stagnant 40% but also was apprehensive of cannibalization in case of portfolio expansion. The team, however, knew that M&M was known for technologically superior product launches based on robust consumer research and had a marketing acumen to build differentiated portfolio.

▶ Consumer Context

The Indian economy was moving into higher growth (8.5%+) trajectory. In addition to steady economic growth, the passenger vehicle industry was benefitting from India's demographic dividend, which was reflected in its young population (50% of population was under the age of 25), steadily improving dependency ratio, growing urbanization, and trend towards smaller, nuclear families. These trends, in turn, resulted in higher savings and increased ability to purchase vehicles. In India, the per capita GDP doubled to US$ 3,270 between 2000 and 2009, while car prices (adjusting for the decline in duties) remained almost at the same level as they were five years back, thereby increasing flexibility to own cars.[5] With over 65–70% of cars being financed in India, availability of financing options at competitive rates was one of factors driving growth.

While these changes led to creating a market with demanding customers, the basic psyche of the Indian buyer did not change. They were still looking for Value for Money (VFM) in terms of low unit cost, operating economics packaged with modern style and robust design. M&M conducted a 100-day study among their consumers to find the gap areas and what they were looking for. Managers and researchers met consumers across segments to know what people wanted, what they thought of utility space and their feelings about the category. The word cloud was prepared to understand "what people wanted?" The team analyzed that customers wanted a large car with distinctive looks & experience pleasure of owning a car that reflected their personality. Functionally, they wanted their vehicle to be spacious, luxurious, and fun with an image that was neither too fuddy-duddy nor too sophisticated. They were looking for "their space"— a car which was comfortable and help them get more from life!

M&M started a customer-centric approach of building a new product, and Xylo was born. This was a MUV which felt as luxurious as a sedan but was young, contemporary, and spacious. Vivek Nayer, Senior Vice-President, Marketing wanted to launch Xylo as a truly multifaceted car with the premium stature of a sedan and the aggressiveness of an SUV. As the technology platform and production was being planned, Vivek with his team were busy looking at marketing strategy decisions and profile the customer for Xylo.

► Consumer Segmentation

In the passenger segment, M&M had two prime offerings—Bolero and Scorpio. Bolero was an entry level UV and Scorpio was the premium SUV. The challenge was to identify a new unexplored space and come up with the customized new offering. M&M conducted opportunity analysis and studied various consumer segments after mapping their preference for various brands. The segments were defined based on "benefits sought" or "what customers look for in their cars". **Exhibit 4** gives the opportunity map and outlines various consumer segments.

Basic Segment: People who were upgrading from two-wheeler to four wheelers and were seeking benefits of good mileage and high value for money. Both cost of acquisition and maintenance were important to these customers.

Value-Seeking Segment: The first-time car buyers or even those who had experienced the basic four-wheeler and were looking for more features and upgrades. They sought value for money with low maintenance cost.

Comfort Seeking Segment: People who wanted greater comfort, features, and upgraded models. For them aesthetics and comfort were more important than low acquisition cost, and hence, they were ready to pay a premium for better comfort and quality.

Individualist: These were young, successful customers with greater ability to pay and were belonging to higher socio-economic segments. They looked at their cars as an extension of themselves, and hence, wanted their cars to have a personality that resonates with their own. This was a less price-sensitive segment.

Status Seeking: Customers for whom their car was a reflection their own status and social standing. These were premium sophisticated customers who wanted known brands and quality experience.

M&M identified the various segments using in-depth consumer research and consumer profile data. Vivek asked his team to classify the various car/UV models available in passenger car segment based on price. These were then mapped to consumer segments based on preference scores and purchase intention. The opportunity map helped the team understand various competition offerings, and hence, the potential in various segments.

▶ Choosing The Xylo Customer: Targeting Decision

The opportunity map emphasized that though price points were not very far away, consumers had distinct needs, and hence, it was critical to build differentiated brands for various segments. The map clearly showed that though Scorpio from M&M was focused on status-seeking consumer, Bolero was spreading thin from basic segments to other high-end segments with its many variants. This strategy was hitting the brand profitability and ROI as its credibility to deliver on their desired needs of high-nd segments was low. Though, the company wanted to position Bolero as an entry level SUV, the map revealed that it was spread thin and was not present in VFM segment. This made the task of brand differentiation and focus more cumbersome as the danger of cannibalization was high.

Rajesh wanted the marketing team to profile the TG for all portfolio brands. The analysis and strategy documents showed that Bolero was targeted at value-seeking segment. The Bolero customer could be defined as one who was youthful, "rooted", value seeker, and progressive. Scorpio was a premium SUV targeted at a status-conscious male who was successful, sophisticated, aggressive, and expected the best from life.

M&M decided to focus on comfort seeking consumer segment for Xylo. It was targeted at males who were young, aspirational, and wanted comfort and space in their cars. He was a young achiever who worked hard but used to party harder. He was socially active, cool, trendy, and indulgent. Based on the target audience and their profile, M&M defined the value proposition for each of its offerings (Exhibit 5). Xylo was positioned as cool, trendy, and spacious car.

Rajesh and his team knew that prime competition in that space came from Toyota. While Toyota's low-end Innova E was priced at Rs. 7.60 lakh, the low-end version of Mahindra MPV, Xylo E2, was priced at Rs. 6.24 and came with greater comforts, including power steering, power windows, and central locking. Toyota's high-end Innova G4 was priced Rs. 9.29 lakh while Mahindra's high-end variant Xylo E8 costed Rs. 7.69 lakh and offered additional comforts including digital drive assist system and flatbed front seats.[6] Rajesh Jejurikar said, "Overall, the brand name, Xylo, implies luxury, high fashion, and technology and was aimed to create a futuristic connect."

The three new platform products were also crucial for M&M to synergize its production strategy. Although Xylo had a new vehicle architecture and component structure, it had similar engine and transmission parts like Scorpio. Xylo and Scorpio assembly lines were not rigid and could increase or decrease the production of one or the other depending on the demand. However, Vivek wanted to replicate the success of Scorpio with Xylo. The target was decided and the value proposition was also identified. But now was a time to find out where these customers were and reach them with a resonating and persuasive communication strategy.[7]

M&M is betting big on Xylo, which packed in a number of bells and whistled like the flat.

► QUESTIONS

1. Analyze the segments identified by Mahindra for utility vehicles? What was the basis of this segmentation?
2. Can you identify any other variable for segmentation which M&M could have used?
3. What were the considerations in choosing "comfort" segment for Xylo?
4. If the company plans to launch another brand, which segment they should be looking at?

► APPENDIX

EXHIBIT 1

UTILITY VEHICLE SEGMENT: MARKET SHARES%

	FY06	FY07	FY08	FY09	FY10	FY11	FY12
M&M	43.2%	40.8%	42.7%	47.1%	55.2%	55.8%	52.6%
Toyota	18.9%	19.8%	19.7%	17%	19.7%	19.6%	20.3%
Tata Motors	19.5%	21.8%	20.3%	18.5%	13%	12.9%	13.4%
Others	18.4%	17.7%	17.7%	17.4%	12.1%	11.7%	13.7%

Source: *SIAM Data; * Till February 2011*

EXHIBIT 2

PRODUCT PORTFOLIO

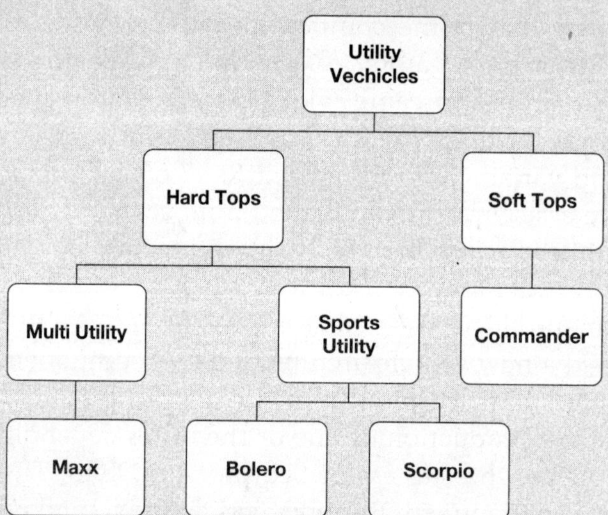

Source: *Company documents*

EXHIBIT 3

M&M BRAND PORTFOLIO AND COMPETITIVE MAPPING

Brand	Positioning	Competitive Framework
Commander	Reliability, Trust	Commercial vehicles
MaXX	Offers more	Passenger vehicles and mini vans
Bolero	Looks and Features	MUV/Entry level SUV
Scorpio	Car plus/Lifestyle	Premium car/SUV

Source: *Company documents*

EXHIBIT 4

OPPORTUNITY MAPPING WITH CONSUMER SEGMENTS

Price Range	Basic	Value for Money	Comfort	Individualistic	Status
1–2.5L	Maruti 800, Omni, Tata Nano				
2.5–4L		Alto, Estilo, Spark, Indica, Santro, A-star	Wagon R,		i10, Honda Small Car,
4–6L	**MaXX, Bolero DI**	Ikon, Indigo	Accent, Aveo, Dzire, **Bolero SLX/SLE**, Punto	Gypsy	Ritz, Swift, Getz, i20
6–8L		**Logan**, Indigo Dicor	Amby, Tavera, Rhino	Fusion, **Bolero Stinger/Vlx**	Jazz, Fabia, Verna, SX4, Linea, Fiesta,
8–10L			Innova, Tata Aria	Getaway, Xenon	City, Octavia, Optra, **Scorpio**
>10L					D segment & above cars, High end SUV's

Source: *Company documents*

EXHIBIT 5

SUMMARY OF TG AND VALUE PROPOSITIONS OF VARIOUS BRANDS IN M&M PORTFOLIO

Brand	Consumer Segment	Source of business	Value Proposition
Scorpio	Status Seeker	High end SUVs/ C-segment cars	Power, Thrill, Adventure, Attitude and Status
Bolero	Value Seeker	Low end UVs/B-C Diesel cars	Fun/Adventure, Youthful, Affordable, Dependable
Xylo	Comfort Seeker	High end MPVs/ C-segment cars	Luxurious space & comfort, Cool & Trendy

Source: *Company documents*

EXHIBIT 6

UTILITY VEHICLES GROWTH RATES-M&M AND NON M&M VEHICLES POST LAUNCH OF XYLO ON 2009

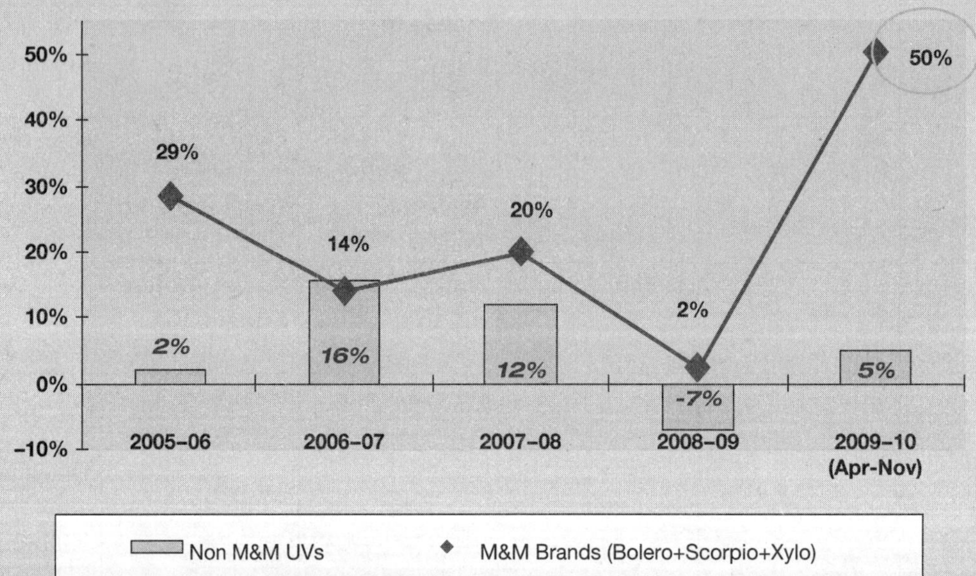

Source: *Company documents*

Indian automobile industry registered a 68% increase in sales at 10.05 lakh units in Dec 2009. Passenger car segment witnessed a growth of 40.27% at 115,268 units and the upward trend was also seen its Sports Utility Vehicles or the SUVs market[8] ICRA report 2010 highlighted that the domestic demand for passenger vehicles grew at 21.2% during the 2009–10.[9] Xylo was awarded MUV of the year 2009 award by CNBC, NDTV and Zigwheels

CASE 10 Kellogg's Cornflakes in India: Finding a Platform that Connects

"Mothers know what they want and when; we can't push our offering to them without giving them a reason they value," the Head of Marketing at Kellogg's India clarified. The Kellogg's cornflakes marketing team was struggling to find an appropriate positioning platform for the brand to increase sales and ensure brand growth. The brand was globally accepted but its journey in India has been bumpy. They had struggled to find a suitable place in consumer's heart and mind, and again they were rethinking the growth strategy.

▶ Breakfast Market in India

The breakfast cereal market in India was pegged at Rs. 12 billion in 2014, an almost 15% growth from Rs. 10.4 billion in 2013, and was expected to grow at a CAGR of 13% over the five-year period. Due to increased health consciousness among consumers, hot cereals and muesli were the fastest growing product categories. Among hot cereals, oats had gained the highest popularity registering a 33% growth in 2014.[1]

Cereal was not a popular breakfast item for Indians, and hence, the market was dominated by international brands from Kellogg's and Pepsico. Bagry's India Ltd and Mohan Meakin were the only two Indian players in the market. Kellogg's India Ltd had the first-mover advantage and was the undisputed market leader with 37% value share in 2014.[2] Regional players had a competitive edge over bigger brands because of their robust distribution network. Competition also stemmed from other FMCG chains that did not necessarily have packaged breakfast as their core product offering, for example, ready-to-eat players like MTR and Britannia with its range of ready-to-cook *upma*, porridge, and *poha*. These products provided consumers with healthy options that were not just quick but also healthy.[3]

▶ Consumer Behavior Towards Breakfast

India did not have the culture of breakfast. A typical, average middle-class Indian family did not have breakfast on a regular basis like their western counterparts. Breakfast was always combined with lunch—"Brunch" as it was popularly called. Breakfast habits (brunch) in India, for the most part, were inclined towards hot, cooked regional items, like flattened rice flakes (*chivda/poha*) in western and central India, whole wheat grits (*dalia*) and *parathas* in northern India along with traditional regional staples such as idli or dosa in the south.[4] In the earlier days, women prepared fresh breakfast for the family. Serving ready-to-eat meals were not part of the cultural norm and such options were also not widely available.

However with urbanization, dual-working households, and lifestyle changes, there was a greater need for convenience. This was also coupled with increasing disposable income and health consciousness. Increasing awareness of health and susceptibility of Indians towards lifestyle ailments like heart disease and diabetes yielded a greater demand for value-added healthy breakfast options.[5] Hence, consumers, especially in urban areas, preferred a quick-fix breakfast and cereals would fit the bill. The influence of Western lifestyles and "eating out" trends also played a significant role in opening the gateway for experimenting with different tastes and varying eating preferences.[6] This transition from traditional to modern breakfast took place among young Indians (24–35 years), mostly from dual income families. Choice of breakfast options was induced by personal factors like time constraint, work timings, social groups, and family members.[7]

► Kellogg's Entry in India

In the late 1980s, ready-to-eat cereal giant and market leader, Kellogg's had reached peak sales occupying a 40% market share in the US. The company had its presence in 18 countries and over 20 plants worldwide with annual sales of over $ 6 billion. However, in the 1990s, competition got tougher and Kellogg's began to struggle when its nearest rival when General Mills introduced Cheerios brand. There was little room for growth in core markets; therefore, the company started looking beyond its traditional American and European countries as a potential cereal-consuming market.[8]

India was a lucrative target market with population of over 950 million, out of which 250 million were middle class and untapped. In 1991, India went through an economic liberalization and removed the barriers to international trade. Three years later, Kellogg's decided to invest $ 65 million towards launching its number one brand, Corn Flakes, in India. "Even if Kellogg's had 2% market share at 18 million consumers they would have a larger market than US itself," said Bhagirat B Merchant, Director of Bombay Stock Exchange in 1994.[9]

► Positioning at Launch

Globally, Kellogg's cornflakes were positioned on the "fun and taste" platform, and they emphasized on the crispiness of its flakes. When Kellogg's entered the Indian market in 1994, it positioned itself to families/households on the health platform, thus emphasizing on the nutritional benefits of the cereal. They tried to communicate to consumers that traditional Indian breakfast options were not as healthy, and hence, cornflakes were a good choice. This was done based on the insight that Indians consumers were not habituated to cereals as a breakfast item and needed to be educated to create acceptance and liking for not just the brand but cereal as a category.

Kellogg's kicked off its India entry with three variants of breakfast cereal: Corn Flakes, Wheat Flakes, and Rice Flakes, packaged with an emphasis on the crispiness of its flakes compared to local cereals. These cereals were best served with cold milk without adding sugar. The tagline to reinforce the positioning was- "Jaago jaise bhi, lo Kellogg's hi" ("No matter how you start your day, start it with Kellogg's"). However, the proposition did not find much credibility with households. Average Indian did not pay much importance to iron/vitamin intake.[10] The nutritional benefit was not a differentiated and strong enough proposition for Indians to change their habits and move away from traditional items as they considered their food to be equally or more nutritious.

The initial sales were impressive but Kellogg's knew that this was a result of one-off purchases. Cereals were a new item for the Indian consumer and after the initial excitement wore off, repeat purchases were few. Another barrier to repeat purchase was the high price.[11] A 500 grams box of corn flakes was almost 30% costlier than its nearest competitor. Indians did not find value in spending so much for an expensive breakfast and often the leftovers from the previous day were cooked or served differently for breakfast next day. In certain households, corn flakes were reserved as a Sunday or special occasions treat.[12] Also, the emphasis on crispy flakes failed in India as consumers were used to hot milk which made cornflakes soggy. This further diluted the Kellogg's brand promise. On the heels of continuous unimpressive sales, Kellogg's realized that their breakfast option was diametrically opposite to what generations of Indians have been eating. The typical Indian breakfast was still hot, home-made, heavy-as-a-meal, and savory rather than sweet. What Kellogg's was offering was ready-to-eat, best served with cold milk, and bland unless you add a sweetener.

In early 1996, defending the company's products, Managing Director, Avronsart said, "Kellogg's India is not here to change breakfast eating habits. What the company proposes is to offer consumers around the world a healthy, nutritious, convenient, and easy-to-prepare alternative in the breakfast eating habit. It was not just a question of providing a better alternative to traditional breakfast eating habits but also developing a taste for grain-based foods in the morning".[13]

Indian consumers did not perceive the Kellogg's differentiators relevant. They were not looking for thicker and crispier flakes with iron and vitamin. They sought basic health and taste which their traditional food and other competitor brands were also fulfilling.

► Repositioning and Product Extensions

Kellogg's saw that Indian households were difficult to target and moved their focus to kids with the launch of two of its highly successful international brands, Chocos in September 1996 and Frosties in April 1997. Chocos were wheat scoops coated with chocolate, while Frosties had sugar frosting on individual flakes. Frosties addressed the shortcomings of plain cereals because they were ready-sweetened which sweeten the milk when it is added to the bowl. Both these variants were not positioned as breakfast items but as snack items on the proposition of fun and taste combined with health. Now the mother was urged to give Chocos as a mid-meal snack to fulfil nutrition requirement.

These variants found feet in the market and targeting kids helped. However, in 1998, Kellogg's again tried targeting families and households by "Indianizing" its cereal range with the "Mazza" brand. Mazza cereals were available in fusion of local flavours like mango-elaichi, coconut-kesar and rose.[14] The variant did not work. Mazza was more to do with the taste of the product and many consumers thought these were too outlandish.[15]

In 1999, Kellogg's began offering fortified cereals. The "Iron Shakti" cornflakes positioned on the nutrient value of cornflakes and addressed iron deficiency in children. The nutrition platform was more focused and relevant here as no other brand or product spoke of iron supplement. This became the differentiator and sales increased by 17%. Making the brand and proposition sound Indian by using words like "Iron Shakti" and "Calcium Shakti" gave it a local feel.[16] This approach was more successful than the brand's previous attempt to imply that the traditional Indian breakfast was not nutritious—messaging which made the Indian housewife rather indignant. The proposition this time was a nutritious and fun breakfast for kids coupled with goodness of iron (which mothers worry about).

Besides positioning, Kellogg's also changed the communication. It removed the rooster which had an integral association with Kellogg's globally from all its advertisements in India. The promotions focused on inducing product trial by targeting schools across the country. In March 1996, the company gave out specially designed 50 gm packs to shoppers at select retail stores, and door-to-door sampling exercise offering one-serve sachets to housewives in the city.[17]

However, the company knew that very few Indians had breakfast and they could grow only by growing the category. In 1997, they launched the "Kellogg Breakfast Week" in Mumbai, Delhi, and Chennai, a community-oriented initiative to create and increase awareness. The campaign focused on making people aware about the prevention of anemia, an iron deficiency disorder, and conducted a series of nutrition workshops to educate individuals and families.[18]

As the brand had sub-segmented the market and offered specific customized variants to each with the relevant proposition, its agency, JWT, wanted to identify the triggers that enabled customers to move towards this category. Their research suggested that though Kellogg's was positioned to kids, they were consumed by the entire family. They also found that healthy afternoon snacking was a large consumer need. Lastly, women in India were becoming more health conscious and desperately wanted to get into shape.

Using these insights, Kellogg's launched Kellogg's multi-grain, fortified cornflakes targeted to adult taste buds. Advertisements also began showing adults eating the cereal, rather than focusing on children alone. The assault on the afternoon-snack segment was led by Chocos. This brand was already popular with children, who were their key consumers for "4 pm munches". The launch communication offered the Chocos variant as a nutritious substitute for chips and other junk food.[19]

► Special K: Get into Shape

In 2008, Kellogg's launched their $1.5 billion "Special K" brand as a weight management cereal targeted at women (25–44 years) who wanted to keep in shape. It was positioned as a low-calorie weight control meal. This was again not categorized as breakfast item but a complete meal. Consultants pointed out that Kellogg's' brand extension strategy helped to increase its relevance across categories. It was a player in the Rs 500-crore weight management market and the Rs 750-crore convenience foods market, apart from the Rs 250-crore breakfast cereal market (which, in turn, was part of the Rs 2,000-crore health foods segment).[20]

The marketing team knew that as against other markets, Kellogg's not only adapted its portfolio to match Indian needs but also made changes to their global positioning to appeal to Indian consumers. Indian market is diverse and unique, and expects the offerings to fit their life pattern. The marketing head at Kellogg's had recently read an article that incorrect positioning was the reason behind 80% brand failures. Kellogg's have been relooking at their 5-year strategy as they have always wanted to be confident on the delivering the promise they have made to its consumers.

EXHIBIT 1

KELLOGG'S IRON SHAKTI TVC

a gang of thieves is seen loading some stolen items in a truck. Just then a man with his family arrives at...

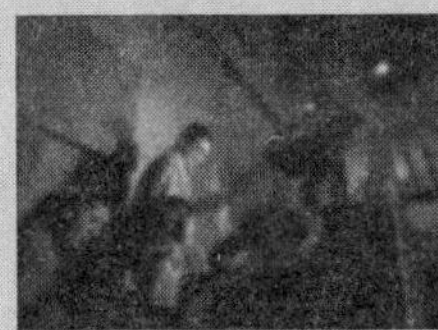

... the scene. Thinking that his neighbor, Pandey *Ji*, is shifting home he does not pay much attention...

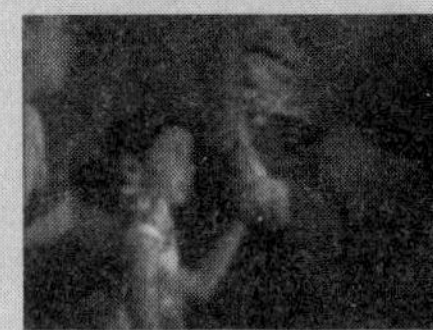

... to their activity. As his daughter worryingly points out to him, "*hamara* TV." our man cools her off by saying, "Pandey *ji ka*".

The little girl gets more disturbed on seeing the thieves with her cupboard. But the father assures her, "Pandey *ji ka*".

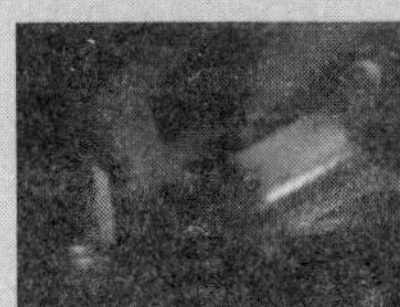

Not able to take any more of this, she vehemently protests on seeing their refrigerator with the stealers. But our ...

... man still reassures her, "Pandey *ji ka*". On reaching home he finds the things missing and realizes everything.

VO: "Iron *kam khaoge toh dimaag kaise chalega. Aapko chaahiye* Kellogg's corn flakes *jisme hai* iron *shakti. Ab poore parivaar ka dimaag chalega* ...

... *nahin daudega*. The ad ends on our man telling his family the thieves' truck number, thereby proving his better memory.

Source: www.agencyfaqs.com

TABLE 1 Sales of Breakfast Cereals by Category: Value 2009-2014

INR million	2009	2010	2011	2012	2013	2014
Hot Cereals	775.05	1,099.09	1,520.88	2,137.94	2,999.65	3,989.47
RTE Cereals	2,919.39	3,605.95	4,306.32	5,254.46	6,361.85	7,689.07
- Children's Breakfast Cereals	166.74	189.05	211.90	250.34	299.75	358.20
- Family Breakfast Cereals	2,752.65	3,416.90	4,094.42	5,004.13	6,062.10	7,330.87
- Flakes	2,328.88	2,848.08	3,358.19	4,028.58	4,782.14	5,666.87
-- Muesli	423.77	568.82	736.23	975.54	1,279.96	1,664.00
-- Other RTE Cereals	-	-	-	-	-	-
Breakfast Cereals	3,694.44	4,705.04	5,827.20	7,392.40	9,361.50	11,678.54

Source: Euromonitor International from official statistics, trade associations, trade press, company research, store checks, trade interviews, trade sources

TABLE 2 Sales of Breakfast Cereals by Category: % Value Growth 2009-2014

% current value growth	2013/14	2009-14 CAGR	2009/14 Total
Hot Cereals	33.00	38.78	414.74
RTE Cereals	20.86	21.37	163.38
- Children's Breakfast Cereals	19.50	16.52	114.83
- Family Breakfast Cereals	20.93	21.64	166.32
- Flakes	18.50	19.46	143.33
-- Muesli	30.00	31.46	292.67
-- Other RTE Cereals	-	-	-
Breakfast Cereals	24.75	25.88	216.11

Source: Euromonitor International from official statistics, trade associations, trade press, company research, store checks, trade interviews, trade sources

TABLE 3 NBO Company Shares of Breakfast Cereals: % Value 2010-2014

% retail value rsp	2010	2011	2012	2013	2014
Kellogg India Ltd	50.20	45.39	41.91	39.10	37.42
Bagrry's India Ltd	13.42	14.06	15.43	16.49	17.36
Frito-Lay India	9.46	10.07	10.50	11.28	12.46
Mohan Meakin Ltd	7.35	7.20	7.02	6.99	6.99
Marico Ltd	-	1.44	3.62	5.06	6.09
GlaxoSmithKline Consumer Healthcare Ltd	-	0.32	1.98	3.81	5.50
Avesta Good Earth Foods Pvt Ltd	1.21	1.52	1.65	1.73	1.78
Hindustan Vegetable Oil Corp Ltd	1.73	1.70	1.74	1.75	1.76

Express Foods Pvt Ltd	1.07	1.27	1.36	1.42	1.46
Avee's Products India Ltd	0.28	0.26	0.26	0.26	0.25
Pantaloon Retail India Ltd	0.09	0.10	0.10	0.10	0.10
Good Earth Foods	-	-	-	-	-
Others	15.20	16.68	14.43	12.03	8.84
Total	100.00	100.00	100.00	100.00	100.00

Source: Euromonitor International from official statistics, trade associations, trade press, company research, store checks, trade interviews, trade sources

TABLE 4 Brand Shares of Breakfast Cereals: % Value 2011-2014

% retail value rsp	Company	2011	2012	2013	2014
Kellogg's Corn Flakes	Kellogg India Ltd	33.43	30.79	28.20	26.69
Bagrry's	Bagrry's India Ltd	14.06	15.43	16.49	17.36
Quaker	Frito-Lay India	10.07	10.50	11.28	12.46
Mohun's	Mohan Meakin Ltd	7.20	7.02	6.99	6.99
Saffola	Marico Ltd	1.44	3.62	5.06	6.09
Horlicks Oats	GlaxoSmithKline Consumer Healthcare Ltd	0.32	1.98	3.81	5.50
Kellogg's Chocos	Kellogg India Ltd	2.28	2.13	2.02	1.95
Good Earth	Avesta Good Earth Foods Pvt Ltd	1.52	1.65	1.73	1.78
Champion	Hindustan Vegetable Oil Corp Ltd	1.58	1.60	1.62	1.64
Kellogg's Mueslix	Kellogg India Ltd	1.45	1.49	1.52	1.52
Express Foods	Express Foods Pvt Ltd	1.27	1.36	1.42	1.46
Kellogg's Frosties	Kellogg India Ltd	0.92	0.87	0.82	0.77
Other Private Label	Other Private Label	0.06	0.38	0.41	0.44
Avee's	Avee's Products India Ltd	0.26	0.26	0.26	0.25
Tasty Treat	Pantaloon Retail India Ltd	0.10	0.10	0.10	0.10
Farm House Breakfast Cereal	Good Earth Foods	-	-	-	-
Others	Others	24.04	20.82	18.27	15.00
Total	Total	100.00	100.00	100.00	100.00

Source: Euromonitor International from official statistics, trade associations, trade press, company research, store checks, trade interviews, trade sources

TABLE 5 Forecast Sales of Breakfast Cereals by Category: % Value Growth 2014-2019

% constant value growth	2014/15	2014-19 CAGR	2014/19 Total
Hot Cereals	13.05	15.74	107.67
RTE Cereals	10.89	11.91	75.49
- Children's Breakfast Cereals	1.78	3.82	20.59
- Family Breakfast Cereals	11.22	12.25	78.17
- Flakes	10.20	10.68	66.13
-- Muesli	13.94	16.99	119.19
-- Other RTE Cereals	-	-	-
Breakfast Cereals	11.70	13.27	86.48

Source: Euromonitor International from trade associations, trade press, company research, trade interviews, trade sources

Questions

1. What was the positioning for Kellogg's cornflakes at the time of launch?
2. Why was the brand not successful? What changes were made to the positioning?
3. What do you think should be the brand proposition going forward?

CASE 11

Nivea – Managing the Legacy Brand

Sunil Gadgil, Director Marketing at Nivea India, was addressing his marketing team at an offsite strategy meet. It was raining heavily and Lonavala looked beautiful from the hills of Northpoint. The team was ecstatic and was eager to contribute in the Nivea journey. Sunil remarked that the market size of India's beauty, cosmetic, and grooming market will reach $ 20 billion by 2025 from the $ 6.5 billion, with the rise in disposable income of the middle class and growing aspirations of people to live a good life and look good.[1] This was surely a huge opportunity for Nivea brand in India.

Nivea had completed 100 years of its existence in 2011. The parent company Beiersdorf AG, Germany was a Rs. 37,600 Crores (Euro 5,750 Million) beauty and skin care MNC. It had affiliates in more than 169 countries, enjoyed market shares of up to 30% and had more than two hundred No. 1 positions in cosmetics categories all over the world.[2] Though Nivea was present in India for over three decades, Nivea India formally started its operations in India in 2006 as a 100% affiliate of global cosmetic company, Beiersdorf AC. Though it had fierce competition from biggies like HUL, Nivea India was finally showing the signs of growth. The deodorant category looked promising and Nivea had the equity of its legacy brand, Nivea Cre'me, to leverage on. Sunil and his team were trying to find solution to the big question—*"What should be the next orbit for Nivea to leverage market opportunity but face the competitive cluttered skin care market?"*

► Background

In 1911, pharmacist and entrepreneur Dr. Oscar Troplowitz and dermatologist Dr. Paul Gerson Unna created the first stable skin cream based on a water-in-oil emulsion. This was named Nivea from the Latin word Nivius meaning "Snow White". When Nivea Crème was first introduced in 1911, it was perceived as a luxury that added to women's limited dress-up routine comprising mere soap and water. and talcum powder.

In 1922, Nivea recognized the skincare needs of men and introduced its first product for male consumers, the shaving soap. In 1936, Nivea promoted sun protection. In 1958, Nivea's Sun Spray was launched; the brand developed Ultra Oil Spray. In 1963, Nivea revolutionized cosmetics with its emulsion concept for Nivea Milk. When weekly baths were replaced by daily showers, Nivea launched its very first shower product in 1978. In 1980s, the cosmetics market was booming and most people had more than one jar of cream in their bathroom cabinet. Thus, in 1982, Nivea Visage united the international brand family by launching a line of face care products. In 1991, Nivea came out with its dual action deodorant to cater to consumers who were beginning to demand high-performance products. The brand's alcohol-free deodorant range matched these expectations by uniting the brand propositions of both protection and care. In 1994, Nivea Soft was launched because young women desired products that carried the proposition of "naturalness" and "lightness". They had a vision to be the number one in skin care. They put together the vision document called "Blue Agenda" in 2012 which defined the path to face the future brand challenges and meet the brand goals.[3] Sunil thought that to get everyone in the team on the same platform, it may be useful to tell the Nivea brand story—right from birth till now—when the brand was mature, had its own aura, and both assets and the baggage!

▶ Nivea Brand Values

Globally, Nivea was known for trust, reliability, and accessibility. The brand positioned itself on "Gentle Care" and "Wellness". The brand was based on four values:

- Care: acting responsibly towards colleagues, consumers, brands, society, and environment.
- Simplicity: striving for clarity and consistency, make decisions quickly, pragmatically, and focus on what iss essential.
- Courage: committing to bold objectives, taking initiative, learning from mistakes, and seeing change as an opportunity.
- Trust: keeping promises and treating others with respect.[4]

▶ The Target Market

Nivea was an aspirational brand and its core target was 18–35 years, modern, socially-developed men and women, belonging to higher socio- economic classes. It was primarily a brand for urban India. Positioning of a mass premium (brands which is aspirational yet is targeting masses) brand made it accessible yet premium in imagery.

▶ Core Brand Identity

Nivea was a fuddy-duddy brand meant for family with the iconic crème at the heart which drove the skin-care category. The brand was positioned as complete caretaker of the skin which ensured universal unisex acceptance.

▶ Brand Design

When introduced in 1911, the dainty art design of Nivea tin was yellow, decorated with fancy green art nouveau tendrils (Exhibit 1). Nivea adopted "Blue and White" color as its brand element in year 1925. These colors represented responsibility, trust, and purity, thus translating intangible brand values into brand design. The blue Nivea color was Ivocart Nivea Blue B 65711. Blue denoted sympathy, harmony, friendship, and loyalty. White represented inner purity and external cleanliness.[5]

The logo was kept simple. Nivea wanted the visual language to offer stronger and clearer expression of the brand values so they based the design and graphic language on the heritage tin and its classic white Bauhaus-era lettering.[5]

In India, Nivea was synonymous with skin cream. Every Indian had memories of having the blue Nivea tin at home mostly bought abroad or gifted by relatives/friends settled abroad. Nivea cream was perceived as a winter cream because of its thickness and oily consistency. Globally, Nivea had been able to do away with this narrow perception, but in India, these perceptions were still strong. In 2006, Nivea has a market share of 19% in the Rs 108 crore skin cream market, which was dominated by Ponds.[6]

► Brand Portfolio and Architecture

Nivea had a systematic, synergetic, and a well-balanced portfolio. It consisted of offerings in skin care, personal care, hygiene, and beauty. The core-essence and decision to expand the portfolio lay in the core brand identity and a question—"Will the extension ensures care and wellness of the skin?".

The lifespan and growth of Nivea brand could be explained through two key factors: the modernization of its flagship product, Nivea cream, and well-managed brand extension using umbrella (sub) brand strategy. But the core driver was still the parent brand, Nivea, which had high-brand equity, and hence, legitimacy to extend its name to other offerings in the skin care category. The architecture was clearly a "sun and planets model" where Nivea Crème occupied the core and other extensions were placed based on their similarity to this core. **Exhibit 2** shows that skin care was the heart of the brand followed by the personal care products.

The little round box of Nivea crème embodied the brand values. It was the first product to be introduced in every country. Next came the extensions, in a pre-established order **(Exhibit 3)**: first were skin care products (Nivea Visage, Nivea Hand, Body etc.), followed by hygiene (Nivea Deo, bath care brands), hair care products, and lastly make-up. The sub-brands expanded these categories, with their specialization based on age (Nivea Baby), purpose (Nivea Sun), gender (Nivea for Men) etc. Nivea had understood its customers well and knew that women were the prime influencers and decision makers regarding skin care and wellness products. Therefore, Nivea launched women's care products before the men's range in every country. Though there was a clear roadmap for extensions, Nivea gave every country organization the freedom to launch/not launch a sub-brand, depending on the market potential.

Each sub-brand was named descriptively and represented a statement of brand's values. Though every extension ensued "Niveaness", there were little differences that made the brand open, living, and non-monolithic. Furthermore, every packaging style reflected a personality and values specific to the sub-brand (Exhibit 5). The aim of each extension was not only to provide for deepening of the core competence (loving care for the skin) and greater penetration in the category, but also promote specific components of the overall image. The farthest extension from the core was Nivea Beauty. This category was away from simplicity and harmony of the Nivea brand. However, in highly developed, sophisticated countries this extension was necessary as it brought young girls to Nivea who grew up to become loyal Nivea customers. This extension added a touch of modernity and "fashion" to the brand.

Nivea managed its portfolio and architecture ensuring coherency and scale. Extensions brought variety to the customers but with any new launch there was a risk of cannibalization. Hence, the key challenge was to ensure perceived distinctiveness from the existing brands. The association with brand Nivea brought its own intangibles and image equities, but they were not enough on their own as physical basis for differentiation was needed.[7] Being the legacy brand with years of communication and experience, customers already formed strong associations with the brand. Exhibit 4 gives the Nivea brand associations before 2013. As Sunil's presentation deck unfolded the Nivea legacy, people present in the room were thinking of their own Nivea moment and interaction with the brand as kids and parents. Everyone remembered the blue Nivea tin with cream used for dry winters and how moms used to dab a finger fun on nose.

▶ Creating Brand Experience and Innovations to Manage Perceptions

The old Nivea videos broke the nostalgia in the room. Nivea India aired their first commercial on television in 2006. It focused on the blue Nivea creme tin and communicated the benefit of soft innocent skin. The integrated campaign was planned by TBWA India and sales of Nivea crème increased by 143.2%. Total Nivea sales grew by 121.8%.[8] Nivea celebrated its 100th birthday in 2011. It rolled out a global campaign, "100 Years better skincare for life", centered around the values that were associated with the brand for generations, namely trust, honesty, reliability, quality, and family. In India, the brand enjoyed nostalgia and credibility besides strong emotional connect. It was remembered as a crème used and recommended by mothers. Nivea followed a "glocal" brand experience strategy. Though the tone and style of brand was kept consistent across geographies, necessary changes were made in the host country for launch.

Nivea roped in Anushka Sharma as its brand ambassador. She embodied what the brand stood for "trust, honesty, international appeal with core Indian values, and high family orientation.[9] She played a central role in the 100-year celebrations and also spearheaded the "Go Sleeveless" campaign which pushed Nivea deo sales. Nivea won 8.7% share of the urban market in 2016 (deodorant category) vs. HUL's 7.7%.[10]

While the company played in all segments, they focused on positions of strength—bodycare, deodorant, and lip care. According to Rakshit Hargave, SVP for Beiersdorf India and Sub-Saharan Africa, since 2011, Nivea India had been the fastest growing affiliate within Beiersdorf's operations and had grown from being an insignificant brand into one of the top three brands in the category. Nivea was regarded to be very strong in the modern trade segment, wresting skin-care business from HUL and Procter & Gamble. The success of Nivea lay in innovation and staying relevant to the consumers.

Nivea entered the men's grooming market with the brand "Nivea for men" in 2007. The men's range was promoted with the tagline " What men want ". In 2013, the brand rebranded its men's range as "Nivea Men". The typical brand user was profiled as the one who tackled things on their own. Nivea till then in India was known more as a female brand. This extension was an attempt to make Nivea a family brand. Nivea commissioned the research which revealed that

- Men were not satisfied with the efficacy of the existing skincare products (which were targeted at women).
- Men were also not interested in visiting products displayed in the women's aisles in the stores.
- While grooming was the end objective for women, men viewed grooming as a tool to get what they want in life.
- 84% of men used products borrowed from the women of their life.
- Most of the men's grooming issues arose out of excessive oily skin and hyper-pigmentation.[11]

Nivea knew that they had to be connect with their male audience and so announced repositioning of its male grooming range with the new tagline, "It starts with you". The new tagline was designed as a call of action that aimed to help men fulfil their everyday potential. Bollywood actor Arjun Rampal was chosen as the face of the brand who lend gravitas and masculine personality to the brand. The brand spoke through all possible touch points and collaborated with IPL Chennai Super Kings to reach out to men in India. For Nivea Men, the key task was to establish the company as a one-stop-shop for end-to-end grooming for men.[10] Nivea Men enjoyed a 28% market share globally and hoped to increase its existing 6–7% market share in India within the moisturizer and facewash category through this repositioning initiative. The men's grooming category in India was primarily defined by deodorant with the largest market share. Skin care was a Rs. 800 crore market and was growing at around 25%.[12]

Globally Nivea was marketing its women products under the strapline, "Feel Closer". Nivea said the Feel Closer line, devised by DraftFCB London, aimed to emphasize the positive impact Nivea had on female relationships by helping them to "feel good in their own skin".

As a part of their 100-year celebrations, a multilevel campaign was planned in key metros focusing on Nivea's skin care expertise through the Nivea skin lounges where consumers learnt more about their skin and got tips on having better skin. The consumer activation program offered a platform to "Meet Rihanna Live" at Hamburg through the "My Skin Moment" contest. Lastly, as part of PLAN "We care & connect" INDIA, Nivea India supports the education of children in the state of Uttarakhand by increasing the school enrolment rate and by improving the quality of education in 40 primary schools.[13]

► Challenges and the Road Ahead

As Sunil was slowly unfolding the Nivea story, there were many consumer stories also being unfolded as almost all team members also had their own "Nivea" moment. Though the extensions were slowly growing and exploiting new opportunities, but the flagship Nivea crème was still stagnant. The value share of Nivea Crème soap was 1.2% in 2016 in bath & shower category when Lifebuoy was at 15.2%, Dove at 4.6% and Lux at 13%. However, in skin care category, Nivea Visage was at 0.6% value share and Dove contributed 0.4%.[14] Sunil pointed out to the Nivea Crème brand manager. Nitika rose and quickly organized her presentation deck. "We all were able to remember our mothers using Nivea or applying Nivea crème from her blue tin on us during winters", she said. It was remembered as "my mother's brand", and hence, there was an opportunity to build the emotional connect with the brand nostalgia and trust of a mother. The brand was using the bond of mother–child relationship to get Nivea crème on dressing tables and to attract young consumers to the brand. Nitika said that their research revealed an insight that "the real strength for mothers to keep going on and keep sacrificing is not something materialistic, but a simple word of gratitude and appreciation or just a silent hug from their kids for all the sacrifices they go through". Using this insight Nivea rolled out TVCs featuring mothers and their kids. The essence of the commercial was that the mother was constantly concerned about her child's safety, health, happiness, and much more. And sometimes, she worried even when she need not. The real reason behind all this worrying was because she cared, unconditionally and that is why mothers trust Nivea as a skin care brand for the family. They launched a CSR initiative which supported and celebrated the sacrifices mothers makes to give their children a better tomorrow. Courageous and underprivileged women were supported by Nivea India in fulfilling their children's dreams.[15].

The integrated campaign was being planned to build the brand around this property. Meanwhile company was constantly looking at product innovation and distribution to increase Nivea market share. The efforts changed the Nivea brand associations (Exhibit 6) but still there was a long way to go!

However, Sunil asked his team "Are current brand associations in line with what we desire? What do we want to add and change and how can we do that?" He wanted a plan to contemporize the brand and make it relevant to today's times, while sustaining and further strengthening its equity in skin-care. He presented some data on brand value share (Exhibit 7 to 12). It showed that Nivea brands still had a small value share in respective categories. How could Nivea increase the brand equity and influence customer behavior in their favor?

► Questions

1. How can company grow and sustain the brand Nivea?
2. How important is legacy in the Nivea brand story?

EXHIBIT 1

Source: https://www.brandingmag.com/2013/01/18/nivea-redesign-yves-behar-fuseproject/

EXHIBIT 2

SUN AND PLANET MODEL FOR BRAND ARCHITECTURE

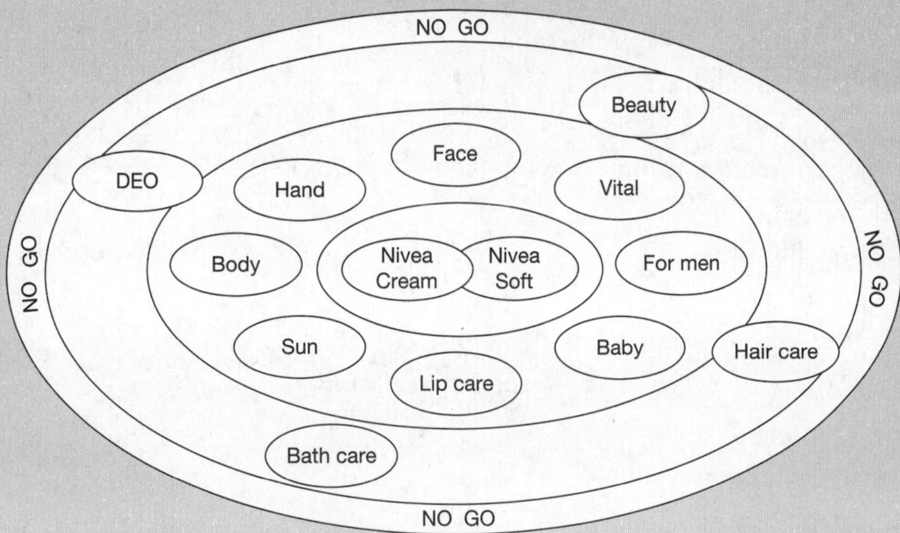

Source: http://www.icmrindia.org/casestudies/catalogue/Simplified%20Case%20Studies/SCMKTG087.htm

EXHIBIT 3

BRAND PORTFOLIO

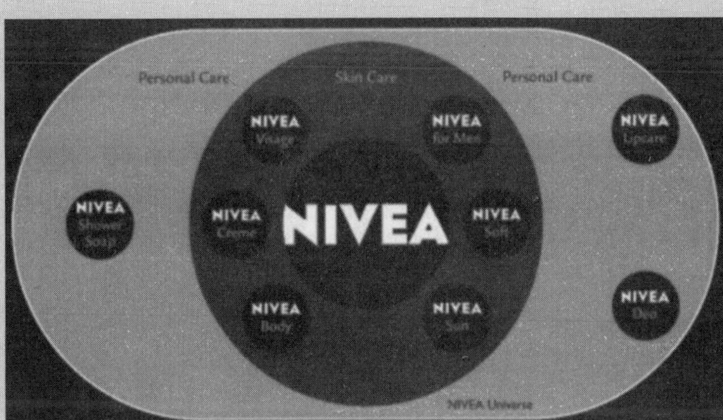

Source: https://uamba.wordpress.com/2012/07/11/umbrella-branding-the-nivea-case/

EXHIBIT 4

BRAND ASSOCIATIONS FOR NIVEA BEFORE 2013

- Cares for skin
- Most strongly associated with the crème
    - Iconic blue tin filled with sparkling white cream
    - My *dadi* (grandmother) used to use it and apply it on me when I was a child
    - My mom applied it on me in winters
    - Unique scent of the cream
- Very good-quality products
- Fuddy-duddy brand
- Meant for the slighter older segment
- Used mostly in winters when skin becomes really dry

Source: Company sources

EXHIBIT 5

PACKAGING – STANDARDIZATION VS CUSTOMIZATION

Source: http://www.afaqs.com/news/story/31209_Nivea-Centennial-celebrations-for-the-Cr232me-de-la-Cr232me

EXHIBIT 6

NIVEA BRAND ASSOCIATIONS 2016

- Presence across categories- deo, body lotions, face wash, men's products like soap, crème, shower gel, lip care
- Not just for my *dadi* (grandma) and mom, but for "me" too
- Slightly premium
- Whitening deodorant / total face clean-up / whitening body lotions
- Anushka Sharma/ Arjun Rampal/ Parineeti Chopra
- Very high quality
- Lots of blue and white
- Products that care for my skin on all body parts and not just the face
- Differentiated products

Source: Company sources

EXHIBIT 7

DEODORANT- % COMPANY VALUE SHARE

	2012	2013	2014	2015	2016
HUL	21.5	14.5	10.1	9.7	9.5
Vini Labs	7.9	12.5	16.9	19.1	20.4
Nivea	5.9	7.5	9.3	10.3	10

Source: Euromonitor

EXHIBIT 8

NIVEA INDIA % VALUE SHARE

NIVEA INDIA	2011	2012	2013	2014	2015	2016
Beauty/ personal care	0.4	0.6	0.7	0.8	0.8	0.9
Bath & Shower	0.6	0.9	1.1	1.2	1.2	1.2
Deodorants	4.5	5.9	7.5	9.3	10.3	10
Men's grooming	0.8	1.2	1.5	1.9	2.2	2.3
Skin care	0.8	1.1	1.1	1.3	1.4	1.4
Mass Beauty/ Personal care	0.5	0.7	0.7	1.1	1.2	1.2

Source: Euromonitor

EXHIBIT 9

DEODORANT – % BRAND SHARE BY VALUE

NIVEA INDIA	2013	2014	2015	2016
Fogg	12.5	16.9	19.1	20.4
Wild Stone	10.9	10.7	10.7	10.5
Park Avenue	3.8	7.7	8	7.9
Engage	4.5	6.7	8	7.8
Axe	11.8	7.4	7	6.7
Eva	5.1	5.1	5.5	5
Nivea	3.9	4.8	5.4	5.2
Nivea Men	3.4	4.2	4.7	4.6
Set Wet	3.8	3.6	3.3	3.3

Source: Euromonitor

EXHIBIT 10

SKIN CARE – % COMPANY VALUE SHARE

	2012	2013	2014	2015	2016
HUL	50.9	49.5	48.6	47.6	46.5
L'Oreal	8	8.4	8.4	8.4	8.4
Himalaya	4.1	4.4	4.5	4.7	4.9
Johnsons& Johnsons	2.5	2.8	3.1	3.3	3.5
P&G	2.7	2.8	2.7	2.6	2.5
Nivea	1.1	1.1	1.3	1.4	1.4
Piramal Enterprise	1.3	1.3	1.3	1.2	1.2

Source: Euromonitor

EXHIBIT 11

BATH & SHOWER – % COMPANY VALUE SHARE

	2012	2013	2014	2015	2016
HUL	44	43.7	43.1	43.6	43.3
Godrej	11.8	10.9	10.3	10.2	10.1
Wipro	8.6	8.3	8.2	8.4	8.5
Nivea	0.9	1.1	1.2	1.2	1.2

Source: Euromonitor

EXHIBIT 12

MEN – % COMPANY VALUE SHARE

	2012	2013	2014	2015	2016
HUL	11	9.3	7.9	7.8	7.7
Gillette	22.5	24.4	24.1	22.9	22.2
Nivea	1.2	1.5	1.9	2.2	2.3

Source: Euromonitor

CASE 12 The Call of the Competition

Competition is a necessary evil in marketing.

Maruti Suzuki (hereafter referred as Maruti or Suzuki interchangeably) has been a long-reigning monarch of small cars in India. It's been more than three decades when India's first Maruti 800 was launched as a modern personal transport, a sense of pride for Indians. Since then, the brand has evolved, adapted and updated itself to changing scenarios, and have had an amazing transformational journey.

With South Asia witnessing rising economic levels, came in shifts in consumer choices. To fit itself aptly into the changed milieu and aspirations of these economies, Maruti has stepped past compact cars and today carries within its stable, models for different upscale segments.

Maruti, for long, established its strong leadership credential in the entry-level segment. From time to time, Maruti Suzuki has faced competition from various players latest being Renault Kwid —posing a major challenge, resulting in market share of Maruti Suzuki dropping from 48 to 40 % in the entry car segment in 2016. The new entrant Kwid took away 20 percent of the segment sales and managed to sell an average of 8,812 units per month.

It is often said, 'When going gets tough, the tough gets going'. Mr. Devendra Chawla, president (Food & FMCG brands), Future Group, once very well summed up about leader brands during such tough conditions by saying, "At such times, market leaders enter newer sub-segments and invest aggressively to defend their turf, which in turn helps in gaining share from fringe players. Also, since a majority of new launches fail in the country, market leader tends to benefit after the challenger brands concede." Invariably, competition leads to increase in market size and leader may end up with stronger position as challenger vacate space.

▸ Brand Equity Fortifies the Position

Maruti Suzuki decided to play its defensive strategy, mainly by protecting its turf on two fronts—one at the entry-level and the other as nation's largest car maker. To take care of the former, Maruti is all set to develop a new-generation Alto, which will be launched by the festive season of 2019 and will strengthen its hold in the entry-car space. The new car is expected to be expressive with great design & crossover look. For the latter, Maruti is making strong headway in the B segment comprising of cars at the premium end of the market—the Baleno, Vitara Brezza, and Ciaz priced between ₹5 lakh and ₹12 lakh. VG Ramakrishnan, managing partner at consultancy firm Avanteum Advisors LLP, strongly credits new product launches for continued strong performance of Maruti Suzuki.

Serious attempts by Maruti to reinvent itself through a surge of upscale launches have helped the company stay ahead and retain the crown of being the country's largest car maker. Overall, the company is sitting on a decade high market share of close to 50% and plans to launch 15 new products by 2020.

The company's market share was 45.9% a year earlier, while its all-time high was 52%, as recorded in November 2016.

The table below clearly shows that eight of the country's top 10 models are from Maruti Suzuki's product portfolio which itself stands testimony to their market share during the month.

Top-10 Models	Jan 2017 Volumes	% Growth
Alto	22,990	7.0
Swift Dzire	18,000	3.0
WagonR	14,900	17.0
Swift	14,540	3.0
Grand i10*	13,010	31.0
Celerio	10,870	52.0
Baleno	10,470	36.0
Hyndai i20*	10,010	4.2
Vitara Breezza	8,932	–
Omni	8,723	48.0

Maruti has all its strategies well-crafted and properly laid to enable it to continue on the winning spree with double digit growth rate. In the first 11 months of fiscal 2017, it sold 13.1 lakh vehicles in the domestic market, a nearly 11% increase from a year earlier. Its announcement to the component vendors to be ready with supplies for production of 17.25 lakh to 17.30 lakh vehicles in fiscal 2018 starting April, talks about its ambitious future plans.

Along with product innovation, focus on consumer preferences and service network, another important factor that contributed to volume gain for Maruti is wide distribution and its continual efforts to expand it further. It is adding about 250 dealerships, including 50 Nexa outlets that sell premium products over next 2 years.

VG Ramakrishnan, managing partner at consultancy firm Avanteum Advisors LLP, says, "The Company has always got right its product positioning and pricing. They have a phenomenal brand appeal. There is nobody who can beat them in the near future." But he also adds a word of caution for the leader to be prepared to face the new intensity in competition once Korean Kia and Japanese Daihatsu enter the Indian market.

► With Competition Evolves the Market

With every new competition, Maruti has only raised the bar of competitiveness. Sometimes, nothing succeeds for market leaders like a little competition. As was once very well put in related to leader brands by Mr. Prashant Peres, marketing director for chocolates at Mondelez India, "When competition intensifies, you either gain share from some of the existing players or grow in a way you create head winds in some segments which outgrow the market."

Maruti Suzuki has, with elan, moved beyond its bailiwick. Company which was largely identified as the maker of no-frills, 796-cc passenger vehicles meant for culturally unsophisticated towns, today has under its umbrella the sedans, crossovers, SUVs, vans along with of course its mini cars and premium hatchbacks. It was successful in identifying most of the potential holding flanks and filled them all with products which are gaining edge over well-entrenched, fancied rivals and global players all around the market place. Table below reflects the dominance of Maruti Suzuki for the year ended March 2017.

MARUTI MODEL	FY17 SALES	COMPETITOR'S MODEL	FY17 SALES
Mini cars Alto 	2,42,635	Renault Kwid 	1,09,341
Premium Hatchback Swift	1,66,885	Hyundai Grand i10	1,46,228
Hot Hatchback Baleno 	1,20,804	Hyundai Elite i20	1,06,180
Sub-4 metre sedan Dzire	1,99,878	Honda Amaze	33,756
Mid- size sedan Ciaz	64,448	Honda City 	57,984
Compact SUV Vitara Brezza 	1,08,640	Ford EcoSport	48,547
Compact MPV Ertiga	63,527	Renault Lodgy 	4,486
Cross-over S-cross	21,417	Hyundai Active i20	20,124
Vans Eeco 	67,263	Tata Magic & Iris	18,949

Source: Industry

The company is also exploring the possibility of introducing a mild-hybrid in the petrol engine which may take the Maruti's famed high-fuel efficiency to the next level. Maruti's expansion covering all gaps in the market has not weakened its traditional stronghold or diluted its image. In the mini-car space, Alto has a strong lead of more than one lakh cars over its nearest rival Renault Kwid in FY17. The premium hatchback Swift was ahead of Hyundai Grand by about 20,000 units in FY17.

Interestingly, despite being as foreign as most of its' competitors, Maruti Suzuki has still managed to retain its' image of "Indianness" and continues to play the card very well.

Are there any flanks which this smart-savvy brand Maruti has left untapped? Hyundai Creta and Toyota Innova are the two leaders in segments where Maruti's presence is not visible at all. The brand has travelled a long road and it has still miles to go and explore new unchartered territories to stay vibrant and alive.

▶ MONARCH'S CLEVER MOVES

Mobile is the only mantra for marketer's success and sustainability. Markets are moving targets and so nothing is constant in marketing. Maruti Suzuki—inspite of the immense love and loyalty showered on it by its customers—could not achieve success when it tried to foray into premium car segment through launches like Kizashi and Vitara. A brand known for its great value, fuel efficiency and huge service network could not fit into the image of a high-end brand. Maruti Suzuki in order to defend its position of being the largest car maker of the country could not afford to leave this wide flank open and uncovered. Complete image makeover was required and in order to defend its leadership status Maruti had to take a revolutionary move. Market broadening and diversification by the brand was the strategic route chosen to keep the challengers at bay.

Not only Maruti Suzuki planned to enter some of the these segments where it was not present but also creation of NEXA led to it creating a new category of affordable premium segments and drive higher profitability. The creation of NEXA was fresh & bold attempt to enter the high-end car segment and is first of its kind premium retail network. The big objective was to cater to the high-end consumers who have gone beyond their first cars and are now looking for an experience. S Cross was the first car launched at Nexa and was quickly followed by Baleno hatchback. Maruti Suzuki launched Ignis through this premium retail in Feb 2017 and has also moved sedan Ciaz to this category. To maintain exclusivity, it was decided that the cars sold from Nexa will not be sold at the popular Maruti dealerships.

▶ STAY AHEAD ON THE CURVE

To understand the automobile market of India and prevailing competition, one brand which deserves a definite mention is Mahindra & Mahindra (M&M)—a brand strongly linked to the SUV segment. The new category of Sports Utility Vehicle (SUV) got created with the launch of Tata Safari in 1998 and got evolved with the launch of Mahindra Scorpio in 2002. The first movers, the stalwarts of this new category ruled undisputedly for many years. Mahindra & Mahindra stated that the company has sold 5 lakh units of Mahindra Scorpio in the SUV segment in India (till 2015).

M&M, which has long been the unchallenged king of the SUV market is now facing heat, due to competition getting intense in the space with rivals Maruti Suzuki and Tata Motors launching new models. In the 4-month period, April–July 2016, as per SIAM data, Maruti has seen its UV sales go up and its market share jumped from 13% to 24%. M&M also saw a jump in sales but only a slight and its market share shrank from 36% to 30%.

"Competition is heating up but we also have a slew of products in the compact SUV space at different price points which gives us better penetration both in cities and rural sectors. Our petrol KUV 100 is a new segment making it possible for the customer to buy an SUV as the first car," said Pravin Shah, president & chief executive (automotive), Mahindra & Mahindra.

M&M is all geared up to face the existing competition and has planned several new launches and is ready to surprise market and competition, upgrading what lies within the fold. It is working very strongly on its strategies to safeguard its brand in the space where it holds power.

In the premium SUV space ranging from ₹15–25 lakh, M&M already enjoys leadership selling 3,000–3,500 XUVs a month, more than all models of other companies put together. It is in the micro-SUV space, where the company is facing maximum heat. Its market share dropped to 29% in the April–December 2016, from 36% in the same period last fiscal year. At the same time, challengers in the segment, Maruti Suzuki and Hyundai both registered strong double-digit growth in SUVs. In order to contain the slide in the micro-SUV segment, M&M is taking host of measures to defend its arena pre-emptively, by attacking before enemy starts its offence.

Firstly on the product front, M&M has focused on bringing out new variants of the XUV 500 and KUV 100. Upgradations in KUV are by improving the aesthetics, fuel economy, and features with no major price increase. Maruti's success is attributed to the strong demand created by Vitara Brezza. And now new entrants Ignis from Maruti and Tata Hexa are seen as posing fresh threat for which M&M has to show its timely preparedness, to save itself from being dethroned. The new KUV variant will come with dual colours for the first time to keep itself competitive against the Maruti Ignis. The KUV will also offer the options of bigger alloy wheels and a host of accessories.

M&M is weaving its winning story around digital technology which is being highly embraced in today's world. It is adding a host of connectivity technologies to make the XUV more feature-packed. It is also experimenting with some of the high-impacting technologies which will revolutionize the segment like the new Eco-Sense telematics feature which will allow real-time tracking of the vehicle, including fuel economy and wear and tear of parts. Mood lighting is another addition on offer.

A new feature of a safety button is being added in the XUV, which will be triggered in the event of any accident and call the stored emergency contact number. It will offer this feature to existing XUV owners as well through a small software upgrade.

To stay ahead of the curve and be relevant, M&M has identified the right gap in the need market. It is the increasing traffic on the road due to which people spend more time in cars and leaves them fatigued. Its connected features and various options offered will add relief by making them gainfully occupied while on road. Mahindra has already tied up with Google and has integrated the Android Auto operating system on the infotainment system of the XUV and is in discussion with Apple to integrate the Apple CarPlay.

Constant reinvention defines the rule of the winning game. Brands have to constantly push their competencies to a level where it becomes difficult for other competitors to reach and emulate. The pie is big enough and the brands can carve out their favourable niche by evolving the category and taking bigger share from it.

▶ Questions

1. An effective marketing strategy calls for maintaining a good balance of consumer and competitor monitoring. Highlight on the basis of the case as to how different brands have been successful in maintaining this balance?
2. Leader brand Maruti Suzuki in order to remain dominant is making efforts to expand total market demand, protect its current market share and also to increase its market share. Explain the various steps and strategies adopted by Maruti to achieve the above.

3. Enumerate on the various challenges being faced by Mahindra & Mahindra, a brand known for SUVs. What strategies should it lay down to fight emerging competition in the SUV segment?
4. As a consultant engaged by Maruti Suzuki, scan the competition for the company. Also identify opportunities and customers, both current and potential for the right strategy build-up of the company.

CASE 13

Fevicol –The Iconic Bond*

► OBJECTIVES

- To identify factors that lead to the development of a strong brand equity
- To identify steps taken to build a strong customer relationship.
- To understand the role of brand extensions in the company's growth strategy
- To elucidate Integrated Marketing Communication components for brand building

► QUESTIONS

1. How has the brand developed resonance with its customers?
2. What steps did Fevicol take to build their brand equity?
3. Analyze the customer relationship management strategy adopted by the organization.
4. What market strategies can Fevicol adopt against competition?
5. Analyze the marketing communication mix adopted by Fevicol, and was it successful?

► FEVICOL: AN ICONIC BOND

The V.P. Marketing of Pidilite Industries, Mr. Dinesh Thakkar was getting ready for a meeting with his CFO. He suspected the company was beginning to lose market share on the flagship Fevicol brand because the competition was extending credit to their wholesale/retail dealer network. Fevicol had diligently stayed away from extending credit to its distributors for the simple reason that the Fevicol brand was very strong for the past 50+ years in India, and had carved out a unique niche in the market. The Board of Directors of Pidilite (the parent company of Fevicol brand) did not want to take on any financial liability on their books by extending "distributor credit". The age-old wisdom in most Indian businesses was "cash is king, sell product for cash". This had worked exceedingly well in the past for most Indian entrepreneurs and manufacturers. The CFO's opinion reflected the same

This case is also applicable for "Designing and Managing Integrated Marketing Communications"

approach when he had told Mr. Thakkar "why extend credit to our trade partners when Fevicol is the only adhesive brand anyone remembers in India? Even the Bollywood movie song praises the power of Fevicol. It's a household name everyone knows and wants".

Dinesh felt while the CFO had a point, and his team's branding strategies for Fevicol had worked very well. However, now a new segment of traders and end users were emerging, they were looking for quick financial gain and might not consider a long-term "value relationship" with the manufacturer. In the adhesives segment, there were a few new emerging brands, mostly regional, who were offering compelling trade schemes and end user promotions, along with various flexible credit terms and discounts to woo the trade and the customers. Fevicol had an iron grip on the market with about 80% market share but he did not want complacency to set in. He knew though the adhesive component was a very small share of the cost of the furniture, majority of the carpenter's preferred Fevicol adhesive to any other brand. The real success of the brand lied in creating the strong belief that nothing is as strong an adhesive as Fevicol. This message had resonated well with everyone in the eco-system—the carpenters, contractors, interior designers, and even the architects. The challenge now was to continue this successful positioning into the future in a fiercely price competitive and changing marketplace and how would they achieve it?

▶ History of the Fevicol Brand

In 1954, synthetic glue for carpenters (applicators) was unheard of in India and was uncommon. Glues were mainly made up of animal fat or starch. B. K Parekh (Founder Chairman of Pidilite) did great deal of work with carpenters to arrive at formulae for synthetic adhesive which met their requirement. This product was then branded as "Fevicol". In the initial years, great efforts were put in to conduct trials on Fevicol with carpenters throughout the country. As this was a proposition which sought to change their established practice of using animal glue and starch, it took great deal of patience and perseverance to get the product accepted by the carpenter community.

The customers that used the product were illiterate and unaware of the superior benefits of the product. To increase brand recognition, he decided to develop a logo that would be symbolic of the performance of the brand. At that time, Mr. P.N. Sarma, the head Ogilvy & Mather (O&M), a leading advertising agency in Indi,a and Mr. Ranjan Kapur were the key executives at the agency. The logo for the brand was to convey "the strength of adhesion". After many rounds of discussion they finalized the iconic logo of two elephants (facing opposite directions) together pulling a plank of wood between them (see Exhibit 1).

Most of the furniture in India was custom-built, hence, the support from the carpenter community was critical for success of furniture-related adhesives like Fevicol. Thus, promoting the interests of the carpenter was of paramount importance. In 1980, they launched quarterly black and white four-page design book called Fevicraft, which they mailed to all carpenters to help expand their business. It had pictures of different furniture designs and line drawings of interior spaces to help the carpenters showcase designs to their clients, thus generating interest in terms of ordering interior designs and new furniture. In 1985, the color version of the book was launched.

In 1989, a hardbound Fevicol Furniture Book was created with superior designs with high utility value which was sold to the carpenters. This Furniture Book became part of the kit of every good carpenter as it started getting them contract/assignments with their clients. It was very popular with the carpenters and helped grow the company's user database rapidly. In 2015, Fevicol Design Ideas book, for residential and commercial purposes, was launched along with an online portal in the same name which would act as a liaison between carpenters, contractors, and architects.

► Focus on Core Benefit

From the very onset the brand built confidence and trust with the trade, offering the best product formulation for furniture adhesives application, achieved through a unique formulation, compared to the messy traditional animal glues. This approach started building confidence amongst the carpenters, the trade, and the end users. Gradually the product quality of Fevicol became the benchmark for the "Best Adhesive".

Thereafter, the company consciously built trade/market-friendly policies, implemented with local sales executive teams to provide genuine services to trade and the end-user customers, thus creating a strong personal bond and trust for the Fevicol brand.

► Overview of Pidilite Industries Ltd

The company was founded by Shri B. K. Parekh in 1959. The determination and vision of B. K. Parekh ensured that in the next few decades, the company kept on introducing new products and built many strong brands. In fact, Fevicol is one of the most trusted and recognized household brands in India today. The market cap for Pidilite Industries Limited was ₹303,350 million as of 31st March 2016. There are 34 brands under its umbrella. The operating profit for the year 2015–16 was ₹ 11640 million and increased by 44.5% over the previous year and net profit at ₹ 7030 million increased by 40.1%. over 2014–15. Sales of consumer products grew by 8.7%, lower than the growth rates recorded in the last 5 years. Sales of industrial products grew at a much slower rate of less than 1% due to weak domestic environment.

The business is divided into various divisions handling adhesives, sealants, art material and stationery adhesives, construction chemicals, pigments, synthetic resins, etc. Out of these, the adhesives and sealants is the largest business contributing to 65% of the company revenue. The brand Fevicol falls under the adhesives and sealants division and is sold in varying pack sizes.

► Overview of the Adhesive Market

The Indian adhesive market is estimated to be around Rs.70 billion per annum and has recorded strong growth during the period 2010–2015. It is one of the fastest growing industries at CAGR 11.9% during 2010-2015 and is expected to grow at CAGR of 15% over the next few years. The increase in demand of adhesives in India is due to the increase in the consumption of adhesives in packaging, furniture, automotive, and construction industries.[3] The major players in the adhesive market are Pidilite, Henkel Technologies, and Jubilant Agri and Consumer Products Limited. (Assume 1 US $ = ₹ 66).

► Existing Players

Jubilant Agri and Consumer Products Limited (JACPL)

Jubilant Agri and Consumer Products Limited (JACPL) has a well-diversified product portfolio that includes consumer products like adhesives, wood finishes, wood preservatives; food polymers; synthetic latex such as Vinyl Pyridine, SBR, and NBR latex; Agri Products like Crop Nutrition, Crop Growth and Industrial Chemicals. JACPL is a wholly owned subsidiary of Jubilant Industries Limited (JIL).

Jubilant Agri and Consumer Products Ltd, manufactures and markets adhesives which are designed to work on multiple substrates, including wood. It caters to the market of both water-based and solvent-based adhesives, which are required for different applications. JACPL also provides specialized adhesives for various applications. The offerings are made through the following brands: Jivanjor, Vamicol, Polystic, and Hero. The Consumer Products division had a network of more than 600 distributors and over 15,000 retailers all over India. It has 10% of the market share.

► New Entrants

Asian Paints

Asian Paints TruGrip Ultra is a water-based, synthetic resin adhesive which was direct competition to Fevicol. It was used for bonding a wide variety of wood-based substrates.

Henkel Adhesive Technologies had a B2B presence in the adhesives segment in India with their Loctite brand and lacked a retail presence for which they entered into a distribution agreement with Asian Paints, which sold the brand at the retail level through a co-branding initiative. Asian Paints had a distribution network spanning 36,000 hardware shops which Henkel wanted to capitalize on. Loctite had been present primarily in industrial adhesives since 2000, and the new retail products were to be manufactured at the factories based in the western region of India, at Kurkumbh near Pune. Their range of products were Asian Paints Loctite Quick, Asian Paints Loctite Rapid, and Asian Paints Loctite Tough.

► Understanding the Pulse of the Customer

Fevicol provided ease of use and the best bonding strength. It offered superior value to the craftsman as compared to its competitors by consistently introducing innovative products in the market resulting in undisputed trust from its customers. As one contractor from Mumbai put it, "I am a loyal Fevicol customer for the past 25 years. Fevicol offers better grip and quality compared to any other brand. Most problems occur due to the laminate, ply, or applicator-related issues and rarely for the product. Though my clients do not ask whether I used Fevicol, it is the most dependable and so I don't compromise and always use it." The training and activities conducted for craftsmen throughout the year, provided him with an opportunity to interact with his fraternity and upgrade his skills on an ongoing basis.

The brand had a critical functionality in the craftsmanship and any compromise on the quality of the adhesive would mean a sub-standard offering. Although the cost contribution of Fevicol to the total expense incurred for the craftsman was marginal (almost 2%) but it assured a good quality finished product safeguarding the rest 98% of the cost.

Not using the right amount of adhesive would lead to a customer complaint and maybe even a loss of business in the marketplace. The company educated and encouraged craftsmen to use the right amount of adhesive in the appropriate manner for optimum results. This enabled the company sales force to continuously build and nurture the relationships locally with the carpenters, to build their confidence in each new product right from launch, and demonstrate each new product's application and benefits. It also enabled the sales force to collect direct feedback from the carpenters.

This model was adopted across the country across the various cities and towns and had a massive appeal for the craftsmen. After the demonstrations, the craftsmen would then place sales orders with the retailer who in turn would then supply to them. Products were usually available in 1kg, 2kg, and 5 kg containers for craftsmen for household buying, and for industrial buying, they were available in large packs of 10 kg, 20 kg, 30 kg, and 50 kg.

Products were available in various packs starting from 50 gms to 200 kg barrel based on the requirements of end users, workshop, joineries, etc.

► Inroads into the Stationery and Craft Segment

Due to the strong brand equity, the brand was able to make inroads in the consumer segment selling Fevicol MR for art and craft needs of induvial customers. The product was sold at stationery shops as a bonding solution for art and craft needs. It could bond cardboard, thermocol, fabrics, wood, plywood, etc. It had strong bonding and was ready to use and non-staining (See Exhibit 3). This ingenious idea gave customers an opportunity to experience the strength, reliability, and ease of use of the Fevicol adhesive.

► Strengthening Customer Relationships

Fevicol Champions' Club (FCC) was a unique initiative started in 2002 by Pidilite Industries to offer craftsmen/contractors an opportunity to network within their fraternity leading to both social and professional growth. It started off small but the movement has grown over the years. The activities organized by FCC are conducted to build goodwill among the community and society. Pilgrimages (taking them to places of worship) are organized for the contractors, socializing activities are planned, skill-enhancing workshops are conducted along with activities with family members. The FCC website helps the contractors get regular updates on the activities conducted by the company across various locations.

One of the important events celebrated by FCC Clubs every year is "Shramdaan Divas". In its fifth consecutive year in 2016, it witnessed participation from 45,100 contractors across 196 towns who donated a day of their labor towards repair work of facilities used by the under-privileged and needy children across the country. *Vriksharopan Divas* (tree-plantation drive), in its second consecutive year, had participation from 15,350 FCC members who planted 19,120 trees.

Similarly, booklets on furniture designs provided to them enhanced their business prospects. The club organized various activities and celebrated the *Vishwakarma Day* which paid reverence to their deity. A huge get-together is organized every year at various locations across India to celebrate this day. The FCC provided insights to the product and marketing teams on the challenges faced by the customers and offered solutions.

The Fevicol Champions' Club (FCC) has provided a platform to the carpenters and other wood-working contractors to come together as a community for their personal and professional growth and also to be recognized for their efforts and imbibe new methods bringing them success, both socially and professionally.. The trust and respect which the brand enjoyed was strengthened by these activities.

▶ Redesigning the Packaging

In 2002, Pidilite decided to revamp the packaging of the brand, Fevicol. The original design of Fevicol was changed once in the 80s. This was the first major change thereafter. To increase the vibrancy of the brand, Mr Amulya Baruah of Plus One Design, was hired to give it a new look. This meant a revamp of the design of the pack as well as the logo. Along with that there was a total revamp of the container which gave the product an entirely smarter and sleeker look with a stronger handle, making it easier to carry a bulkier pack, as shown in Exhibit 4

▶ Market Challenges for Retaining Customers

The brand enjoys a huge fan-following from its users who have across years and generations only used Fevicol. The durability and reliability that the brand offers is second to no other player in the market. The brand, in fact, has been very successful in consumer, bazaar (trade), and industrial market segments.

The brand is synonymous to the adhesive category and has enjoyed unprecedented position as a leader in the category. It is only the customers who are extremely price sensitive who move to unbranded synthetic adhesives, thereby compromising on the final product.

As adhesives is a low-involvement product, and the final wood-work does not show any traces of the brand of adhesive used, many a times even when the carpenter has not used the product they still claim that they have to gain credibility with clients and also get a better price for their work.

In fact, in one of their campaigns "Mataji" released in 2006 by O&M in their usual style of satire addressed a very important matter of customers buying readymade furniture without checking whether Fevicol has been utilized. It communicated to the readymade furniture makers the risk of not using Fevicol. According to "India Furniture Market Forecast and Opportunities, 2019", the country's furniture market is projected to grow at a CAGR of around 26% during 2014–19. Home furniture segment is the leading contributor, followed by office and institutional segment. The western region of the country is expected to be the highest revenue contributor in the India furniture market, followed by southern region, due to the presence of large number of industrial hubs and upcoming infrastructure developments in these regions.[6]

▶ PRICING AND DISTRIBUTION

Premium pricing is adopted in line with the product image and offering. This has helped the brand consolidate its position in the market. To fortify Fevicol's presence in both the B2B and B2C areas, Pidilite had set up a "Rurban" division to concentrate on the distribution in the semi-urban and rural regions. Being focused on the semi-urban and rural areas could open up new revenue streams through higher volumes for Fevicol.

The adhesive segment has a robust and wide-spread distribution channel across India. It is manufactured at the plant and then dispatch to the Carrying and Forwarding Agent (C&FA) from where the goods are distributed across the country to various distributors, who then further distribute the product to the retailers. The ply-wood retailer stores across the country stock Fevicol and all its variants. In fact, in the earlier days, these ply-wood shop owners would keep the 5 kg Fevicol container right at its entrance to enhance the store image because it was the only branded product they had in their store among mostly unbranded ones. In fact, a loss-leader pricing was adopted by these store owners as they were willing to give huge discounts on Fevicol to urge customers to buy plywood from them.

A separate identity, "Rurban sales development", was created for a section of Tier 3 markets where treatment and strategy to promote business was different. Here the type of customer and the furniture made were also different, but it was important to address their specific needs as well to expand the market.

▶ SALES PERSON SELECTION AND TRAINING

Each of the company's salesperson was selected based on initiative and self-motivation. He was trained to take pride in selling Fevicol to the customers and catered to all types of ply-wood stores to sell the product. The sales person was always encouraged to tackle all customer complaints and empowered to solve them in favor of the customer. The sales person was fully trained and well versed with the product attributes and benefits and was given consistent training on new and existing product.

▶ INTERNATIONAL PRESENCE

The company has global presence in 14 countries across the globe. In Bangladesh and Egypt, the company has manufacturing facilities. There has been a significant increase in exports of consumer and craftsmen products in order to achieve sustained growth. This has been possible because of the expanding distribution network in various countries and deploying additional manpower.

To facilitate better global networking, Pidilite has established offices/subsidiaries in several countries, including Singapore, USA, Brazil, UAE, Indonesia, Egypt, Bangladesh, Kenya, Sri Lanka, Thailand, Ethiopia, Myanmar, and Ghana. Most of their products are manufactured in-house with the help of a strong, research-driven innovation overlaid with consumer insights. A well-equipped and well-staffed R&D center continuously develops and enhances products for consumers, craftsmen, and industries. Pidilite has also established a state-of-the-art research center in Singapore that is now a member of Singapore Chemical Industry Council (SCIC).

The operational teams in each country had customized and transferred the brand's "success formula" from India to those countries, and successfully implemented the brand extensions as well. In Bangladesh, Fevicol had completely displaced an incumbent Japanese brand and commanded the brand awareness and popularity levels at par with that in India. Pidilite had set up manufacturing facilities for Fevicol in Bangladesh, Egypt, and soon after, in Sri Lanka. The international operations at the company is on a fast track and poised for major growth

► Integrated Marketing Communications

In 1987, B. K. Parekh and M. B. Parekh felt the need to design an advertising campaign for Fevicol and requested Piyush Pandey of O&M to conceptualize it. Initially, the "Dum lagake haisha" (put all your might into it) was conceptualized for Fevitite, but the brand slogan was so appealing that it was applied for the Fevicol campaign. After this success, Piyush Pandey and his team have worked extensively with the brand and won accolades for their creative execution. The brand captured the hearts and minds of consumers thanks to its engaging and humorous Integrated Marketing Communications and its never-dying appeal with the masses. "The earthy humor in Fevicol ads brings a smile to everyone's face. The ads have even made our other clients think of life beyond selling products and ending up connecting with the audience better," says Piyush Pandey, executive chairman of O&M (India and South Asia), the agency which brought Fevicol to the center stage in the 1980s with the "Dam laga ke haisha" (put all your might into it) television commercial. The brand advertised heavily during the cricket world cup and IPL season. The brand exposure increased hugely due to the viewership.

The Bollywood movie, "Dabangg 2" had a dance number starring two very famous actors that dramatically emphasized the strength of the Fevicol bond.

In 2009, Pidilite Industries and O&M got together to celebrate 50 years of adhesives brand, Fevicol. This culminated in a film entitled "Moochwali". A young girl performed a male role in a play, wearing a moustache stuck on with a dab of Fevicol. It never came off. She grew with it, lived with it, and died with it. She even reincarnated with it and the nation of a billion-plus loved it. It was an irreverent, smart, and funny advertising that one would not necessarily associate with a B2B (or business to trade, at best) advertising until two or three decades ago. It is what we today call "the Fevicol kind of advertising".

The brand's film involving the overcrowded open bus is a pride of India (see Exhibit 5) and relates to everyday life of the common man. The advertising campaigns whether in film or in print emphasize focus on the strength of the adhesive by a metaphorical representation.

For Fevicol Marine, the campaign was so devised that it would communicate the strength of the adhesive even when immersed in water for longer periods of time. "Wahi mazboot jod, paani mein bhi" (the same bonding strength is also possible under water) was the tagline .

Fevicol won the Silver EMVIE in the Best Ambient Media in 2013–14 category for an innovative "free store" activation at a city mall in Mumbai wherein 87 wooden items of all shapes and sizes were on display. Visitors were offered the opportunity to pull off any of these items and walk away with it. However, none of the wooden items could be removed, thereby reinforcing Fevicol as the ultimate and most reliable glue. See Exhibit 7 for more Fevicol print ads. Another publicity event was when Fevicol participated in the Standard Chartered Mumbai Marathon in 2013, where a group of people wearing the Fevicol branded shirts were doing a "standing run", which is running on the same spot as if they were glued to the place. This funny behavior at a marathon attracted huge attention from all the participants and the media coverage created quite a stir in the press and TV.

In 2016, the Company received the "Most Promising Company of the Year" at the CNBC-TV18, 11th India Business Leader Awards (IBLA).

The company hosted the prestigious Pidilite Awards for Excellence (PAFE) ceremony to felicitate meritorious students of architecture and interior design. The company believes that talent and excellence are paramount and both should be rewarded and recognized. A Pidilite Knowledge Series was initiated where leading architects and interior designers participated and shared their knowledge and experiences with each other. This lead to building stronger customer relationships not only amongst contractors but also amongst interior designers and architects.

Fevicol Design Ideas was launched on the digital platform in 2013 with a new website and a mobile application. This website connected home-owners to professionals like interior designers and contractors. There are 10,000 interior designers and 15,000 contractors on the website and showcases approximately 50,000 design ideas.

▶ Segmenting, Targeting, and Positioning

Understanding customer needs and developing offerings that suit their needs has been the formula for success. Their customer-centric approach and focus on innovative products has made it an undisputed leader in the market.

Demonstrations on new product usage and queries on existing products are solved at the FCC (Fevicol Champions Club) meet by the sales person. This inculcates a sense of confidence about the usage of the new product amongst the users who ultimately then land up buying it for the use in their wood work.

The R&D of Pidilite launched innovative brand extensions for Fevicol. One of them being Fevicol Marine, which had an exceptional bonding strength and was an ideal adhesive for bonding wood, plywood, laminates, veneers, particle board, kitchen units, wall units where exposure to water and humidity was high.

Fevicol Marine was a specialized waterproof adhesive that protected furniture from de-bonding even when exposed to water. A piece of furniture was subject to a lot of stress due to change in weather, moisture, infrequent, and continuous exposure to water. This often resulted in opening of joints and de-bonding of laminates in spite of using good quality material. The special chemical properties gave a superior bonding result along with waterproofing. The product ensured that bonded plywood would remain intact, even if it is kept in water for 48 hours, or in boiling water for up to an hour. Moreover, this adhesive was very useful for making furniture in areas like kitchen, bathroom, balcony, and roof-top terrace where exposure to moisture was high.

Fevicol Marine enjoyed great success in the market and was able to capture a sizable market share across the country. The variant—though launched for a specific end use—turned out to be even usurping their veteran brand Fevicol SH. Fevicol SH was a synthetic resin adhesive intended for wood working and binding plywood, laminate, veneers, MDF, and all types of boards and cork. It was also used to manufacture sporting goods and book binding. Fevicol SH achieved handling strength in 8 to 10 hours, fully curing in 24 hours. Earlier on the applicators (carpenters) were using Fevicol SH, but after Fevicol Marine was launched, a majority of the applicators started using Fevicol Marine due to its versatile properties.

The brand came into existence when the demand arose from the consumers to have a faster-setting adhesive which would be equally effective when exposed to water. The brand extension was conceptualized and launched in 2010

Fevicol Speedx was devised to provide handling strength in 2 hours which improved productivity and was cost effective to the user. Fevicol SH Xtra was conceptualized to enhance the offering of Fevicol SH and provide superior tack development, early-handling strength development, and faster-setting time.

Marketability of the finished wood work was pivotal to the users of the brand. Clients would often request for new age materials like PVC or Acrylic sheets to be used in the wood work. For this purpose, the applicators required an adhesive which would meet this need, and along with it, provide a factory-finished look to carpentered furniture.

The essence of the brand and the brand extensions continued to focus on the changing consumer preferences, and hence, were successful and gained market popularity.

► Next Steps

So, after the brief review, Mr. Thakkar was now ready to discuss the next year's marketing plans with the CFO before presenting it to the Board of Directors and the CEO.

Fevicol reigned supreme as a market leader and enjoyed remarkable trust from its customers. If the rumor was true about the big paint company entering the adhesives market, then the marketing team needed a strategy which would further strengthen Fevicol's brand equity and capitalize on the brand extensions to face a potentially formidable competitor.

EXHIBIT 1

OLD PACK AND LOGO OF FEVICOL

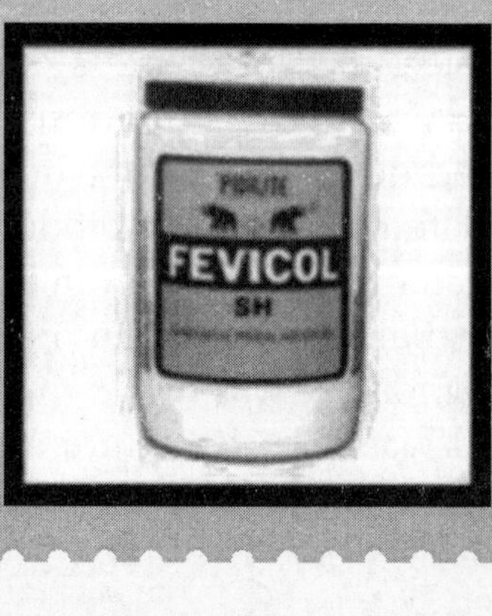

FEVICOL

EXHIBIT 2

FEVICOL FURNITURE BOOK

EXHIBIT 3

FEVICOL MR PACK FOR ART AND STATIONERY

EXHIBIT 4

FEVICOL NEW LOGO AND PACK

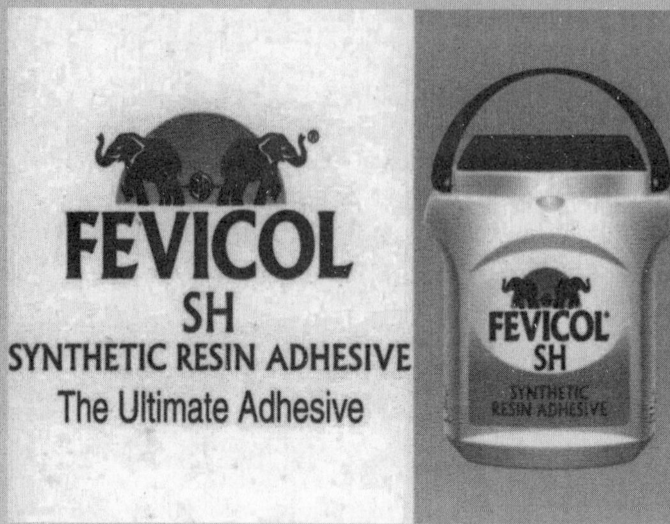

EXHIBIT 5

OGILVY AND MATHER PICKED UP A SILVER LION IN THE FILM CATEGORY FOR 'FEVICOL BUS' IN 2002.

EXHIBIT 6

VARIOUS ADVERTISING CAMPAIGNS OF FEVICOL

a. Another classic "pakde rehna chodna nahi"

b. Fevicol celebrating the marriage bond

c. The "Yamraaj" (God of death) idea.

d. During election time they came up with "clever chair" campaign, which was a major hit.

e. The moochwali campaign celebrated 50 years of their existence.

f. The brand enjoyed immense popularity when it was featured in a song enacted by leading Bollywood starts for the feature film "Dabangg 2."

CASE 14 Designing and Managing Services

▶ Mirchi & Mime-A Perfect Jugalbandi of Contemporary Fine Cuisine and a Unique Service

"A well-crafted case that succinctly captures the truly unique characteristics of Mirchi & Mime and beautifully blends them with the core dimensions of superior customer service. It constitutes a very interesting and rich context for demonstrating to students how creative design and superior service, coupled with concern for society at large, can contribute to marketing excellence and sustainable competitive advantage." **Dr A Parasuraman, Professor of Marketing & Holder of the James W. McLamore Chair, University of Miami (author SERVQUAL Model)**

▶ The Premise

This unique 110-seater bar and grill restaurant in Hiranandani Gardens, Powai (in Mumbai), was started by Prashant Issar and Anuj Shah, alumni of the Henley School of Business (UK). Prashant had 22 years of experience in the food and beverage industry while Anuj has 15 years in the corporate administration world. Both were eager to put their entrepreneurial abilities to the sword. Both had peaked very early in their professional life and were bored with enjoying the "good life" of doing nothing challenging. As they were looking for investment avenues, two potential investors suggested the concept of Signs, a Toronto-based restaurant, which was hailed for its innovative approach of employing the deaf. This duo, then, decided to bring the unique and novel concept to India.

Their vision was to take this concept further with a total of 21 mime concept restaurants in India, London, Dubai, and Singapore by 2018. Driven by the values taught to them by their alma mater, the two believed in two core values that shaped the inception of this unique restaurant nestled in the heart of Powai, Mumbai:

1. *Integrity and commitment are more important than capability and skill.*
2. *It is important to generate wealth for society in addition to generating wealth for the individual.*

Diversity in culture, societal gap, and acceptability of this concept in India inspired them to meet the people who would go on to become their most popular brand ambassadors for "Mirchi & Mime".

▶ The Journey

Before opening the restaurant, Anuj and Prashant first studied sign language and recruited staff from the Rochiram T. Thadani High School for Hearing Handicapped located in Chembur east, Mumbai.

They spoke with not just their prospective employees, but with their families as well. They explained that the job would provide lasting, viable means of employment, and that would not only provide sustenance to the employee but in most cases bring economic stability to their families as well. The pre-requisites for a job at this restaurant were a radiant smile that came from the heart, focus in endeavour, a hunger for progress, and an uncanny intuitiveness for service to please others. The duo believed that integrity and commitment (internal values) are more important than capability and skill (external values), which can be developed.

Once the staff was recruited, they were trained for eight weeks by experts from Dr. Reddy's Foundation with support from NASEOH. The module was led by Clyde and Ranjan, who joined the core team. The program comprised of introductory modules on life skills, job readiness and the English language, followed by an extensive basic hospitality skills module. Furthermore, the entire core team of Squaremeal Foods, including the chefs, were taught basic sign language by a certified tutor. The transformation of the team under Clyde & Ranjan's guidance was ground breaking.

With the staff trained and ready for service, the team felt that this was certainly do-able. Going by the saying "A restaurant can last forever but the concept cannot", the team realised that it was food that would have to lead the concept and service was only value addition and the icing on the cake.

They managed to put together a team of two young chefs with contrasting experience in world food and classical Indian cuisine. This led to a culmination of an unusual and exciting compilation of dishes, which defines their strength and brand proposition, "Good food served quietly".

► Integration of the SERVQUAL Model in Defining the Service Philosophy

As firm believers of the saying by Donald Knuth, "The best practise is inspired by theory", this duo has spent considerable amount of time to build the core ecosystem of the restaurant. The SERVQUAL model—developed by Parasuraman, Zeithaml, and Berry in the 80s (popularly known as the PZB Model) and assimilated by Prashant and Anuj during their Henley Business School days—was used as the fundamental model and facilitator to measure, evaluate, and manage quality analysis of services in the restaurant.

The five dimensions—as used in the SERVQUAL model—were profoundly studied to arrive at the exclusive check list to build this unique fine-dining experience.

- **Tangibles** refer to physical facilities, equipment, and appearance of personnel—the packaging for the delivery of the service.
- **Reliability** is the firm's ability to perform the promise service accurately and responsibly every time a customer interface is encountered.
- **Responsiveness** is the firm's willingness to help customers and provide prompt, effective service.
- **Assurance** is knowledge and courtesy of employees and their ability to inspire trust and confidence.
- **Empathy** is caring and individualized attention paid to customers—service delivered from the heart.

Careful attention was given to each of the above five dimensions at each and every stage to make this conceptual dream a living reality

Tangibles

The team believed that tangibles in a restaurant business are highly important as a poor design gives rise to apprehension. A clear and simple brief was given: design was to be atypical of an Indian restaurant with a comfortable dining space which is contemporary, and has a stylish and contemporary cutting-edge design.

Minnie Bhatt of Minnie Bhatt Design transformed the bare shell into a stylish international space with carefully planted moments of truth. The restaurant is quirkily decorated, with a semi-private dining area settled under a wall decoration of mix and match, vintage culinary utensils, and with bell jars covering objects spread across the restaurant that exudes a bistro like charm. One wall boasts of a collection of traditional Indian recipes from an anonymous cookbook written in the 1900s, thus giving the customer a hint of what cuisine he/she can expect.

Some of the key points considered while executing the design were:

1. An open-door design layout was picked over a closed curtain layout as the team believed that it is the openness to accept and portray talent in the form of service that would help them excel in achieving their vision of wealth creation for the society.
2. Critical attention was to given to ensure that it was a restaurant and not a gimmick. Nothing that portrayed the concept of mime or silence was encouraged nor shown.
3. The tangibles were kept as generic as possible which did not give a hint to anyone about the concept of mime.
4. Special care was given to the sensitive nature of the staff's disabilities. The menus were designed to visually show the customer what dish to order.
5. The menu layout is in a matrix format and easy to order. Instructions for sign language are illustrated and explained on the menu.

Reliability

The dimension of reliability was brought across the table with the quality of food and experience. The team worked upon making food the compelling reason to revisit coupled with service being a value-added experience.

Responsiveness

The inherent quality of responsiveness is evident among all the members of the team at Mirchi & Mime. Even during the afternoon hours when the restaurant remains closed, a visitor is welcomed with a smiling face and is promptly offered a glass of water by anyone who sees him approaching the closed doors. A feeling of warmth resides within the four walls of the restaurant, and it is this culture that persuades a visitor to step in again to enjoy the splendid culinary experience.

Within only four months of the launch, the restaurant was flooded with long queues, social media buzz, blogger reviews, and testimonials and reviews by visitors on Zomato. Responsiveness to the team had a different meaning. None of the visitor comments were liked, shared, or responded to by the team. Instead alterations in the menu, cuisine, and design were made based on the customer's comments but without a response online. With the massive flow of reviews online, the team believed that responding to comments would eventually result in creation of a template response that would act as an expectation ground for the masses.

Assurance

The staff went through a rigorous training module which included sessions on Life Science, job readiness, simple English, and service skills. This training was not only given to the 27 servers but also to the others in the team to build understanding and relevance in a holistic manner.

Stock options for employees were given to all who completed one year of service, which further boosted the morale of the team and led to newer heights of customer delight. Mirchi & Mime was a second home for the employees that rewarded them richly for delivering a great service to the customers.

Empathy

The training helped build a sense of confidence and achievement within them, which indeed led to their abilities being used effectively and honoured. The line on the T-Shirts read "I know sign language. What's your super power?" instilled the rightful reason for being employed.

The service gap is defined as the difference between what the customer expects and what is delivered. This gap was bridged by eliminating any kind of expectations from the customer. There was no buzz created at the time of launch with the sign boards, concept, or cuisine. The team believed that when there are zero expectations, the experience is equal to the expectation, and it is this experience that will bring back the customer. Thus, the entire business model revolved around serving the best quality food silently and effectively.

▶ The Experience

The concept of Mirchi & Mime is pretty simple. Diners are greeted at the entrance by a hostess who points to the reservations-of-the-day book. Reserved diners scan the book for their names and point, while walk-ins can simply shake their heads and, well, walk in! Once seated at their tables—with illustrated menus in their hands—diners can, once again, simply point and indicate the number of portions. An easy-to-follow gesture glossary is also appended to the menu for diners to indicate other eating accoutrements like cutlery, crockery, salt, pepper, spices, etc.

Manager's intervention takes place at various touch-points in the service delivery process. The first one occurs with the host introducing the concept to first-time diners. Sign language is demonstrated to the diner to help ease the service experience.

Hello | Welcome to.. | Mirchi | & Mime

My name is | Point to your name plate | My sign name is...

My manager's sign name is... | Thank you | Welcome | Positive or negative satisfaction

After a 10–12 minute wait, dishes start making an appearance on the table accompanied by tiny signboards indicating what each dish is, and the rest is as simple as sitting down to a meal at any other "regular" restaurant. And once you're done, a simple chin tap with your right hand conveys your appreciation—a gesture enthusiastically appreciated by the server. It conveys that you have made their day. This is followed by bill payment and thanks.

► Experience Speak

An anonymous review on Zomato is an indication that the philosophy of the Mirchi & Mime team is understood, appreciated, and loved by all. The reviewer stated, "The numerous positive reviews of this place finally made me get to Mirchi & Mine on a busy weekday. The guys running this place were kind enough to get us a place promptly. Let me start with the wonder I had when I saw all these guys serving all the customers with a huge smile on their face. An absolutely amazing concept! I am glad someone thought of this. But mind you, it's not just about the Mime, it's all also about the Mirchi, the food'.

► Scalability

The team plans to open 21 mime concept restaurants in India, London, Dubai, and Singapore by 2018. With immense scope and availability of resources to pursue this dream, the venture is likely to face challenges at every stage of their journey. The Mime chain has now opened 2 restaurants in Mumbai with 52 mime servers and hopes to scale this unique fine-dining restaurant concept across major cities in India and globally.

► Questions

1. Discuss the pros and cons of the unique Mirchi & Mime fine dining concept.
2. In this new era of shifting customer relationship, how has Mirchi & Mime forged a strong internal and external customer-based engagement using customer empowerment and customer co-production to deliver compelling value to the relevant stakeholders?
3. What are the challenges you foresee for the team on their journey to build and expand to 21 restaurants by 2018?
4. Keeping the SERVQUAL model in mind, what are the gaps seen in the restaurant service industry? How has Mirchi & Mime managed to bridge these gaps?
5. The restaurant was designed to give a unique dining experience to all. What is your response to expanding the mime concept into a home delivery service? Will this lead to exploitation of the specially-abled community or increase the revenues for the business dramatically? Will this concept work? Can the unique experience of the restaurant be replicated in the home delivery mode of service delivery? If you were the decision maker in the Mirchi & Mime team, what decision would you take?

► Acknowledgement

Ms Trisha Parekh-Phd student in NITIE, Mumbai and former Research Associate at K J Somaiya Institute of Management Studies and Research, Mumbai for content building and drafting the case study.

CASE 15

Aachi Masala – Entering the North Indian *Masala* Category

Aachi Group, the South Indian multi-product, multi-brand conglomerate, has entered the highly competitive North Indian *masala* (spices) segment. Aachi Masala, the power brand of the group, has become a household name in the southern belt for its South Indian range of *masalas*. Created by Mr. A.D. Padmasingh Isaac, the Chairman and Managing Director (CMD) of Aachi Group, this group is now more than two decades old and has gradually grown from being just a *masala* brand to an FMCG company and enjoys a considerable mind share in South India, especially in Tamil Nadu. In 2015, Aachi Masala forayed into North Indian *masala* range as a part of its expansion strategy. Mr. Isaac was wondering if the brand, which has predominantly been catering to South Indian taste buds, will be able to earn and enjoy a similar position with its North Indian versions.

► The Industry at a Glance

The food processing industry of India **(Exhibit 1)**, accounts for more than 32% of the total food market of India and is growing at an average annual growth rate of 11%.[1, 2] It is ranked 5th in terms of production, consumption, and exports. It accounts for 14% of India's GDP and 13% of total exports.[3] As per Confederation of Indian Industry (CII) estimate, the food processing industries have the potential to attract more than US$ 33 billion of investment over the next 10 years.[4]

The sector is primarily divided into three broad segments.[5]

1. Primary food processing comprising sorting, grading and packaging of fruits and vegetables, milk, rice, spices, etc.
2. Secondary processing of food comprising of food re-shaped for ease of consumption includes flour, oil cakes, tea leaf, and beverages powder.
3. Tertiary processing of food (or) value-added food segment includes processed fruits and vegetables, juices, jam and jelly, etc.

The primary and secondary segments accounts for more than 60% of processed foods in value terms and the value-added food segment holds around 40% share in the total processed food market.

► Aachi Group

Aachi Group was established in the year 1995 by Mr. A.D. Padmasingh Isaac, a first generation entrepreneur hailing from Nazareth in Tirunelveli District of Tamil Nadu. After a stint in Godrej in sales and marketing positions, Mr. Isaac's entrepreneurial journey began with liquid blue brand, Twinkle. He launched it in pocket-friendly sachets catering majorly to the semi-urban and rural markets in Tamil Nadu.

Mr. Isaac attributes the idea of Aachi Masala to his mother Mrs. Flora and his wife Mrs. Thelma, whose cooking skills, especially the use of *masalas* inspired him to venture into this business.[6] Making women's work easy was also another inspiration behind the idea of Aachi, as per the company website.[7]

Aachi products are sold in more than twenty-five states in India. The brand has nearly 200 products with over 700 Stock Keeping Units (SKUs) as in the beginning of 2016.[8] The total employee strength of the group is in excess of 20,000. Latest company sources indicate that Aachi Group is growing at a CAGR of 30% over the last three years, which is higher than that of the industry average. The company is eyeing a turnover of ₹1200 crores for the year 2017–18. Over the years, Aachi group and Mr. Isaac have won many awards and accolades.

► All in the Family

Aachi group is a family-owned undertaking. While Mr. Isaac steers the group as its CMD, his sons Mr. Ashwin Pandian and Mr. Abhishek Abraham also play important roles in the management of the organization.

The Aachi Group comprises of the following companies

- Aachi Masala Foods Private Ltd – The parent company selling its core products, *masalas*[9]
- Aachi Spices & Foods Pvt Ltd – Division that concentrates on ground spices and food products
- Aachi Special Foods Pvt Ltd – Newly launched; includes packaged drinking water

Brands under Aachi Group:

Aachi Masala: The core brand comprising a gamut of packed ground spices.

Twin Birds: a special product for non-vegetarian pickle and curry items

Frispoo: The snack range

Twinkle: The home cleaning range

Tanjus: The bottled fruit juice range

Aachi packaged drinking water

Ponnii: a range of edible vegetable oil

Sabash: Herbal cosmetic brand

Blesso: Cough syrup

▶ Aachi Masala Division

The Aachi Kulambu Chilli Powder is the flagship product of Aachi. Despite being a failure during the early phases of the product launch, the product picked up and is currently one of those products that keeps the cash registers ringing for the company.

Red chilli is the main ingredient in most of the Aachi Masala products. The portfolio includes blended *masalas* for generic vegetarian and non-vegetarian South Indian recipes such as sambar, rasam, biriyani, vathal kuzhambu, tamarind rice powder, lemon rice powder, etc., in the vegetarian segment, and chilli chicken, pepper chicken, chicken 65, egg curry, fish curry, mutton curry *masala*, etc., in the non-vegetarian *masala* segment. The ground spices range includes the flagship kuzhambu chili powder, red chilli powder, coriander powder, turmeric powder, etc.

Company sources say that for new product development and manufacturing, Mr. Isaac's everyday morning walks provided him with the insights. It is said that he used to give a quick scan into the dustbins during his walks to understand the consumption pattern in his neighbourhood, based on the empty product wrappers thrown. This helped him to learn and study the food habits, product usage, and preferences of people in that locality and create new products. The core raw materials, red chilli and turmeric, are procured directly from farmers. For instance, chillies are sourced from Guntur, turmeric from Erode, coriander from Rajasthan, pepper and cardammom from Munnar, cumin and mustard from Madhya Pradesh, and so on.

The manufacturing facility of Aachi is located at Keel Ayyanabakkam, 15 km from Chennai in Tamil Nadu. It has a manufacturing capacity of 120 metric tonnes of spice powders and spice mixes per day. Production of some *masala* variants is outsourced for cost efficiency, but sources say that the company adheres to strict quality control system to ensure quality of the finished products. For quality testing, the group invested in an exclusive testing services entity, Scientific Food Testing Services (P) Ltd., for following food standards in the products based on biological and chemical content.

The manufacturing process is governed by the Food Safety Management System with ISO 9001:2008 Certification. The R&D Team coordinates with the manufacturing units in developing new products, packaging material, food labelling, product shelf life, and suitability of new products for human consumption.

The spices and spice mix powders are packed in automatic packing machines. Packs are ensured to be tamper proof and sturdy enough to retain the aroma and flavour for a longer shelf life. The dispatch is done with the company's own trucks. The distribution is supported by a sales team, which is monitored directly by the CMD.

Over the years the brand has extended into categories likes ready-to-cook range with products such as gulab jamun mix, rava idly mix, pal ada payasam mix, rava kesari mix, etc., It also manufactures rice paste varieties such as biriyani rice paste, tamarind rice paste, tomato rice paste, etc., and pickles in a wide range from lemon, mango, tomato, mixed vegetable, garlic, citron, etc., Ghee and jams are also being manufactured. The brand currently has over 250 products in its range.

Aachi's products are available in different package sizes ranging from 100 grams to 5 kg packs, catering to different buyer segments. Apart from this, the regular ground spices are also available in sachets priced at ₹2, ₹5, and ₹10 to target the lower-middle income segments. Most products have a shelf life of 24 months, which again is higher than that provided by competitors which ranges from 9 to 18 months.

Aachi's products reach the consumers through 5000 agents and 12 lakh retailers. The product range is classified into 8 divisions for easy distribution. As per the company sources, Aachi offers more than 20% gross margins to retailers, which again is higher than the market standards which ranges from 8–14 %.

With a view to serve small retailers in towns and villages, Aachi used the Hawker Sales Distributors, whose everyday responsibility is to go all around and sell Aachi brand of products in the remotest corners of markets across India.[10] The project began in April 2014 and currently there are around 700 hawker sales force distributing Aachi brand of products in the markets.

Apart from the conventional distribution network, Aachi also opened Aachi Model Shops to stock and sell the entire range of Aachi group products. The company believes that this model can enable customers to choose from a wide range of products, including those that may not be available in their neighbourhood stores such as toiletries and health products. The Aachi range of *masala*s and food products are also exported to USA and the Middle-East. The company received the Export Excellence Award for 2016 from FIEO – Federation of Indian Export Organisation.

From the initial stages, Aachi has been investing on above-the-line (ATL) promotions. The TV ads of the brand are very popular. During the launch of Aachi Kuzhambu chilli powder, Aachi roped in Devayani, a leading Tamil actress to promote the product. Actors like Satyaraj were also featured in TV ads promoting non-vegetarian *masala* line. In the most recent TV advertisement of the brand, Mr. Isaac himself promotes the brand, showcasing the procurement and manufacturing practices and the motto of the organization. Below-the-line (BTL) promotions like quantity purchase schemes with the objectives of achieving a reasonable level of distribution and a good deal of shelf/string space in retail outlets is also done alongside ATL for better reach and coverage.

► North Indian Masala

Unlike the South Indian *masalas*, where red chilli is a dominant ingredient, the North Indian *Masala*s have a unique taste and flavor where a distinct combination of spices are used. Spices such as bay leaves, cinnamon, pepper, cloves, cumin, fennel, *kasuri methi* (dry fenugreek leaves), mango powder, mint, pomegranate seeds, etc., form important ingredients in North Indian *masala*s alongside *lal mirch* (red chilli), giving it the distinctiveness.

Aachi Masala forayed into the North Indian *masala* segment in 2015 as a part of its expansion strategy. The product range includes Garam Masala—the universal *masala*, which is used in most of the North Indian dishes in two varieties, Royal and Super Garam Masala, Kitchen King Masala—another universal *masala* which can be used both in vegetarian and non-vegetarian dishes, Chaat *Masala*, Channa Masala, Pani Puri Masala, Jal Jeera Masala, Paneer Tikka Masala, etc. The package sizes of North Indian *masala*s are 15 grams and 50 grams for most of the products. The company believed that its unique packaging strategy, which gives its products a longer shelf life, and a pocket-friendly pricing strategy will be able to take its range successfully to the northern and eastern regions of the country.

► The Competition

The major competitors in the category are Everest and MDH at the national level.[11].

Everest is India's largest spices brand based in Mumbai. The brand is stocked by 400,000 outlets in more than 1000 towns across India. More than 3.705 billion packs of Everest are sold each year. There are more than 42 varieties of *masala* blends under the Everest brand name.

MDH (the Mahashian Di Hatti Limited) specializes in several unique traditional blends of spices suitable for different North Indian recipes. The company was founded in 1919 by Mahashay Chuni Lal as a small shop in Sialkot, and has since grown in popularity all over India. The MDH brand name is very well known throughout India.

Apart from these, brands like Catch and Ramdev Masalas also enjoy a considerable market share in the North Indian masala Category.

At the regional level there are players like MTR, which has a very strong presence in South India. MTR was established in 1924 as a restaurant chain by the Maiya family in Bangalore.[12] Apart from its South Indian masala range, the company has a wide range of North Indian masalas and ready-to-cook range, and targets the northern and eastern markets, and also the global markets.

State-level player, Shakti Masala has also got a decent market share in the *masala* segment.[13] The company has been operating from Erode, Tamil Nadu since 1975. The brand offers a wide variety of South Indian and North Indian *masala* range.

► Road Ahead

Aachi Masala's core differentiators are affordability, shelf life, distribution, and retailer friendliness. It has found itself a distinct place in Tamil Nadu households, especially in the last decade. With a brand name that resonates with the Tamil-speaking market segment, it also enjoys a considerable mind share and brand recall, as per the company sources. Despite being seen as a strategic move to establish itself as a national brand, its expansion into the highly competitive North Indian *masala* range and other new products that cater to the pan-Indian customers, has its own challenges. The brand presence of the competitors in the North Indian markets and brand loyalty of the customers are the major challenges apart from the logistics and retailing challenges. Only time can say if Aachi is able to taste success in its product and market expansion strategy, especially in the North Indian *masala* range.

EXHIBIT 1

FOOD PROCESSING

Sector Snapshot - FOOD PROCESSING
Sector Contribution To Emplyment Generation

CARG: 11.8%

Sector Contribution To Emplyment Generation

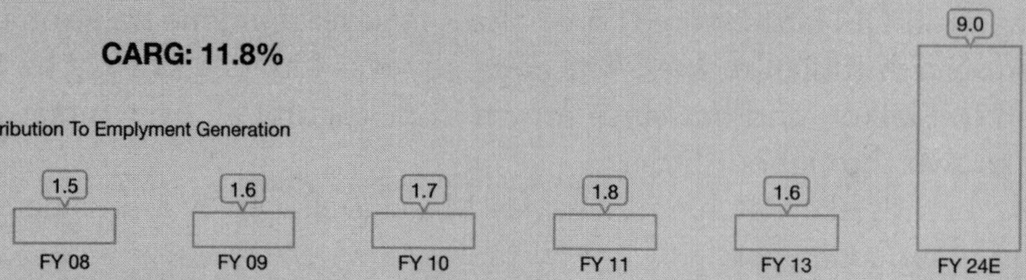

Key Policy Initiatives

Infrastuctures	Food processing sector has been assigned priority status for bank credit 60 Agri Export Zones (AEZ) have been set up across the country
Investments	In FY16, Ministry of food processing industries granted funds worth U$D18.81 million for the ongoing Mega Food Park Projects
Join Ventures And Tie Ups	Many global and Indian companies are getting into joint ventures to make global products available in India. Starbucks and TATA Alliance, The largest joint Ventures

Processed food exports from india rose at a CAGR of 21.5% during FY11-16, accounting for USD19, 337.4 million in FY16

Surge in demand for fruits and vegetables witnessed with shift in consumption. Change in production pattern also notified with growing demand

By 2024, food processing sector to employ 9 million people inIndia

Sector Advantages

2016: Market size of food processing industry is USD258 Billion

Import duty scrapped on capital goods and raw materials for 100% export-oriented units Excise duty exemption of 100% for goods used in installation of cold storage facilities

2020F: Market size forcast to reach USD482 Billion

Source: www.ibef.org

EXHIBIT 2

AWARDS CONFERRED ON MR. A.D. PADMASINGH ISAAC

Sl. No.	Name of the Award / Award Constituted by	Award Given For	Year
1	National Award	The Best Employer Award	2016
2	Most Influential Leader	ERTC	2017
3	Asia's Most Promising Brands	World Consulting & Research Corporation.	2017
4	Centennial Legacy Award	LIONS Clubs	2017
5	International Achievers Conference	Fatest Growing Indian Company Excellence Award	2016
6	Confederation of Indian Industry	CII - 5S Excellence Awards	2016
7	Export Excellence Award - FIEO	Export Excellence Award	2016
8	Fast 50	India's Fastest Growing Brands	2016
9	WCRC Leaders	Power Leaders	2016
10	The Brand Trust Report	India's Most Trusted Spice	2015
11	Mayan Awards (Vista India Communications)	Helping Hand to Humanity	2015
12	Indian Institute of Materials Management	Significant Sontribution to SCM field	2015
13	Comniscient	India's Most Attractive Brand	2015
14	Corporation Bank	Best Entrepreneur	2015
15	WCRC Leaders Summit 2014	Asia's Fastest Growing Marketing Brands	2014
16	ABK - AOTS DOSOKAI	Sustenance Award	2014
17	Lions Club International	Worlds No 1 Masala Products	2014
18	TEA Award	Best Spices Advertisements "Aromatic Kings' Award	2013
19	ABK - AOTS DOSOKAI	ABK - AOTS CDISSIA 5S Trophy & Certificate	2012
20	Lions International	Life Time Achievement Award	2012
21	FICCI Tamil Nadu State Counil	CSR Excellence Award	2012
22	MEGA TV	MEGA Womens Award	2010
23	TIE Chennai	Extreme Entrepreneur Award	2010
24	Times Group	Trialblazers	2010

CERTIFICATIONS HELD BY AACHI GROUP OF COMPANIES

- Mr. Isaac is committed to supply high quality food products to satisfy the expectations of millions of customers globally through strictly adherence to Food Safety standards. Aachi products are made under ISO and HACPT certification.
- Most Aachi products are packed at their own manufacturing units. To have control on Quality and Food safety standards. Aachi relies on the CQAT. It is headed by a General Manager having rich experience in Food Processing. Testing and Food Safety. CQAT has QA Analysis at each and every manufacturing unit. CQAT Members are trained on HACCP. Consumer Affairs. Legal Metrology, Packaging Technology, Six Sigma, 5S Tools, Global Food Safety Initiative (conducted by US AID) etc.
- To comply withthe Food Safety Managment System (FSMS / ISO 22000:2005), all incoming Raw materials and Packaging are tested for compliance to set specifications. All produc flows are monitored on-line as part of Quality Assurance. Quality Analysts keep close vigil on Process Flow for compliance to Standard Operating Procedures and Regulatory issues.
- CQAT monitors the on-going productions to fulfill the high quality expectations of Aachi. CQAT recommends Imporovements in Process. Automation, Modernizing present facilities and implementing latest testing methodologies to check Food Adulterants. Quantity inherent properties of Process Ingredients and Human Health Pathogens to the Top Management.
- Vendors, Audits are made to identify best suppliers of repute. Aachi CQAT bears the moral responsibility in achieving the Vision and Quality Policy of Aachi, It strives hard to protect the 'Aachi' brand name and secure its reputation.

Source: www.aachigroup.com

CASE 16 SliceRooms: A Slice of Time, a Cut of Profits!

"I usually travel to Delhi and Mumbai for impromptu meetings which may be for two to three hours. I would take a morning flight and return to Chennai the same day. We would meet in the board room of a hotel or at times meet in the lobby of a five-star hotel depending on the time availability. As a hotelier myself, I am able to connect to the idea that business travellers are in dire need of hotel rooms for a short stay of two or three hours."

A Laxman, concept owner, SliceRooms.com

A 2 p.m. check-in and a 12-noon check-out is the dominant hotel industry practice across the world. This two-hour window enables the hotel to make the room ready for the next guest. In practice, it would take less than 30 minutes to have a room ready and that would vary depending on the size of the room. It is also seen that in practice, around 10% of the guests check out early in the morning. "Given this situation, around 10% of the hotel rooms in a hotel would be vacant from around 8 a.m. to 2 p.m. daily. These rooms are the inventory for SliceRooms," muses Laxman.

The availability of such unutilized inventory and the required need of business travellers inspired Laxman to launch slicerooms.com as a virtual marketplace designed to connect supply with demand from travelers with unmet day-stay needs.

► What is Micro Stay?

The concept of providing rooms on hourly basis is called micro stay. Based loosely on the concept of capsule hotels, micro stays also go by the name of day stay, short stay, capsule stay, and transit stay. Micro stays work well for the traveler who otherwise has to wait it out in the airport departure halls while some have access to airport lounges. A note on the Frotels website also highlights the poor state of public washrooms in India.

This could serve as an additional motivator for the harried business traveler to seek micro stays. Today, online booking platforms and apps like Stay Uncle, 6 Hourly, and Chatur Musafir make available various options for micro stays. Yet, some of the aggregators and hotels refuse to entertain unmarried couples. Frotels alludes to the stigma of short stay as a substandard activity.

"It's probably not fun to ask a hotel receptionist to give you a room for a few hours in the afternoon. The receptionist will assume you want it for a romantic assignation and will look at you in a certain way. You will feel embarrassed for one of two reasons: a) your business meeting has been horribly misconstrued and you can't now face going up to the room with a client; or b) you have been found out", notes the Economist blog.

RA Christopher, General Manager - Operations, SliceRooms adds that micro stay is a popular concept in developed markets. However, the micro stay market in India faces multiple challenges like resistance from hoteliers and stigma attached to micro stays. According to NG Ramesh, this concept works best for the business traveler who travels back the same day to the originating city.

► Does it Make Business Sense for Hotels?

In a highly competitive environment in which the hotel industry operates, achieving profitability and a decent ROI is a nightmare. On an average, hotels offer a discount of up to 25% on the rack rate (which is the published tariff). It is also common practice to offer an agency commission of about 20% to OTAs (online travel agents). Christopher of SliceRooms avers that the variable cost of a room typically ranges from 8.50% to 10% on the rack rate. This variable cost includes amenities, linen and laundry, guest supplies, cleaning, and expenses on other optional services like fruit basket, turndown service, and mineral water.[1]

The hotel industry norm is to project 70% to 80% of the published tariff as budgeted Average Room Revenue (ARR) after offering an average discount of 20% to 30% to both FIT and corporate clients.[3, 4] Laxman says that "the hotels can sell the same room twice a day and this additional room revenue accompanied with very negligible additional cost, would add both to the bottom line and top line of the hotel". This would further enhance the projected ARR. Therefore, there is no doubt that short stay or micro stay makes immense business sense for the hotels.

► The Target Customer

Our target customer is the business traveler who returns the same day to the originating location or travels to different locations in a day, and the pilgrim who visits multiple places of worship in a day. But reaching out to them seems to be a challenge according to Christopher. He wonders if social media is the best option to reach out to them. He also hopes that once demand picks up, the hotel industry would embrace this concept enthusiastically.

Apart from these travellers, corporate clients could also embrace the micro stay concept to conduct quick meetings, which may also increase revenue for other hotel services such as the restaurant, coffee shop, and bar.

Currently, the metros and tier II cities have the potential to attract such target customers. In addition, some of the tier III cities and pilgrim centres are also likely to generate interest and demand. For such travellers, SliceRooms fulfils the unmet needs of a good room to take rest for a while before a meeting or visit, and a private place to freshen up and unwind in between journeys or work.

► The Micro Stay Market

Globally business travel has increased phenomenally and India is no exception. In India, Tier II and Tier III cities are growing and business is expanding. Based on industry sources, Laxman estimates that about two lakh business travellers fly back to their originating city the same day, in addition to about fifty thousand pilgrims.

There are 10,000 organized hotels all over India, which approximates to seven lakh rooms on sale every day. About 10% of the room guests check out early morning. This translates to 70 thousand rooms vacant between the early departure and the next guest arrival (unutilized room times). Be it an early arrival or delay in transit, the frequent business traveler is seeking limited hours of hotel stay.

With the estimated available inventory of 70 thousand rooms at an expected ARR realization of INR 1,500 per sliced room, the potential revenue per day translates to about INR 3,800 crores per year. However, Christopher values the micro stay market in India at around INR 600 crores currently, But expects it to grow 20% every year. This could mean that revenues on the micro capsule stay concept may reach INR 3,000 crores in five years and add about INR 2,400 crores to the bottom-line of the industry.

► How Does it Work?

SliceRooms.com is a virtual marketplace that facilitates to connect both demand (travelers' unmet day stay needs) and supply (unutilized room times). It facilitates optimal utilization of idle room inventory for hotels; customers can book hotel rooms for anywhere between 2 to 6 hours and need not pay for entire day stay if they stay for fewer hours. SliceRooms currently charges a 10% commission fee per booking to the hotel.

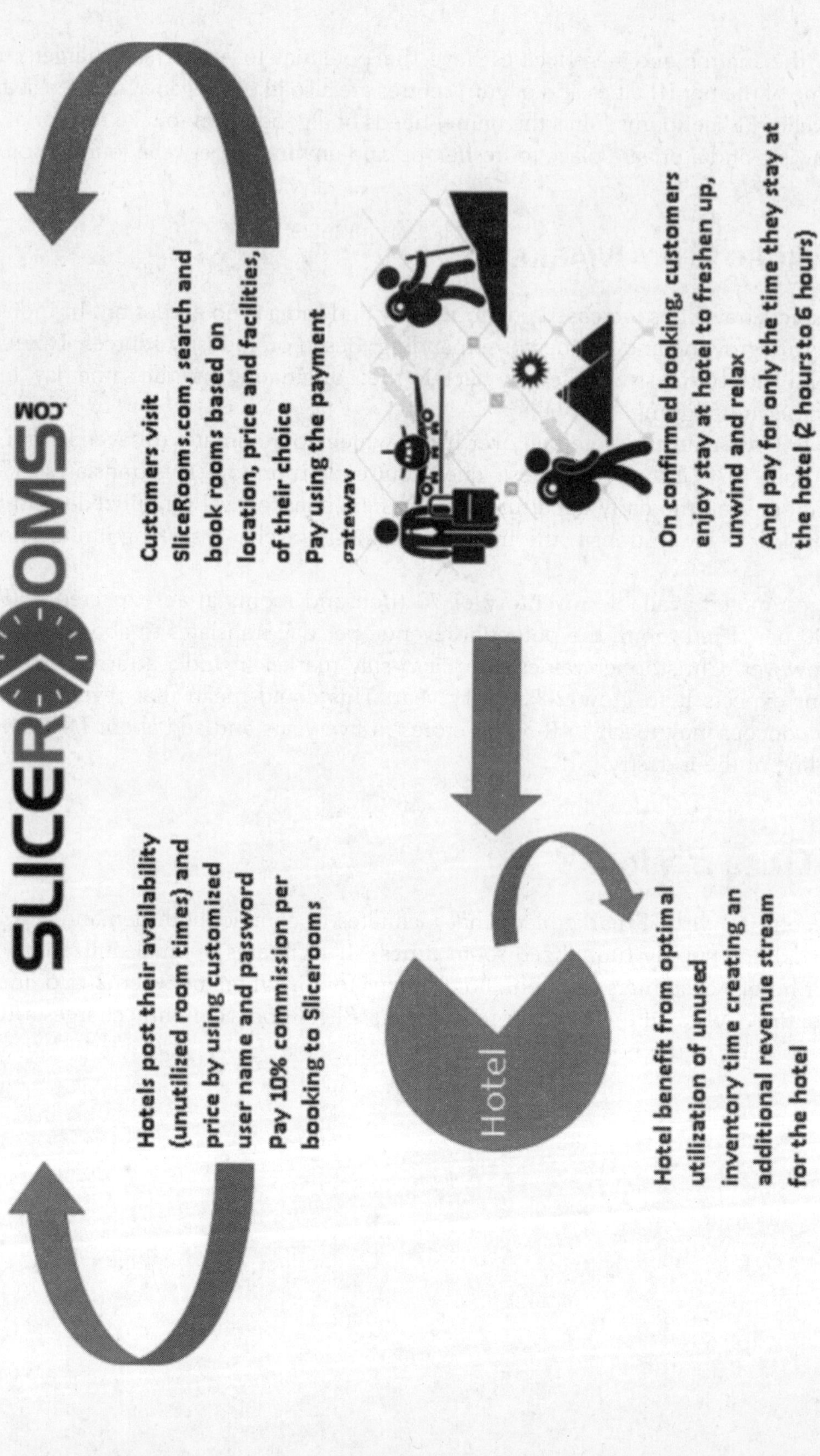

Fig. 1: How Slicerooms works

SliceRooms has a robust, asset-light business model with no inventory buying or a minimum guarantee with hotel owners. Dynamic pricing of tariffs on an hourly basis provides the customer with the comfort to pay only as per use. It is also examining tertiary revenue streams like banquets and marketing tie-ups for lead generation which would further enhance its own revenue. The potential to scale up with minimum investment is significant. It already has a presence in over 20 locations with a considerable footprint in South India. It has currently tie-ups with 400 hotels.

Hotels register themselves on the SliceRooms website to allow listing of their rooms and reach a wider customer base. Every hotel in the SliceRooms network is advised to follow a dynamic pricing methodology.

SliceRooms operates through a website which lists hotels in the SliceRooms network with an option for any new hotels to tie-up through an "Add your hotel" button. Based on the customer requirement selected via a custom search, hotel rooms with a rating of 1 to 5 stars are displayed with details of facilities. The first-two-hour pricing with pictures of the property are also shown. Customer makes bookings as desired and pays only for the duration of stay and not for the entire day. On confirmation of time of arrival and departure by the customer and confirmation of availability by the hotel, rooms are allotted and tariff is paid through an online payment gateway. As mentioned earlier, a 10% commission fee per booking is charged on payment (via online payment gateway/on arrival/check out), which is the primary revenue for SliceRooms.

► The Dilemma

The prognosis for micro stays is promising. That the concept of micro stays has caught popular imagination is not a mirage. Hotels have realized the addition this would make to their bottom line. For instance, Lemon Tree Hotel, Chennai displays the tariff prominently for a day-use room on their website. The 4-hour package for a business room with free Wi-Fi is on offer at INR 1,699/- plus taxes and the 8-hour package at INR 2,199/-. Contrast this with the non-refundable tariff of INR 3,999/- with free Wi-Fi and buffet breakfast.

SliceRooms is aware that marketing efforts have to be expended on multiple fronts. There is a need to sign up with hotels for inventory and build a consensus on pricing and the commissions, even as they reach out to the target customer.

Laxman now ponders what should be the go-to-market strategy. Among other decisions, he is debating the duration of the slice / micro stay. Should it be any number between two and six hours? What base rate should be charged for the micro stay? What then should be the duration of the extended stay beyond the base duration? What price should he charge for the extension? He also notes that while upscale and upper-upscale hotels in developed nations have adopted the micro stay concept, India is yet to catch up. But he is confident it will!

Rooms & Rates

Your Stay 6/19/2017 6/20/2017
Guests 1 Total Adults
Modify

Review Your Stay

View By Offer View By Room

enlarge

Day Use Room

• King/Queen beds • High speed WiFi
More about this room
From 1,699
INR / Night Excluding Taxes & Fees
Add To Compare

4 Hours Package

Stay between 8 a.m to 8 p.m for 4 hours. Includes: Free WiFi 24X7, 500 Bonus Points
Read more
Policies:
1,699
INR / Night
Excluding Taxes & Fees View Price Breakdown
Add To Compare

8 Hours Package

Stay between 8 a.m to 8 p.m for 8 hours. Includes: Free WiFi 24X7, 500 Bonus Points
Read more
Policies:
2,199
INR / Night
Excluding Taxes & Fees View Price Breakdown

Your Stay 6/19/2017 6/20/2017
Guests 1 Total Adults
Modify

Review Your Stay

View By Offer View By Room

4 Hours Package

Stay between 8 a.m to 8 p.m for 4 hours. Includes: Free WiFi 24X7, 500 Bonus Points
More about this Rate
Policies:
From 1,699
INR / Night Excluding Taxes & Fees

8 Hours Package

Stay between 8 a.m to 8 p.m for 8 hours. Includes: Free WiFi 24X7, 500 Bonus Points
More about this Rate
Policies:
From 2,199
INR / Night Excluding Taxes & Fees

Pay For Room-Free WiFi & Breakfast (non cancellable)

Pay for only your room and get additional 10% off. Includes: Free WiFi 24X7, Buffet breakfast, 500 bonus points
More about this Rate
Policies:
From 3,999
INR / Night Excluding Taxes & Fees

Pay For Room Only-Free WiFi and Breakfast

Pay for only your room and get: Free WiFi 24X7, Buffet breakfast, 500 bonus points
More about this Rate
Policies:
From 4,443
INR / Night Excluding Taxes & Fees

Pay For Room-Free WiFi, Breakfast & One Major Meal (Non-Cancellable)

Pay for only your room and get additional 10% off. Includes: Free WiFi 24X7, Buffet breakfast and lunch or dinner, 500 bonus points
More about this Rate
Policies:
From 4,447
INR / Night Excluding Taxes & Fees

Pay For Room-Free WiFi, Breakfast & One Major Meal

Pay for only your room and get: Free WiFi 24X7, Buffet breakfast and lunch or dinner, 500 bonus points
More about this Rate
Policies:
From 4,893
INR / Night Excluding Taxes & Fees

Business Package

Includes: 2 way airport/railway transfers, 2 pieces of laundary, Free WiFi 24X7, Buffet breakfast, 500 bonus points
More about this Rate
Policies:
From 5,043
INR / Night Excluding Taxes & Fees

DOUBLE YOUR HOTEL'S REVENUE!
www.slicerooms.com
support@slicerooms.com
+918015025044 / 044-65556755
SLICEROOMS.COM™

DOUBLE YOUR HOTEL'S REVENUE!
Introducing Slicerooms, the latest online platform that offers the few hours of room vacancy that arises in a hotel before a full time guest arrives to a short stay guest. It is a win-win concept that helps hoteliers earn more per room, while helping guests looking for just few hours of stay spend less on hotel bills.
Slicerooms has already joined hands with a wide range of hotels across India including star hotels to meet growing customer demand. It is now, your turn to register on slicerooms.com and let a winning concept in hotel business take you to the next level.
SLICEROOMS.COM™

NO MORE
Waiting on the
AIRPORT COUCH!
www.slicerooms.com

https://www.slicerooms.com
BOOK A ROOM
FOR FEW HOURS
Save on hotel bills
Type destination city
Type City Name
Choose Your Location
Choose Location
Hotel
Choose Hotel
Adult
1
Children
0
Check in date
27 October 2016
Time From
03 pm
Time To
05 pm
Search
STEP 1
FILL IN YOUR DETAILS!

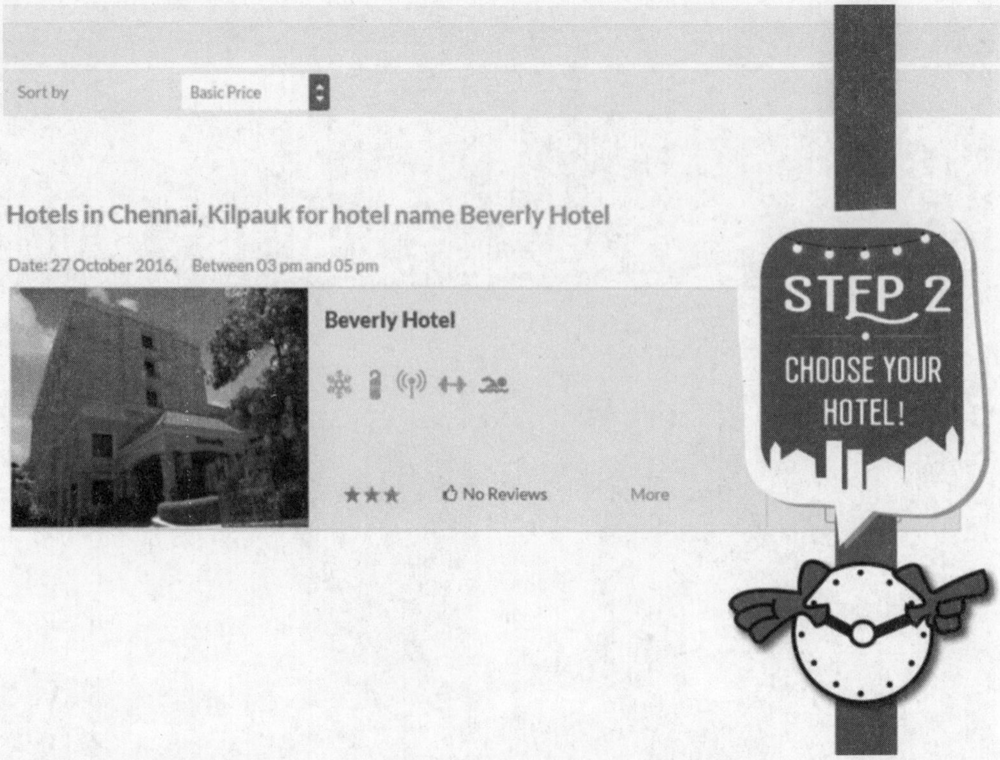
Sort by
Basic Price
Hotels in Chennai, Kilpauk for hotel name Beverly Hotel
Date: 27 October 2016, Between 03 pm and 05 pm
Beverly Hotel
No Reviews
More
STEP 2
CHOOSE YOUR HOTEL!

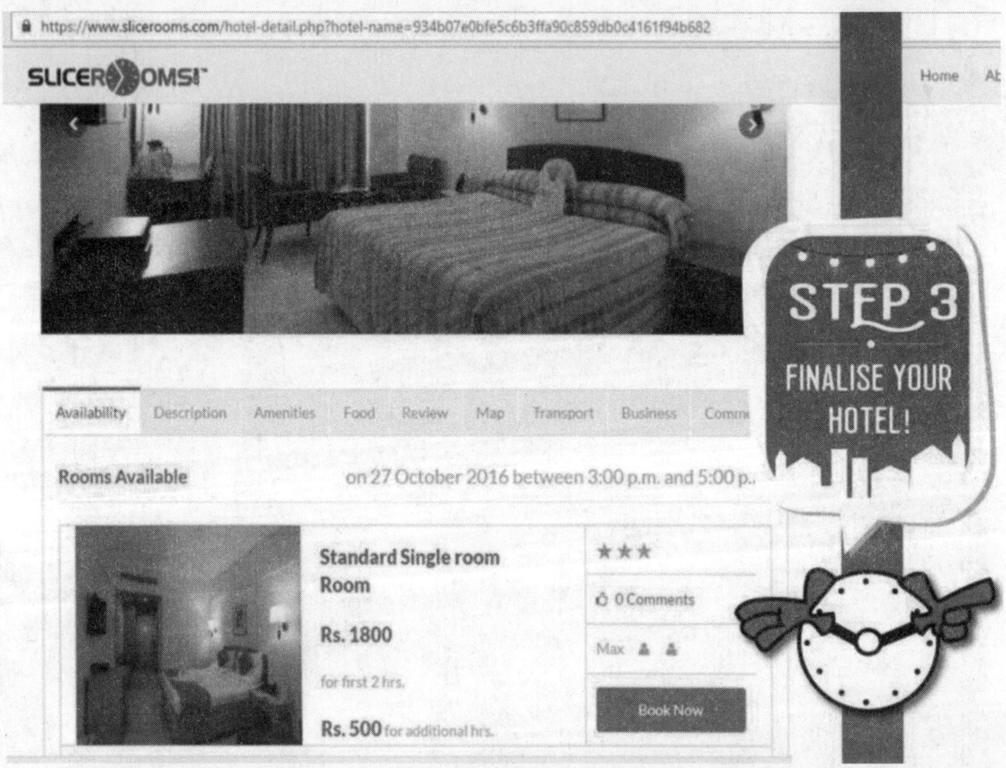
https://www.slicerooms.com/hotel-detail.php?hotel-name=934b07e0bfe5c6b3ffa90c859db0c4161f94b682
SLICEROOMS
Home
Availability
Description
Amenities
Food
Review
Map
Transport
Business
Rooms Available
on 27 October 2016 between 3:00 p.m. and 5:00 p.
Standard Single room Room
Rs. 1800
for first 2 hrs.
Rs. 500 for additional hrs.
0 Comments
Max
Book Now
STEP 3
FINALISE YOUR HOTEL!

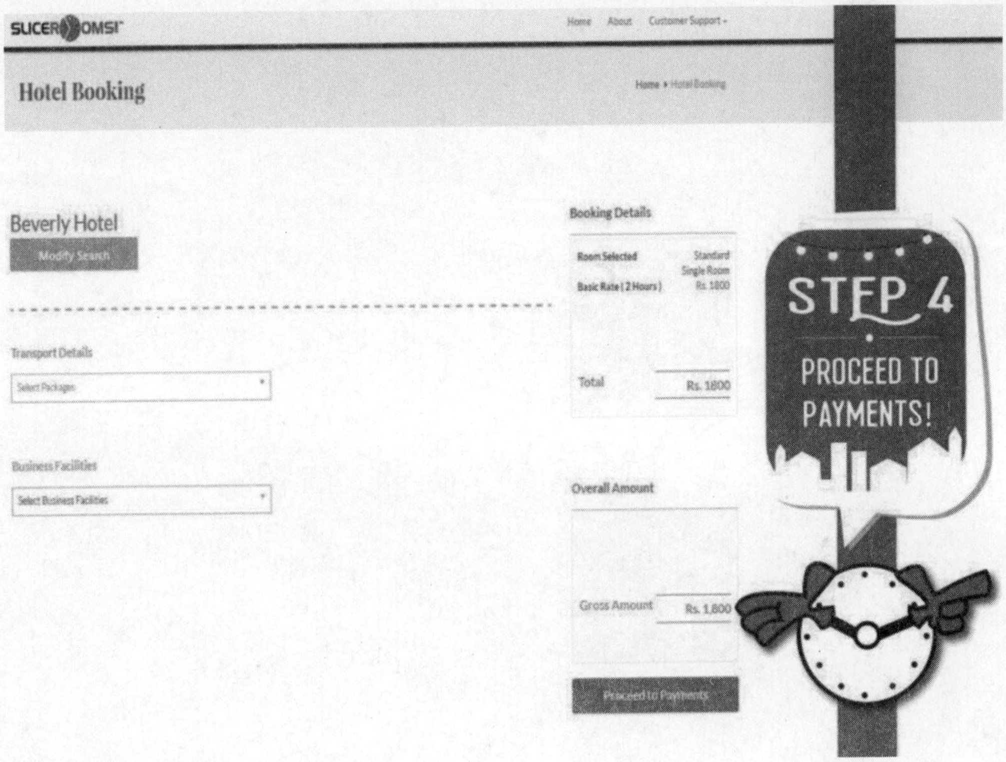
Home
About
Customer Support
Hotel Booking
Home ▸ Hotel Booking
Beverly Hotel
Modify Search
Transport Details
Select Packages
Business Facilities
Select Business Facilities
Booking Details
Room Selected
Standard Single Room
Basic Rate (2 Hours)
Rs. 1800
Total
Rs. 1800
Overall Amount
Gross Amount
Rs. 1,800
Proceed to Payments
STEP 4
PROCEED TO PAYMENTS!

CASE 17

Oreo in India – Launching and Establishing A Global Brand in India Using Integrated Marketing Communications Effectively

► Introduction

For most of its 100-year plus existence, Oreo was consistently America's best loved cookie, but today it is a well-established global brand. Mondelez International moved it into emerging markets quickly learning the rules of success in these hitherto unfamiliar markets, changing and refining the brands strategy and ultimately triumphed in winning over consumers. This case demonstrates how Oreo brand's successful entry into the Indian market was well orchestrated using the Communication Mix elements such as Advertising, Sales Promotion, Events and experiences and Public Relations to establish the brand during the launch phase and subsequently stabilize and grow the brand in India.

► Background and Company Profile

The "Oreo Biscuit" was first developed and produced by the National Biscuit Company (today known as Nabisco) in 1912 at its Chelsea Manhattan factory in New York, US. This factory was located on Ninth Avenue between 15th and 16th Streets. Today, this same location of Ninth Avenue is known as "Oreo Way."

On March 6, 2012, the famous cookie brand, Oreo, celebrated its 100th birthday. From humble beginnings in a Nabisco bakery in New York City, Oreo has grown to become the bestselling cookie brand of the 21st century generating $2 billion in global annual revenues. Currently owned by Mondelez International, Oreo is one of the company's dozen billion dollar brands. (Source: __https://www.warc.com/content/article/India_Twists,_Licks,_Dunks_with_Oreo/97608)

Until the mid-1990s, Oreo largely focused on the US market – as reflected in one of its popular advertising slogans from the 1980s, *"America's Best Loved Cookie"*. But limited growth opportunities in the US Market spurred the company to turn to emerging markets like China and India. Mondelez International, launched Cadbury Oreo in India in March 2011. *(Ref Annexure 1)*

▶ Market Background and Brand Strategy in India

Mondelez was present in India in the Chocolates, Beverages and Candy categories. The company entered the Rs 17,000 crore, competitive India Biscuit market with their lead brand Oreo in 2011. The Biscuits category was growing at 17% in India (Nielsen Survey, 2010). While the Oreo launch presented opportunities, it also posed great challenges. From being a leader in the Chocolates category in India, Mondelez was now a challenger in the Biscuits category.

The challenge was to launch Oreo and peg it against three Biscuit category titans – Parle (41%), Britannia (26%) and ITC (8%), who dominated the biscuit market with a total of 75% market share. These players had been present in the market for many years and had a strong portfolio of established household brands. And the Biscuit category was a very competitive market - only two brands (Parle-G and Britannia Good Day) in a pool of about 1000 brands had garnered more than a 5% market share. Even established brands like Hide and Seek, Monaco and Bourbon had less than 2% market share. This shows the seemingly insurmountable task that a new brand had to circumvent to establish its credentials in this category in India. *(Ref Annexure 2) (Source: Nielsen Survey 2010)*

Cream biscuits are primarily consumed by households with children. Cream being the central component and biscuit just the shell, the focus for a brand was obvious and undisputable – Cream! It was also known that consumers did not find any differentiation between brands. Therefore, the key challenge for Oreo was to decide on how to get a firm foothold in a fiercely competitive category ruled by familiar household brand names with firmly entrenched buying and consumption habits.

Oreo was launched in India in March 2011. It entered the market as Cadbury Oreo because Cadbury is a strong brand name in India, and initially focused on generating awareness and rapid trials. The key objectives of the launch were:

1. Gain a 1% share of the Biscuit category in the first year.
2. Build awareness, 40% trials and 40% repeat purchase in priority markets.

▶ The Marketing Mix Imperatives: Oreo in India

The product was fine-tuned to suit the Indian palate and Mondelez leveraged the retail stores reach acquired with the Cadbury acquisition to build distribution.

Oreo launched its traditional chocolate cookie with vanilla cream centre at Rs 5 for a pack of three to drive impulse purchase and trials, Rs 10 for a pack of seven and Rs 20 for a pack of 14 for heavy consumption segment. The cookie design was the same as its international counterpart – a part of the consistent brand imagery of Oreo.

The company maintained the heritage of the two decoratively embossed chocolate cookies filled with sweet vanilla cream to stand out from me-too products and meet customer expectations of having the real Oreo.

▶ Focus on Distribution & In-Store Presence: Launch Phase

Early launch focus was on building strong distribution and adequate availability in Traditional Trade & Modern Trade. However, availability with an emphatic presence at Point of Buying was the need of the hour for Oreo to break through the highly cluttered and fiercely competitive Biscuit Category. In Traditional Trade, a host of unique Point of Purchase (POS) devices were developed to ensure Oreo stands out when stocked within the category. And for the first time, POS devices were executed that brought Oreo outside the category into the front-of-store in a Traditional Trade store. Counter-top POS devices ensured the brand stands out and is easily spotted by the shopper.

In Modern Trade also a similar strategy was followed. Emphatic in-category presence combined with clutter breaking out-of-category POS visibility was executed. This virtually created a **"Wall of Blue"** effect in the trade channel emphasising and enhancing the brands compelling presence. The primary focus during the in-trade launch was on building the presence of brand Oreo and hence no promotions for trade or consumer were executed in the launch phase. All trade investments were focused on improving the on-shelf presence for Oreo.

▶ Oreo Brand Advertising and Communication

Communication and advertising have been consistent across many markets as the core customer and the brand truths remain the same. The company focused on using the "moments of togetherness" proposition for Oreo in India, with television forming the main medium of communication. In addition, other media platforms were tapped as well. Oreo was present in digital media as well with the Oreo Facebook page adding fans at a rapid rate. The company also created an "Oreo Togetherness Bus" which toured 9 cities and brought alive the Oreo togetherness concept with consumers. A similar campaign was also run with Vans in smaller towns. Oreo strategy was to drive point-of-purchase sales with store displays and in-store consumer activations to generate trial and build consumer preference for the brand.

The brand touch points used for communication included packaging, TV (Spots and programme Sponsorships), Radio spots (including radio programme content), Digital website and social networking sites, host of Out-of Home advertising activities such as hoardings, at airports, in transit communication and billboards. Merchandising, POP, sales promotion, retailtainment to build brand trials and ambient marketing was used to create buzz around the brand launch.

▶ Communication Strategy that Addresses the Mother

In the cream biscuit segment, mothers are the buyers and household with kids form a majority of the consumption. The insight that was leveraged was: mums value the opportunity to create simple, delightful moments for the family to be together. There is nothing that warms the mother's heart more than seeing her kids share a joyous moment, a smile or a hearty laugh with their dad, siblings or grandparents.

► Advertising Theme: Bringing People Together Through the Oreo Ritual of 'Twist, Lick and Dunk'-TLD

Rituals play a central role in the lives of Indians, and they follow them with zeal and enthusiasm. Rituals also help in bringing people together. So this created an opportunity for Oreo to bring families together. The Oreo ritual of 'Twist, Lick and Dunk' became a platform to connect with people beyond the product, and bring about taste, joyousness and family bonding.

Oreo's communication message focused on creating:

1. A **'Ritual of Pleasure'** for the child, centred on the joy of consumption.
2. A **'Ritual of Emotion'** for the parent, that sparks these slowed-down moments of togetherness and enhances the bonding between child and parent.

► Implementing the Brand Communication Strategy

Creating simple, everyday family bonding moments became the trump card of the brand's creative strategy. Therefore, the big idea was: *'Oreo's eating ritual elicits childlike delight and creates family moments of togetherness'.*

► Father-Child Relationship the Most Unique

Unlike the mother, the father spends far lesser time with the kids. So when the father is around, kids want to grab every opportunity they can to spend time with him. Children do this by constantly engaging with the father and bringing him into their world. Fathers, in turn, join in and cherish these delightful poignant moments by becoming childlike themselves and giving in to the kids' requests.

The Oreo launch TVC captured the nuances of this relationship. The TVC depicted an everyday situation in the home, where Oreo fostered simple family bonding moments through the 'Twist, Lick, Dunk' (TLD) ritual that elicited childlike delight.

Oreo twisted, licked and dunked its way into Indian hearts. The communication medium were selected based on their affinity with mothers who were the TG for the communication. *(Ref Youtube link*: https://www.youtube.com/watch?v=xr2Qkd8ucfQ*)*

► TV Campaign

Oreo TV campaign was launched in March 2011. The first wave of trials happened based on strong in-store presence of the brand. This trade presence was further amplified with the TV investments scaling-up. The brand had one of the highest SOV (Share of Voice) on-air during this phase in the Biscuit category. The brand's communication also created disruptive aston (ticker) bands and pushback banners during highly popular Cricket World Cup and IPL series to grab attention and create brand saliency amongst the viewers. This further fuelled the fire at the retail trade level through enhanced brand trials.

▶ Outdoor

Billboards, bus wraps, seat backs and handles, backlit boards inside malls and train wraps were swathed in Oreo blue and TLD messaging. Oreo packet-shaped bus shelters strikingly caught the passer-by's attention. Oreo 'Twist, Lick and Dunk' ambient innovation on mobile vans showed the Oreo cookie being dipped into a glass of milk to bring alive the TLD ritual *(Ref Annexure 3)*

▶ Ambient Innovation

Oreo 'Twist Lick Dunk' Innovation on mobile vans showed the Oreo cookie being dipped in a glass of milk to bring alive the TLD ritual

▶ Point of Sale (POS) Activities

Best-in-class presence in Modern Trade stores using dispensers, floor shelf units, standees, vinyl's on walls and spectacular displays. High visibility in Traditional Trade with branded counter-top outers, sleeve hangers, communication windows and inflated pack danglers to aid purchase. *(Ref Annexure 4)*

▶ Shopper Activation

Oreo engaged thousands of families with fun games and TLD-based sampling in malls and modern trade stores. *(Ref Annexure 5)*

▶ Oreo 'Togetherness Movement'

Oreo initiated a 'Togetherness Movement' through activities like TQ Quiz, TQ Survey, Togetherness Pledge and TQ Bus, to encourage parents and kids to spend time together. The Oreo Togetherness Bus visited 9 cities across India. The bus gave families an opportunity to bond over the 'Twist, Lick and Dunk games', a cookie corner to sample Oreo, a photo corner to capture fun family moments, and a Togetherness wall where parents and kids could make a pledge to spend more time together. *(Ref Annexure 6)*

▶ Digital Engagement

Activities were shown on the Oreo India website, on Facebook and online TLD games and contests created fun moments for people to engage with Oreo.

▶ Brand Performance Against Objectives

Brand Share

Oreo's target 1% share was achieved within the first 6 months of its launch in the market. (Source: Nielsen Survey, 2011) *(Ref Annexure 7)*

Building Brand Trials and Repeats

Brand trials and repeats exceeded targets for both children and adults within four months of the brand's launch. (Source: IPSOS Brand Tracking Study, 2011). *(Ref Annexure 8)*

Brand Awareness Scores

Oreo Brand Awareness beat other cream biscuits brand's awareness. (Source: IPSOS Brand Tracking Study, 2011). *(Ref Annexure 9)* and Oreo performed better than norms on brand linkage. (Source: IPSOS Brand Tracking Study, 2011). *(Ref Annexure 10)*

With a strategy focused on rapid brand awareness and extensive distribution, the Oreo India launch story has been a success so far.

▶ Oreo Launch - Facebook Results

Oreo among TOP 30 brands on Facebook in India
Oreo India Facebook Community crossed 45,000 members in just 9 weeks
Within 5 months of the launch, the Oreo India Facebook had 5,00,000 fans

▶ In Conclusion

Oreo has been able to get a very firm foothold in the highly competitive biscuits market in India by creating compelling differentiation at every level - in product offering, in-store in the Traditional and Modern Trade channels, in leveraging a unique consumer insight, in addressing consumers' desires and in establishing a new ritual. This differentiation was amplified and communicated to the target consumers using a plethora of cherry-picked integrated marketing communications tools and techniques- mass media advertising, consumer contact programmes, radio, bill boards, POS material to generate trials and brand conversion, social media networking sites, creating buzz through ambient media communications, exploiting the brand's website, Out-of Home media etc. All this has been orchestrated to single-mindedly create differentiation at the consumer level for Oreo brand. Thus making Oreo a part of the consumers' repertoire in a highly crowded and fiercely competitive biscuit market in India.

In sum: *To be different. You have to be seen as different.*

ANNEXURE 1: HISTORY OF OREO GLOBALLY

1912
The first *Oreo* is produced at Chelsea Market bakery, Manhattan, NY, U.S.

1920's
First advertisement showing the "twist" appears on trolley cars. *Oreo* exported to several countries in Central and Latin America.

1930's
The name "*Oreo* Sandwich" is changed to "*Oreo* Créme Sandwich."

1940's
Oreo introduced in Canada.

1950's
Oreo design adds the *Nabisco* colophon emblem.

1960's
Oreo launched in Venezuela.

1970's
Oreo Double Stuf Chocolate Sandwich cookies introduced in the U.S.

1980's
Oreo celebrates its 75th birthday; *Oreo* brand "Cookies 'N Cream Ice Cream" created and Fudge Covered *Oreo* Sandwich cookies introduced in U.S.

1990's
Oreo available in more than 30 countries, including China, Brazil, Spain, Portugal. White Fudge Covered *Oreo* cookies introduced as holiday seasonal product in U.S.

2000
Oreo cookies are enjoyed by 9 out of 10 households in the U.S. Mini *Oreo* cookies in convenient on-the-go packs introduced.

2004
Golden *Oreo* launched. Reduced Fat *Oreo* cookies are reformulated to have zero grams of trans fat per serving.

2006
Oreo becomes China's #1- selling biscuit.

2007
Oreo becomes a billion-dollar brand; *Oreo* lauched in Greece, Denmark, Norway and Sweden; Snack 'n Seal packaging introduced in the U.S.

2008
Oreo launched in UK, Netherlands and Italy. First-ever global *Oreo* campaign lauches, Global Moments.

2009
Oreo Fun Stix and Golden Double Stuf launched. *Oreo* biscuits are the subject of the world's largest blind taste test in Madrid, Spain.

2012
Oreo celebrates its 100th birthday and asks the world to celebrate the kid inside.

2011

Oreo becomes a $2 billion brand. *Oreo* introduced in Poland, Germany and India.

2013

Oreo debuts its "Wonderfilled' animated marketing campaign-focused on how sharing an Oreo can bring a change in perspective.

2014

Oreo partners with Paramount Pictures for the global release of Michael Bay's "Transformers: Age of Extinction", the brand's first-ever global movie partnership covering over 35 countries.

2016

Open Up with Oreo global campaign debuts in more than 50 countries more open to those around them and, as a result, make new connections.

2017

Oreo Dunk Challenge global campaign launches in over 50 countries, inspiring fans to dunk *Oreo* biscuits in milk as a way to re-connect with their inner child.

ANNEXURE 2: MARKET SHARE OF BRANDS IN THE BISCUITS CATEGORY. (NIELSEN 2010)

Rank	Brand	% Value share
1	Parle-G	19.9
2	Good-Day Regular	8.7
3	Parle Cream	4.2
4	Marie Gold Regular	4.2
5	Parle 20-20	3.5
6	Sunfeast Special	3.5
7	Tiger Glucose	3.
8	50-50 Regular	2.5
9	Sunfeast Glucose	2.3
10	Tiger Creams	2.
11	Milki Bikis Regular	2.
12	Parle Krack Jack	1.6
13	Parle Monaco	1.6
14	Parle Hide N Seek	1.4
15	Britannia Bourban	1.4

ANNEXURE 3: OUTDOOR (MAY 2011)

ANNEXURE 4: POS ACTIVITIES (MARCH 2011)

counter tops

dispensers

shelf in shelf units

communication windows

Other elements

ANNEXURE 5: SHOPPER ACTIVATION (JUN 2011)

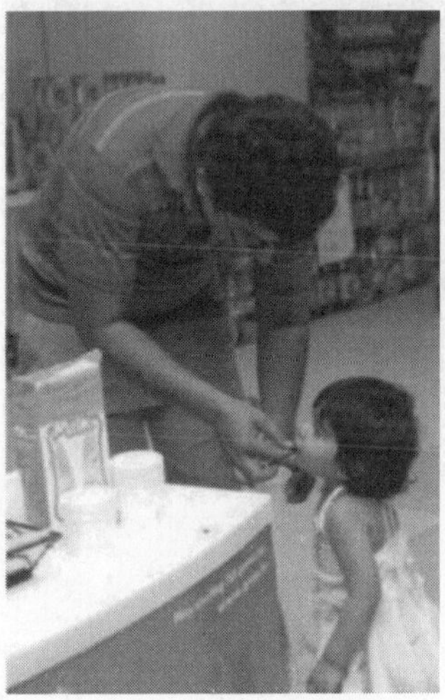

ANNEXURE 6: OREO TOGETHERNESS MOVEMENT (JUNE 2011)

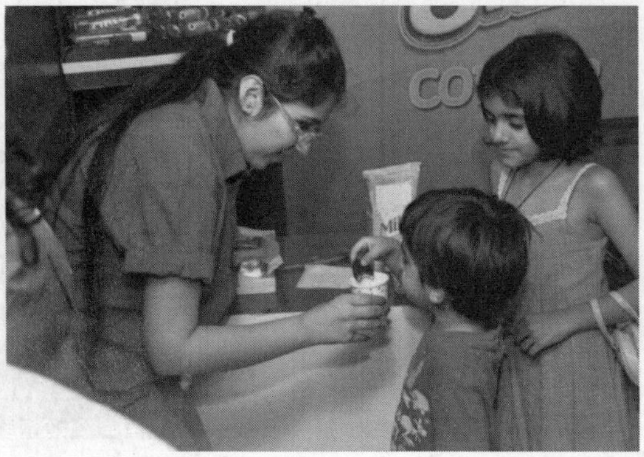

ANNEXURE 7: BRAND SHARE

Brand Metrics	Year 1 (March 2011 – March 2012) Target	Achieved in June 2011
Value share (%)	1	1

(Source: Nielsen Survey, 2011)

ANNEXURE 8: BUILD TRIALS AND REPEATS

Consumer Metrics	Year 1 Target	Achieved in June 2011-Adults	Achieved in June 2011-Kids
Trials	40 %	50 %	75 %
Repeats	40 %	73 %	70 %

(Source: IPSOS Brand Tracking Study, 2011)

ANNEXURE 9: BRAND AWARENESS SCORES

	Oreo	Parle Kreams	Bourbon	Dark Fantasy
Adults				
TOM+ Spont	23	2	22	1
Total Awarness	77	83	86	47
Kids				
TOM+Spont	47	3	33	6
Total Awarness	93	85	94	53

(Source: IPSOS Brand Tracking Study, 2011)

ANNEXURE 10: BRAND AWARENESS SCORES

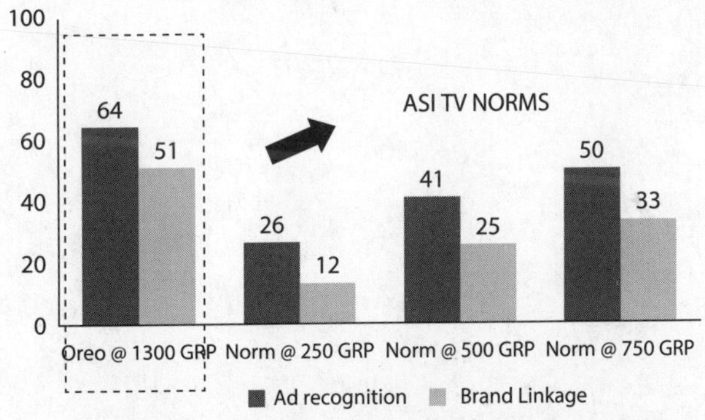

(Source: IPSOS Brand Tracking Study, 2011)

► Questions

1. Analyse and discuss the competitive scenario in the Biscuit's category in 2011. Do a SWOT on the competing brands and Oreo.
2. Elaborate on the communications strategy developed for Oreo in India. Do you agree/disagree? Why?
3. Discuss the various elements of the Integrated Marketing Communications campaign developed and executed for Oreo launch. Emphasis on the major focus on distribution and In-store presence of Oreo prior to the launch of the TV Campaign?
4. According to you what has been the most critical factor(s) that contributed to the brand's success during the launch phase in India?
5. Develop and discuss the next phase of the Brand's Integrated Marketing Communication programme.

► Acknowledgements

- Ms Trisha Parekh- Phd student in NITIE for content building and drafting the case study.
- Ms Arthi Basak-Associate Vice President –FCBINTERFACE

CASE 18

Wonder Cement – Building a Strong Brand Through Digital Marketing

"There is a way to do it better – Find it"
– Thomas Edison

► Introduction

Durability, strength, and power are some of the propositions on which most of the cement companies in India are positioning themselves. But, there exists a brand that seems to be looking beyond the functional attributes of cement—Wonder Cement.

Possessing a towering ambition to be known as the leading national player, Wonder Cement harbors a proven track record and is greatly affiliated with a rich heritage. Belonging to the R.K Group, Wonder Cement is a cutting-edge cement manufacturing company that greatly emphasizes on quality, trust, and transparency. organization emerge as one of the very superior players in the marble industry. In the words of Ashok Patni, the Chairman of Wonder Cement, "Cement is the foundation upon which we construct our lives, our homes, our roads, and our societies. Our structure will not only serve the generations of tomorrow but will also carry our legacy as they stand the test of time". These words aptly put forth the group's obedience towards its core values—the 3 Es, namely efficiency, excellence, and eminence. The entity has already acquired the distinction of being one of the best quality manufacturer of cement in the country by end users' endorsements. It has been set up in technical collaboration with ThyssenKrupp and Pfeiffer Ltd in Germany, the world leaders in cement technology. The unit in Nimbahera produces cement at par with international quality standards.

R. K Marble Group owns a cement plant in Nimbahera, city located in Chittorgarh district in the state of Rajasthan. The unit is involved in manufacturing Portland Pozzolana Cement (PPC) and Ordinary Portland Cement (OPC). It is one of the first fully-automated plants in India, bulwarked by the state-of-the-art German technology under strict quality assurance at all stages of manufacturing. The involvement of the "ROBOTIC (POLAB)" system has also been instrumental in the advancement of the plant's manufacturing and quality control procedures.

► Background of the Industry

The cement industry is the second largest producer of cement in the world. There are more than 85 cement companies and 200 plants in India. The growing real estate market, the on-going infrastructure development, the influx of FDI are some the key drivers of the industry. Owing to the presence of companies like Lafarge, Ultratech, and Wonder Cement, and their high-capacity plants in Rajasthan, the state occupies the position of being the highest producer of cement. Wonder Cement is a part of the list that comprises of the top five cement players in Rajasthan

► Brand Proposition

Cement is an intermediary product and is characterized by low involvement and low interest. In this category, it is often difficult to facilitate differentiation, and hence, the task of creating a strong brand recall becomes essential. Wonder Cement understands this and has righty stayed away from the stereotypes. The cement company has positioned itself in such a way that will make them reap long-term benefits owing to the presence of positive emotions and elements that signify much more than just the products' functional factors.

It all started with the new campaign accompanied by the hash tag "#EkPerfectShuruaat", and the creation of a state-of-the-art website in contrast to other cement-manufacturing companies. The inclusion of interactive features on the website to showcase the cement-making process helped Wonder Cement hit the bar. The energy and spirit of the company was captured by featuring stories of leaders and the management. The "Shuruaat Sahi Toh Har Baat Sahi" campaign revolved around the idea of supporting new beginnings and the aspiration to become "Number One". Social Media workshops were organized for internal employees with a view to bring about a digital revolution at Wonder Cement.

► Saath7 Cricket Mahotsav

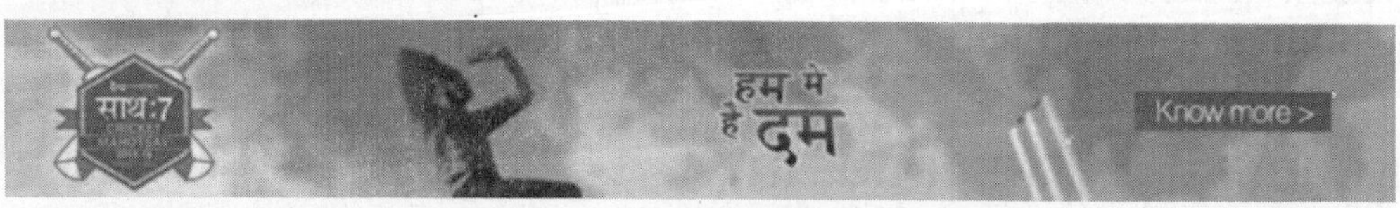

To amplify online activities, an offline route was chosen through cricket tournaments. "Saath7 Cricket Mahotsav" was a seven-overs per inning, seven players per team cricket tournament which covered 248 locations, 33 districts, and 9894 villages. The competition was inaugurated by Kapil Dev in November 2015. Saath7 helped Wonder Cement increase brand awareness in the rural markets.

With the purpose of improving women's participation in sports, the company decided to award an additional seven runs to the team that featured a female player in their playing seven.

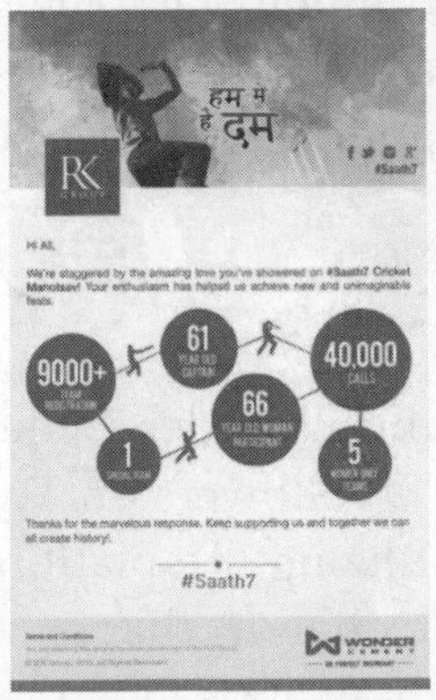

After 15 hard-hitting and exciting matches between the 16 shortlisted teams, the winning team would emerge as the "Team of the Tehsil". The Tehsil teams would face each other at the district level to shortlist the best district team. 33 district teams converged at 6 zones from Rajasthan and helped narrow down 6 zonal teams.

Anyone over the age of 15 and a resident of Rajasthan was permitted to play in the tournament at zero cost of registration.

To complement this offline activity, a micro site of Saath7 was designed to simplify the registration process. The site garnered 32,427 page views and helped 550 people get hold of the live coverage of the Saath7 Launch event, along with 13,617 micro sites visit and 1,465 downloads. Kapil Dev's association with the tournament was leveraged to the greatest extent. During the launch, the organizers managed to reach out to more than 4 lakh people via Facebook. Real-time match updates, produced via various social platforms, generated more than 7 million impressions and more than 10 thousand tweets accompanied by the hashtag "#Saath7" on Twitter. Influencers, sports-oriented bloggers, sports portals were also instrumental in getting the result achieved. #Saath7 trended on Twitter during the launch of the campaign. It was seen to be trending on the 1st position for 4 hours during the grand finale. The campaign received more than 1 lakh video views on YouTube.

► CSR

The "Swach Jal Sabka Haq" (Everyone has the Right to Safe Water) campaign was initiated with an objective to provide free, clean, and cold drinking water to people across 70–90 locations in 29 districts. The process was undertaken to help capitalize on the broader view of providing relief to over 16 lakh people in Rajasthan, Madhya Pradesh, and Gujarat. This CSR activity of Wonder Cement was promoted on digital media and received overwhelming results.

► Digital Footprints

As per the data provided by the company, Wonder Cement has more than 174,274 likes/reach on its Facebook page and more than 6600 followers on Twitter. The company has disregarded the stereotypical image of a B2B brand by utilizing the platform provided by Instagram and has more than 1200 users following the handle. The analysis that explains the fan reach on Wonder Cement's social media handles is a key indicator of how appealing the content is to the social media audience. Wonder Cement leads in the engagement metrics on Facebook, surpassing all other industry players owing to its novel and relevant content. An engagement metrics measures the level of engagement that a piece of created content is receiving from an audience from users who are active on platforms during a day/week/month. It shows how much people interact with the content. Factors that influence engagement include users' comments, shares, likes, and more.

Being a leader in the engagement metrics also reflects on how the content is triggering interest among the followers. The social media campaign experienced more than 330% growth of new visitors on the website, with more than 110% visitors returning on the website. As compared to the previous year, 2016–2017 has seen a 120% increase in the social media traffic. The website of Wonder Cement epitomizes the 7 Cs model of a website design conceptualized by J. F. Rayport and B. J. Jaworski.

In Search Engine Optimization (SEO), measurement is critical to success, and keyword rankings are a great measure of SEO. Higher keywords ranking signifies more traffic. This was achieved using Google Analytics. It is a freweb analytics service offered by Google that tracks and reports website traffic. It is now the most widely used web analytics service on the Internet. It is possible to monitor effectiveness of online marketing campaigns right from user demographics to geographic locations, user platforms (desktop/mobile) to behavior/content consumption habits. Thus, it helps to optimize campaigns in a much more effective manner. Through ongoing optimization, Wonder Cement has seen more than 300% growth in traffic that comes to its website every single month. These results are a combination of organic searches and paid ads.

Year	Keywords ranked on the first page of Google	Total keywords ranked on Google	Backlinks
2015–16	25	100	600
2016–17	80	450	2000

Backlinks are incoming links to a webpage. It is one of the major elements responsible for the ranking of a web page because a page with a lot of backlinks tends to be ranked higher on all major search engines. Backlinks help search engine bots discover links to a site and crawl the site effectively. It also helps in faster discovery and indexing of the site. The success mantra for the digital strategy of Wonder Cement is the original content and a seamless engagement plan for internal and external customers.

▶ Engaging Internal Customers

Wonder Cement also developed the #PeopleOfWonder initiative, a campaign that strongly dealt with the idea of new beginnings. It captured the energy and spirit of the company by featuring stories of leaders and management. The cluster of events kick-started with photography, bolstered by a profile campaign on digital media that covered everyone at Wonder Cement. An internal e-mailer was circulated to all the employees of Wonder Cement about the new campaign and urged them to participate in the campaign to make it a grand success. During this phase, the total engagement on Wonder Cement's Facebook page included 182,109 users and a reach of 958,100 was observed. A dedicated section on the Wonder Cement website was made where all the stories of the employees were listed. Twitter influencers promoted the stories of Wonder Cement employees on the channel and promoted the campaign, resulting in 270 tweets, 3,818,026 impressions, and the reach of a staggering 1,023,646 on Twitter.

In the second phase of the digital strategy, it unleashed the #WonderOfCement campaign, showcasing the Wonder Cement plant and its immense knowledge affiliated with construction. Cinema graph and slow-motion video campaigns on digital media were deployed to cover the Wonder Cement plant and technology. Video testimonials of consumers, engineers, architects, and contractors were created. On Facebook, this campaign generated a reach of 3,637,400 users, video views of 831,701, and an engagement of 320,952 users. On Instagram, video views were observed to have reached 288,342 and an engagement involving 165,691 users was noted. On YouTube, 303,254 video views and 97,487 video banner clicks were generated. On Twitter, the influencers promoted the videos and testimonials on the channel, resulting in 535 tweets, 7,081,979 impressions, and a reach of 1,252,040.

► Engaging Dealers and Intermediaries

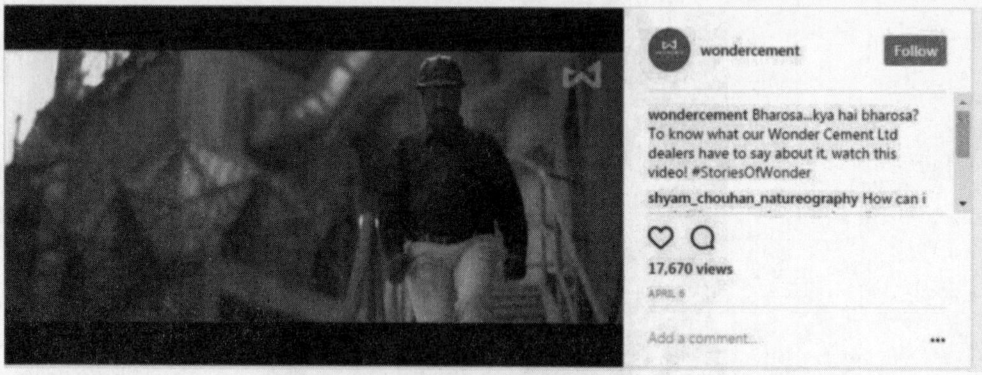

In the third phase of the digital strategy, a new perspective was added by engaging the dealers. The rationale for this revolved around the theory that although dealers are an integral part of the construction business, they are rarely given the opportunity to talk about themselves, their abilities, their achievements, and their aspirations. Through the #StoriesOfWonder campaign, dealers were given the opportunity to express themselves through a series of digital films. A dedicated website was created for the #StoriesOfWonder campaign, which was hosted on the Wonder Cement domain. This resulted in a total reach of 677,608 users, 95,278 video views, and a total engagement of 90,508 users on Facebook. Similarly, on Instagram, 44,337 video views, an engagement of 44,912 users were recorded. 65,510 video views were observed on YouTube.

► Press Coverage

Samachar Jagat, a local daily, created a section for Wonder Cement on its website to promote all the dealer stories. In similar fashion, Rajasthan Khabre, a local website, popularized all the dealer stories with help of its online influence. Wonder Cement celebrated all the festivals on digital platforms and wished everyone for the "Perfect Shuruaat" (perfect beginning). Employees, via e-mail, were informed about all the events, functions, and management-oriented news related to Wonder Cement.

► Tracking Digital Marketing Strategy with Sales Growth

In a nutshell, the digital marketing strategy of Wonder Cement has always focused on brand building and creating mass awareness rather than pushing for online sales. This is because India's digital consumption behavior does not give good insights on people buying cement in the online space. Moreover, internet penetration is low in the predominant target groups in the key distribution markets of Wonder Cement. Their strategy has always emphasized on showcasing the brand's philosophy of trust, transparency, and "people first". Through all the mentioned campaigns, attempts were made to showcase the culture of Wonder Cement. This culture reflected the manner in which everyone across the board, ranging from the sales and marketing teams to the dealers and the contractors, are treated equally. All the campaigns have delivered the desired results of higher engagement rates across all social media platforms, thus making Wonder Cement one of the most organically engaged brands in the cement industry in India. In the words of Mr. Tarun Chauhan, the management advisor, "Every content piece/idea has connected the consumer back to the company's philosophy and broken the content stereotype". While the campaigns have shown success in creating mass awareness and have helped build the brand online, their sales have shown significant y-o-y growth with 3.5% spike in sales in 2014–15, 24.5% in 2015–16 and 25.05% in 2016–17.

▶ Accolades

The results of the strategy were path breaking. With 6900 followers on Twitter, it out- performed its competition. It was ranked first in organic engagement (total number fans v/s total number of likes, comments and shares on each post) on Facebook, surpassing all other industry players. It had the third largest following on Facebook after ACC and JK Laxmi.

Social media is a crucial element of any brand's communication plan. Wonder Cement has created new benchmarks for a B2B brand with regard to digital strategies. The company won the best Social Media award by under the cement category. This award is an acknowledgment by Social Samosa, a one-stop shop for all the social media information in India Wonder Cement was listed on the Campaign Asia website and found its place among the 10 best brands that excelled on social media. Its content revolving around social causes and employee engagement essentially a high-involvement concept created the relevant impact. Summarizing everything, Wonder Cement has been highly successful in showing the human side of the brand and in maintaining a commendable connection with its target group.

▶ Questions

1. Critically evaluate the radical digital marketing communication strategy used by Wonder Cement. List out the pros and cons of Wonder Cement strategy vis-à-vis the traditional communication strategy followed by the other cement brands in Rajasthan?
2. Explain the role of owned content in leveraging the digital marketing strategy of Wonder Cement? Discuss the online and offline customer engagement strategy used by Wonder Cement and its synergistic impact on brand building.
3. Evaluate the social media marketing strategy of Wonder Cement-both for internal and external stakeholders. Explain the rationale for both stakeholders.
4. Amongst which critical stakeholder could this digital marketing strategy have gone wrong? Why?
5. As a communication consultant to Wonder Cement, what could be your suggested strategy for the ensuing festival season?

► Acknowledgements

- Ms Jinal Shah – Coordinator & Assistant Professor-Bachelor of Management Studies, SIES College of Commerce and Economics, Mumbai for content building and drafting the case study.
- Mr Vivek Patni – Director, Wonder Cement
- Mr R S Mohnot – Management Advisor, Wonder Cement
- Mr Tarun Singh Chauhan – Management Advisor, Wonder Cement
- Mr Zahid Khan – Branding Head, Wonder Cement
- Ms Bhagyashri Pokharana – Sr Officer-Branding, Wonder Cement

CASE 19 A Case Study on Direct Marketing of Wedding Return Gifts

Wedtree.com is a start-up based at Chennai, India, whose core business focus is wedding take-away[1]. The company is using social media campaigns and other direct marketing efforts to build and retain its customer base. Anand Krishnamurthy, co-founder and CEO of the company, has over the years expanded his business across categories. The market is seasonal, but the growth prospects are promising. With more competitors eyeing the segment and marketing challenges on the path, Anand is beginning to contemplate strategies that will help him grow and sustain in the industry, while keeping his niche focus intact.

► The Indian Wedding Industry

In recent years, India is witnessing a new trend, which is making the entire world look at the country in awe. The trend is "The big fat Indian weddings". When Lakshmi Mittal, the steel baron, made headlines—not for his acquisitions but for his daughter's wedding—the world stopped and watched. The beauty of Indian weddings was also showcased in an English movie, "Monsoon Wedding".

The Indian wedding industry is a whopping Rs. 1 lakh crore industry and growing at an annual rate of 30%.[2] It is observed that people spend anywhere between Rs. 5 lakhs to Rs. 5 crore on weddings, on an average. There have also been instances of tax raids triggered by very high wedding spends in recent times.

With the transforming Indian economic scenario, the rising middle-class incomes, and with half the population under the age of 30, the demography also supports the industry. Industry pundits predict that the marriage market[3] is set for a stupendous growth in the next five to ten years.[4]

On an average about 10–12 million weddings happen in India every year. The scale and grandeur, however, depends and varies based on the social and cultural factors. As diverse a country like India is, the customs and traditions followed in weddings are also varied. While culture and tradition still dominate how weddings are organized and conducted across the country, modern and contemporariness are also visible recent times.

Most weddings are three-day events in India; in a few states it even runs up to five days. Traditionally, weddings are organized by the brides' families and partial to full expenses are borne by them. Indian weddings[5] involve multiple events; most of them are pre-wedding events. Though it differs across regions, the most common are: Engagement, *Mehndi, Sangeet*, Main Wedding, and Reception.[6]

In the olden times, all the aspects involved in the wedding were organized and managed by members within the family. Each member of the family would typically be involved in a micro event, supervised by the head of the family. They took pride in getting personally involved in organizing the events. By doing so they believed their affection towards the bride/groom and the togetherness that runs within the family is better felt. Today, due to paucity of time and changing psychographics in the community, the event—which once was a closed family event—has opened up into a multi-billion-dollar industry with an ecosystem, which is perennial and prospective. Thus, the boom of wedding planning industry[7] emerged. The industry is pegged at $ 40 Billion as of 2015–16.[8]

Though originally unorganized and fragmented, in the last few years, it is observed that the wedding planning industry is increasingly becoming organized since start-ups began entering the fray. There are the traditional *tentwallas and* food catering companies, who still prefer to go with the customs and traditions. But creative wedding planners have found their niche due to their efficiency in end-to-end management of the event, which includes guest hospitality. But the cost ranges from Rs. 5 Lakhs for a budget wedding to up to Rs. 5 crores for a grand extravaganza. As a result, the weddings are beginning to wear a more corporate look and feel, moving away from the traditional theme.

Emerging trends in Indian weddings:

1. High spend per guest, in terms of personalized invitations, hand-picked cuisine, and lavish take-aways.
2. Increased interests in décor, food, and themes. Destination weddings are gaining importance, major attractions being Turkey, Europe, Maldives, Sri Lanka, Mauritius, etc. Use of colors in the décor and multi-cuisine spread are a few interests.
3. The wedding planners do a lot of experimentation to carve a niche for themselves. A strategic blend of tradition-meets-contemporary is striking a cord with the Indians.
4. Growth of allied industry—beauty salons, jewelry, apparel, tourism, etc., is happening alongside the growth of wedding industry

The Wedding Spend Pattern

The major expense heads in Indian weddings are food and jewelry. Destination weddings are also a trend with Goa, Jaipur, and Udaipur being the most popular, and average spend ranging from Rs. 1–2 crores. Food costs are anywhere between Rs. 500 to Rs. 1300 per person, pandal decoration costs range from Rs. 5000 to Rs. 25,000, goes upto one lakh for themed pandals. While the bridal salree cost ranges from Rs. 10,000 to Rs. 3 Lakhs, the wedding invitation costs anywhere from Rs. 100 to Rs. 5000 per card based on customization. The bridal make-up in another spend area, which goes up to Rs. 50,000 per session, and *mehndi* costs anywhere between Rs. 500 to Rs. 5000 per person (For *mehndi* event alone, there are families that spend anywhere from Rs. 50,000 to Rs. 10 Lakhs)

The Allied Industry

Many allied industries like jewelry, apparels, durable goods, etc., depend on wedding industry. The following table provides details of the allied industry at a glance and their worth.

Alongside the allied industry, the online portals like Shaadi.com, Bharatmatrimony, etc., make revenues up to Rs. 250 crores annually from match-making alone annually. Fashion designers,

TABLE 1 The allied industry and its worth[9] as of 2015–16

Markets	Worth (in crores)
Gold and diamond jewelry Market	Rs. 60,000 crore
Apparel market (wedding)	Rs. 10,000 crore
Durable goods market	Rs. 30,000 crore
Hotel and other wedding related	Rs. 5,000 crore
Pandal and venue decoration	Rs. 10,000 crore
Wedding invitation card market	Rs. 10,000 crore
Bridal Mehndi market	Rs. 5000 crore
Others (Dhol, bands, camels, elephants, lighting etc)	Rs. 5000 crore

Source: www.retail.franchiseindia.com, 2015

florists, confectionery makers, and event managers are also making big bucks from the flourishing wedding market. The cuisine in modern Indian weddings are not purely Indian; anything from Lebanese to Italian or Mexican is found in the spread. For invitation cards, the trend is moving towards event-wise cards with exclusive themes for each event like separate cards for *sangeet, mehndi*, cocktail, reception, or main wedding, and card makers who have understood this trend, differentiate themselves creatively. They also personalize them at a premium.

► Significance of Wedding Return Gifts

While return gifts form a part and parcel of all festivities in the country, wedding return gifts enjoy a unique significance owing to the sheer spend involved in the activity. Wedding take-away or return gifts are given as parting gifts to the guests who had attended the wedding as a gesture of thanking them for their presence. A huge amount is spent on return gifts across the country. Return gifts that are given during weddings and other auspicious events are commonly called as *Tambulya or Tambulam.*[10]

It is also a common tradition across the country to give clothes as return gifts, especially to close relatives and friends. Modern weddings are beginning to witness unique gifts such as figurines of Gods/ Goddesses, wall hangings, jewel boxes, etc. However, the rich and famous do give expensive gifts that could range from silver ware to expensive watches, gold coins/figurines, etc.

► The North-South[11] Divide

As compared to the lavish and extravagant nature of North Indian weddings, the South Indian weddings are low key in terms of spend and grandeur. South Indian weddings mostly go on for 2–3 days only, with focus majorly on traditions and customs rather than fun that generally dominates the North Indian weddings. In recent times however, the South Indian weddings have also undergone some major transformation with respect to the number of events that take place during the weddings.

The predominant difference between North and South Indian weddings is the time at which the main wedding is held. While in the North it happens in the evenings, in most parts of the South, it happens in the mornings.

The other events such as engagement, main wedding, and reception look almost the same in both the regions, except the bridal attire and a few differences in the customs and procedures. Events such as *sangeet* and *mehndi* are new found additions in South Indian weddings, largely in the last decade or so.

▶ About Wedtree.com

Wedtree.com is an online return gifts portal based in Chennai.[12] The company was founded by the husband-wife team, Anand Krishnamoorthy and Brindha Padmanaabhan, engineers by profession. While Brinda handles the product and vendor development and their management, and stores, Anand focusses on marketing, sales, and administration.

It was in June 2014 that the couple decided to quit their high-paying jobs, like many first-gen entrepreneurs in India and start wedtree.com with the saved funds. Anand says that the idea was to start a "one-stop merchandise platform/brand for wedding and personal events". They went on to build an innovative web and app-based portal and began by selling invitations, sarees, fashion jewelry, sweets, and gifts. It took them almost a year to reach an annual turnover of Rs. 1 crore.

The business model is based around a web-based platform. For their website, the search engine is optimized for "Seer Bakshanam"[13] and return gifts, which the founders believe has given them a core differentiating points.

▶ The Product Strategy

The initial product mix included wedding invitations, gift sarees, fashion jewelry, sweets and savories, and other gifts. As the product pool majorly constituted of private labels, bringing new products under the umbrella needed a massive effort. The pricing and delivery time of private labels became the easy referral points for customers as they were also available in regular channels.

▶ Product Categories

Invitations: Wedtree.com offers a wide range of invitation options to the customers. The invitation branches out into sub-categories: Welcome boxes[14], formal invitations, trousseau packing, luxury wedding invitations, and casual invitations. Welcome boxes have a wide range of options viz., decorative ones using silk/satin fabric and ethnic brocade designs, chocolate boxes, nut boxes, velvet boxes, etc. The price ranges from Rs. 96 to Rs. 490 per piece. There are more than 100 options of formal wedding invitations in the price ranging from Rs. 14 to Rs. 120 per piece. Trousseau packing[15] consists of decorative trays in wide variety of fabrics from velvet, satin, raw silk, etc., in ethnic and contemporary motifs, and the price ranges from Rs. 80 to Rs. 490 per piece. Luxury wedding invitations range from Rs. 80 to Rs. 158 and causal invitations has price ranging from Rs. 14 to Rs. 158 per piece.

Return Gifts: Return gifts category has the widest range of products with more than 2000 options for a price ranging from Rs. 1 to Rs. 7980. The sub categories **(Exhibit 1)** are: favor bags[16] in the price range Rs. 5 to Rs. 1500, utility return gifts, which includes saree covers, jewelry bags, mobile pouches, etc. Return gifts by occasion category is customized across a range of festivals and occasions and the Wedtree collections category includes Minakari[17] collectibles and gifts made out of German silver, marble, wood, brass, palm leaf, etc. The category also displays special collections, budget-friendly gifts, combos and on-sale items that are heavily discounted.

Apparels: The apparels category predominantly consist of sarees. More than 700 sarees are on display and updated on a daily basis. The collection includes the traditional silk, cotton, tussar and mixed fabrics, the contemporary crepes and chiffons, kalamkari and art silk varieties, dress material, and traditional outfits for young girls. The sarees come under the brand name Prashanti Silks. The price ranges from Rs. 730 to Rs. 9840.

Fashion Jewelry: The category includes bridal jewelry, armlets/*vanki*, traditional jewelry, bangles bracelets and *kada*, earrings, *jhumkas*[18], necklace, silk thread bangles, antique oxidized jewelry gold-plated jewelry, etc., in the price ranging from Rs. 291 to Rs. 14, 074

Party Supplies: Wedtree has partnered with Todzzle brand to provide theme-based birthday party supplies to its customers in price ranging from Rs. 20 to Rs. 940.

Wedding Sweets: This is the unique category of products offered by wedtree.com. Anand and Brinda said that they did a thorough research before designing the combos under the category. There are also other sub categories such as sweets, snacks and seer backshanam[19] catering to different needs of the customers in the price ranging from Rs. 10 to Rs. 292.

► The Direct Marketing Model

"The web and app-based marketing model drives social product discovery and idea exchange", says Anand. He feels that the main factors acting in favor of wedtree.com are lack of competition in the product segments considered by them as the market was not very organized. There was also a need for a focused market research effort to venture into segments of this sort because of the high level of customization needed. Due to paucity of time, customers wanted the return gifts options to be provided under one umbrella, which can facilitate both customization and personalization, not only for big occasions like weddings but also for small family occasions and festivities. This resulted in a felt need for an online portal for return gifts with focus on regional[20] traditions, customs, and practices.

Though there were product specific portals like returngiftcart.com for return gifts and indianweddingcards.com for invitations, a plethora of saree portals and many models which are wedding focused like weddingz.com, wedmegood.com, Anand realized that there is a segment unexplored—a one-stop portal for all return gifts needs that is specific to Tamil traditions and customs. Wedtree.com was successful in understanding this need and the focus is on "affordable products delivered with no compromise on quality".

Apart from website and Search Engine Advertising (SEA), Wedtree.com also invested on social media campaigns mainly through Facebook. For SMM campaigns, segmenting and targeting the customers is done based on demographic and interest searches made by the prospects. They use the targeting tools available on Google and Facebook to target their prospects. For example, women in Bangalore in the age group of 21–35, working in IT/IT, has shown interest in ethnic/art-related products/gifts. They also segmented prospects based on their behavior in their website post visiting the same. Parameters such as number of sessions, time on page, span of attention on individual categories/items, frequency of visits, carting patterns, buying preferences, etc., were used for targeting the prospects. Re-targeting on social networks is also done for re-checking on interests and to prevent leakages. Anand says, "We have strong tools for engaging and re-marketing. The conversion is better on retargeting and shallow when we acquire new users in the platform", because of which they are able to do 0.5% conversion. Anand, however, is not able to discriminate accurately between digital and manual conversions because they happen simultaneously for products of this nature.

With the website and app-based marketing model, the brand has also been able to reach out and serve international customers, especially in the USA, Middle East, Singapore, and European markets.

As regards the delivery of products to the customers, the company promises shipment in 15 days and 3 days for transit, both for domestic and international customers. However, the average is around 12 days. Anand says that they have been able to manage the delivery schedules pretty decently due to good inventory and logistics management strategies.

Wedtree.com brings together many private label brands for invitations and gifts and they enjoy decent margins because of special pricing and a decent credit period. One challenge that the company faces in terms of logistics, is with respect to international shipments. For overseas shipments, the invoice needed special explanation, and sometimes the customer gets an import duty bill. This is primarily because the return gifts and invitation orders are generally shipped in quantities of 50s or 100s or more and is generally mistook by the customs as a commercial transaction, specifically in Europe, Singapore, and Dubai, where the company had to intervene and provide necessary explanations for smoother transactions. Anand feels that it is a lot better while dealing with USA.

▶ The Alternative Channels

In August 2015, Anand and Brinda decided to create an alternative offline channel as they felt that for products like this, customer touch-and-feel experience would enhance the brand value and trust in the long run. Anand says that their online customers trust them more when they say that they have a retail outlet in Chennai. So, with a small funding raised from a family friend, they opened their first retail channel in Thiagaraya Nagar, Chennai. The outlet showcases gifts and invitation options alone. Pop-up promotions for the brick-and-mortar store is facilitated on Webtree.com website, thus the company ensures that people who visit the site can walk in to their outlet for the touch-and-feel experience. No separate promotion campaign was done for the outlet. The outlet, in fact, has its own share of exclusive walk-ins being located in the trade and commercial hub of Chennai. Currently, the outlet contributes 15% of the total revenue of the company.

The other offline outlet is the chain of carrying the brand name, Prashanti Silks.[21] Prashanti Silks specializes in traditional wear for women, predominantly sarees and dress materials along with ethnic kids' wear. They specialize in silk cotton, mixed raw silk, tussar, etc., which are patronized by the locals and also their customers spread across the globe, as they were considered as affordable and lighter alternatives to pure silk. The store also sells pure silk apparels for women. The brand has existed for a decade now in Chennai and Banglore. There are currently four Prashanti outlets, 3 in Chennai and 1 in Bangalore. Wedtree.com acquired Pranshanti Silks in November 2016 to provide their customers with the option to view a vast range of sarees and other garments. As the brand had in the market for a long time, it also has its own set of regular customers. Currently, Prashanti alone contributes 35% of the revenues.

► Current Status and the Road Ahead

From Rs. 1 crore a year, the company is now seeing a revenue of Rs. 1 crore a month, thanks to the bold expansion and acquisition decisions taken by the promotors. They are currently addressing about 800 to 1000 events a month (customer who purchases a return gift/invitation/sweets/bulk sarees). They also cater to individual and non-event customers (customer who purchases singe saree/jewelry), about 1200 a month. There is a huge scope for expansion in the international markets due to fact that Indians living abroad in recent times are planning events in their own locations, due to time constraints, and also because of the costs involved in travel.

Acquisition of Prashanti Silks increased the sales and also helped them to set foot into a new market, Bangalore. Anand plans to expand his business city wise, with physical stores supporting their online platform. While on the product side, the company plans to expand into categories such as bridal wear, footwear, etc. On the customer-support front, they are building micro apps, such as the invitation tracking app, which will help customers to track their invitations, RSVPs, guests, gifts, etc.

The biggest challenge, however, is the investment. The founders have been able to manage the business with personal and family funding so far, which enabled them to enjoy higher freedom and peace of mind. For expansion, they may be forced to look at external agencies for funding, which has its own risks and compromises. On the other hand, the founders are highly knowledgeable with respect to South Indian markets, specifically Chennai and Bangalore markets, due their proximity and acquaintance with these markets for a long period of time. The new markets, especially the North Indian markets, could pose its own challenges in terms of cultural diversity and competition. The company should look at investing on market research in order to better understand the opportunities and threats involved in new markets. Another challenge could be competition. With better pricing and options, there are possibilities that new or existing startups may eye the space, posing a threat to Wedtree.com. Wedtree.com should constantly be looking at bringing nuances in the range and combinations of the product to stay ahead and be relevant. While offline channels do promise revenues, how much of profit will be negotiated in the process is something that needs deep contemplation, especially for the new ventures.

With alluring prospects and challenges umpteen, time can only say if Anand and Brinda will be successful in their market and product expansion ideas.

EXHIBIT 1

SUB CATEGORIES – RETURN GIFTS

- **Favor Bags**
  - Potli Bags
  - Jute Bags
  - Paper Bags
  - Exclusive Potli Bags
- **Utility Return Gifts**
  - Saree Covers
  - Clutches and Purses
  - Hand Bags
  - Decorative Trays
  - Jewellery Holders
  - Travel Kits
  - Mobile Pouches
  - Kum Kum Holders
  - Dry Fruit Boxes
  - Key Hangers
  - Diyas
  - Shoulder/Sling Bags
- **Return Gifts by Occasion**
  - Diwali Return Gifts
  - Navaratri Return Gifts
  - Baby Shower Return Gifts
  - Housewarming Return Gifts
  - Upanayanam Return Gifts
  - Wedding Return Gifts
  - Birthday Return Gifts
  - Arangetram Return Gifts
- **Collections**
  - Minakari Return Gifts
  - Divine Return Gifts
  - German Silver Return Gifts
  - Wooden Handicrafts
  - Brass Return Gifts
  - Marble Return Gifts
  - Metal Handicrafts
  - Silk and Kalamkari
  - Jute Return Gifts
  - Home Decors
  - Palm Leaf Return Gifts
  - Blouse Bit
- **Specials**
  - Premium Return Gifts
  - Budget Friendly Return Gifts
  - On Sale
  - Return Gift Combos
  - Ready to Ship
  - Silk Thread Jewellery
  - Dry Fruit Packs

CASE 20 Selling Process in Animal Nutrition and Health Industry

Vamso Biotec Pvt Ltd is a company set up by Dr.O.P. Agarwal way back in 1969. It all started as a small-scale operation based at Sirsaganj, Uttar Pradesh, and now it is a pan-India business operations employing more than 300 people. Being a veterinarian, Dr. Agarwal wanted to uplift the standards of rural animal husbandry practices with his innovative herbal supplements, and today, Vamso caters to the therapeutic and supplementation needs across all the species segments like cattle, poultry, and companion animal health care. From the very beginning, the sales model has remained almost unchanged—face-to-face sales call with prescribing doctors or farmers and promoting the benefits of the products. With almost 5 decades of operation behind them, Vamso has been operating in the same industry for 47 years with same model but the stake holders (customers, channel partners, prescribers and influencers), everyone is a whole new generation. It is an entirely different ecosystem now. Mr. Mukesh Agarwal, the Managing Director of the company feels that a lot more can happen in Vamso's *"go to market'* strategies and it becomes all the more necessary as the industry is poised to grow further significantly over next decades. The company is considering ways to address different species segments with dedicated and focused business strategies, be it in product offerings or its selling model.

▶ The Industry

The Indian animal health (AH) industry has played a vital role in safeguarding the animal husbandry interests of the nation. The Indian animal healthcare market was estimated to be around 42,000 million INR (2014) and is projected to be around 60,000 million by 2018. The species share in AH market is 50% for livestock, 40% for poultry, 5% for companion animals, and rest 5% for other remaining animals. Though there are no published data, INFAH (Indian Federation of Animal Health Companies) anticipates the contribution of various categories of animal health products as 40% for feed supplements, 17% for antibacterial, 15% for biosecurity, 13% for antiparasitics, 5% for hormones and biological, and 10% for other categories. There are nearly 50 major companies operating in the animal health market in India, though the market is dominated by top 10 players.

The regulation of animal health products in India is under the Department of Animal Husbandry under the Ministry of Agriculture (MOA). The Drug Controller General of India (DCGI) regulates and licenses, products for veterinary use. Department of AYUSH is responsible for bringing regulations for herbal and contemporary medicines meant for animal use.

Animal husbandry in India has undergone magnificent changes over the years, thanks to the adoption of innovative technologies used for prevention and cure of farm and companion animals. There has been a paradigm shift in the business approach of animal health companies that have evolved from therapeutics to preventive to productivity enhancement, and now to overall healthcare of the animals.

EXHIBIT 1

AH INDUSTRY: FUTURE IS FEED

March 18, 2015

The recently concluded VIV Asia in Bangkok from 11–13th of March 2015 re-confirmed the premixes to be the most important segment of animal health industry now. Out of a total of 871 listed exihibitors – an overwhelming majority to the exihibitors were feed ingredients/additives, feed premixes, feed products and feel milling companies.

Through new approaches and advancements, the animal health industry has evolved and propelled the animal husbandry to new heights of glory. India's surge to the top of milk and egg production reinforces the significance of animal health Industry.

EXHIBIT 2

DAIRY

State-wise Milk Production in India (2007–2008 to 2012–2013) (In'000 Tons)						
States/UTs	**2007–08**	**2008–09**	**2009–10**	**2010–11**	**2011–12***	**2012–13***
Andhra Pradesh	8925	9570	10429	11203	12088	12762
Bihar	5783	5934	6124	6517	6643	6845
Gujarat	7911	8386	8844	9321	9817	10315
Haryana	5442	5745	6006	6267	6661	7040
Himachal Pradesh	1007	1026	971	1102	1120	1139
Jammu and Kashmir	1519	1565	1592	1609	1614	1631
Jharkhand	1442	1466	1463	1555	1745	1679
Karnataka	4244	4538	4822	5114	5447	5718
Kerala	2253	2441	2509	2645	2716	2791
Madhya Pradesh	6572	6855	7167	7514	8149	8838

Maharashtra	7210	7455	7679	8044	8469	8734
Odisha	1625	1598	1651	1671	1721	1724
Punjab	9282	9387	9389	9423	9551	9724
Rajasthan	11377	11931	12330	13234	13512	13946
Tamil Naidu	6540	6651	6787	6831	6968	7005
Uttar Pradesh	18861	19537	20203	21031	22556	23329
Uttarakhand	1221	1230	1377	1383	1417	1478
West Bengal	4087	4176	1300	4471	4672	4859
India	**107935**	**112182**	**116424**	**121844**	**127904**	**132430**

Source: Ministry of Agriculture, Govt. of India.

$: figure are estimated based on livestock census, 2007 and rate of concerned Neighbouring State.

#: Indicate Milk production decreased in 2012–13 compared to 2011–12 due to high rate of urbanization and is based on latest census.

EXHIBIT 3

POULTRY

Statewise production of eggs in India(2013–14)		
Sr. No	**Region**	**Annual egg Production (million)**
1	Tamil Nadu	11933
2	Kerala	2237
3	Karnataka	3677
4	Andhra Pradesh	22297
5	Maharashtra	4566
6	Gujarat	1455
7	West Bengal	4711
8	Odisha	2322
9	Punjab and Haryana	8025
10	Rajasthan	1033
11	Uttar Pradesh	1707

12	Bihar & Jharkhand	1261
13	Madhya Pradesh	871
14	J & K	671
15	Chhattisgarh	1370
16	Himachal Pradesh	106
17	Others	1481
	Total	**69730**

Source: Industry sources

EXHIBIT 4

ANIMAL FEED

Placement status of broiler birds 2013				
Sr. No	**Region**	**Avg. Placement in millions/ week**	**Annual broiler production (Million No)**	**Annual Feed requirement in MMT**
1	Tamil Nadu	7.05	348	1.18
2	Kerala/Tamil Nadu	1.21	60	0.20
3	Karnataka	5.24	259	0.88
4	Andhra Pradesh	7.59	375	1.27
5	Maharashtra	7.32	362	1.23
6	Gujarat	1.21	60	0.20
7	West Bengal	6.69	330	1.12
8	Odisha	1.62	80	0.27
9	Assam	1.37	68	0.23
10	Punjab and Haryana	5.27	260	0.88
11	Rajasthan	0.98	48	0.16
12	Uttar Pradesh	3.77	186	0.63
13	Bihar & Jharkhand	3.41	168	0.57
14	Madhya Pradesh	1.16	57	0.19

15	J & K	0.55	27	0.09
16	Chattisgarh	1.19	59	0.20
17	Himachal Pradesh	0.72	36	0.12
18	Uttarakhand	1.07	53	0.18
19	Others	1.65	82	0.28
	Total	**59.07**	**2918**	**9.92**

Source: Industry estimates for December 2013

Most of the poultry integrators manufacture their own feed. Some of them purchase Premix. Specially feeds or concentrates. Most of the independent poultry farmers buy feeds from commercial feed millers.

Current egg production is around 69 billion eggs (2013) and is anticipated to reach 93 billions by 2020. 85% of the feed required is made by farmers at the fsarm by using basic feed mill structure (grinders and mixers). 15% of the total feed is sold by commercial feed millers. State-wise layer feed requirements per year is given in following table.

In the animal nutrition and health industry, the major product categories are animal feed, pet food, feed additives, veterinary medicines, and herbal formulations. Animal feeds are sold through rural agri-inputs and feed distribution channel, and sales personnel's mostly meet the channel partners and organizes periodic customer events. Pet foods are sold mostly through FMCG channels today, whereas the category started through prescription channel more than 2 decades back, which they are still continuing to cater. But their primary focus has shifted to modern trade. Feed additives, veterinary medicines, and herbal formulations are still very similar to pharmaceuticals sales model, and the sales personnel visits prescribers, channel partners, end users based on the primary target segment for respective product categories.

► The Organization

Vamso Biotec Pvt. Ltd. provides research-based, efficacious and quality-assured natural, biotechnological, and allopathic products for health and productivity needs of variety of animal species through its group of companies—Cattle Remedies India Ltd. (CRIL) and Vamso Biotec Pvt. Ltd. (VBPL). The company focuses on its resources for the development of unique solutions for cattle, poultry and pet healthcare.

Vamso Biotec Pvt. Ltd. is an ISO 9001:2008 & GMP- certified company having two manufacturing units at Dehradun (Uttarakhand) and Sirsaganj (Uttar Pradesh) in India with the state-of-the-art R&D at Dehradun (Uttarakhand). The manufacturing and R&D is equipped with modern and most sophisticated instrumentation facility & machinery to maintain high quality standards during product development and manufacturing.

Mukesh Agarwal

Managing Director, Vamso Biotec Pvt. Ltd.

"From the very first day, we are dedicated towards providing quality-assured, value-added, and cost-effective solutions for farmers and animal health care professionals. We are committed to provide unmatched service to our customers through our specialized manpower resource. Our endeavour is to provide need-based solutions for livestock, poultry, and pet health care. We commit ourselves to shoulder the responsibility for overall development of livestock, poultry and pet industry. We look forward to achieve greater competitiveness, more profitability, and higher values through innovative products."

EXHIBIT 5

SALES & MARKETING ORGANOGRAM

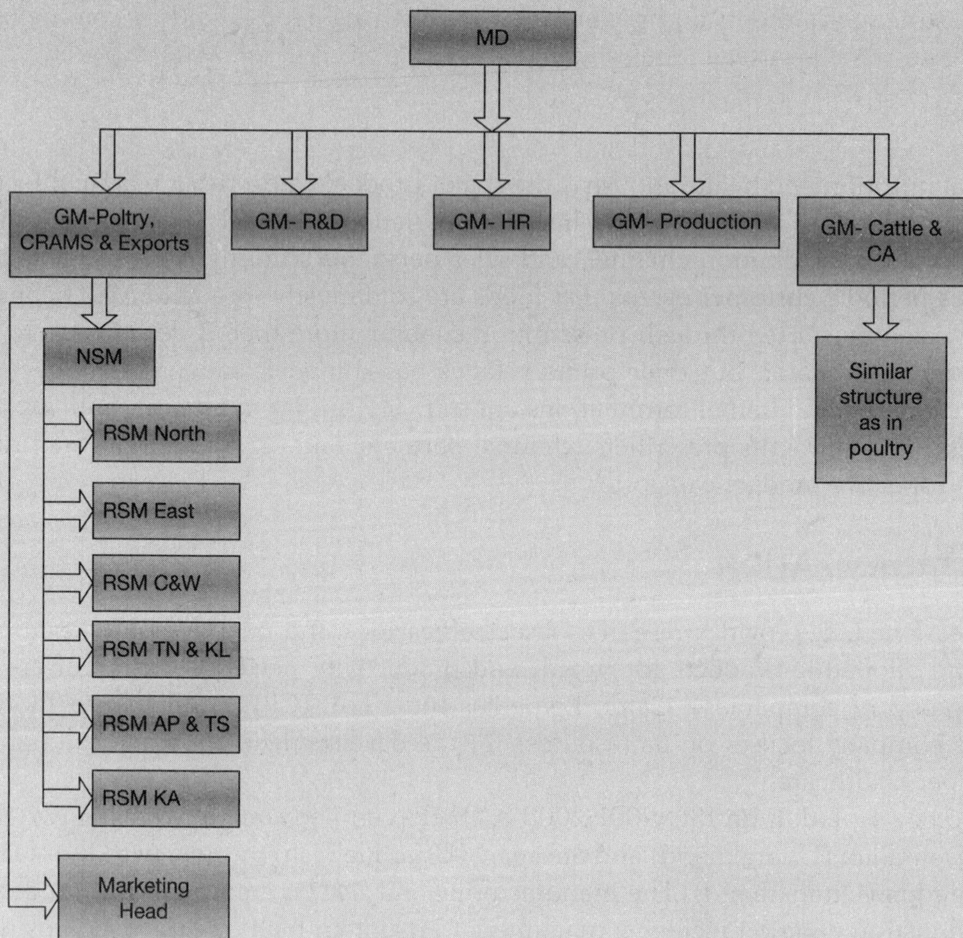

▶ Exclusive Sales & Marketing Force for Targeting Each Species Segments

Vamso had realized from the very beginning that poultry, livestock, and companion animal segments require dedicated focus. Accordingly, it has developed exclusive sales and marketing teams to cater to the needs of different species segments. This brings sharp focus on customized selling approach, and also enables to bring out need-based product offerings and relevant services for each segments.

Poultry customers comprise of broiler, breeders, and layers sub-segments, and they can also be further classified into farmers, integrators, and feed manufactures. Vamso primarily caters to this segment with its supplements and additives product range which consists of phytochemical and chemical formulations, and biosecurity products as well. Poultry supplements and additives are growing at an estimated CAGR of 6–8%. It comprises almost 50% of the animal nutrition and health market. Vamdia Forte, an intestinal function modulator for poultry, is the largest selling Brand of Vamso and also the brand leader in its category.

Livestock team primarily caters to the needs of cattle and buffaloes and it is mostly a prescription market. The sales team meets the veterinary doctors and paravet staff employed by state and central governments, and dairy co-operatives. Almost all the state government's animal husbandry department have recruited large number of artificial inseminators to enhance the spread of cross-breeding program to remote villages. They are regularly met by sales representatives as now inseminators are present almost in every villages providing round-the-clock veterinary services to cattle farmer at their doorsteps. Vamso offers its herbal and synthetic products catering to the therapeutic needs of the prescribers and also the supplemental requirements of a dairy farmer. Uterotone is the largest-selling uterine tonic in livestock market. Initially when it was launched 3 decades ago, it was a prescription drug go and is now an OTC (over the counter) product for care of fresh cows. To reinforce the market penetration of its leading brands and other upcoming brands, Vamso has recruited a large field force to ensure its representation in each and every district of the country.

EXHIBIT 6

NUMBER OF SALES EMPLOYEES IN DIFFERENT SEGMENTS

	POULTRY	LIVESTOCK	COMPANION ANIMAL
SALES REPS	22	140	5
TEAM LEADERS	6	30	0
LEADER'S MANAGERS	2	8	0
SALES HEAD	1	1	1

► Personal Selling Model: One Size does not Fit All

A poultry representative typically works in a customer circle that uses Vamso's product as an "Input" to his business either by mixing in feed or water for birds, especially when it comes to farmers or integrators (end users). The customer is very much focused on Return on Investment (ROI) and demonstrates a fair degree of rational-buying behaviour. In addition, there are products in Vamso's range which are used as a supportive solutions for treating birds. The prescribing veterinarians (fewer in number unlike in the livestock segment) also want to be very sure about the efficacy of the product because they are in turn accountable for ROI to end users. On a typical work day, the representative takes an appointment early in the morning and plans his/her day based on confirmation of the same. For large corporate accounts, mostly appointments are taken by email 2–3 days in advance. He/she meets the customer individually and sometimes with the respective line manager or a technical support (a veterinarian appointed by Vamso) personnel. or occasionally with product managers or senior personnel from the head office. Most of the important corporate customer calls (as the stakes are high) are done jointly by sales and support team.

EXHIBIT 7

VARITEY OF INFULENCERS IN PURCHASE DECISION

POULTRY	LIVESTOCK	COMPANION ANIMAL
NUTRITIONISTS	VET DOCTORS	PET DOCTORS
CONSULTANT VETS	PARAVETS	DOG BREEDERS
KOL* FARMERS	KOL* FARMERS	DOG TRAINERS
ACADEMICIANS/ RESEARCH SCIENTISTS	RETAIL CHEMISTS	RETAIL CHEMISTS/ PET SHOPS

* KOL= KEY OPINION LEADER

EXHIBIT 8

% OF CALLS TAKE PLACE AS PER APPOINMENTS CONFIRMED BY CUSTOMER

POULTRY	50%
LIVESTOCK	80%
COMPANION ANIMAL	90%

A representative in the livestock team fairly adheres to a pre-decided plan of work for the day, week, and even months. He has a master tour plan which is reviewed and approved by the line managers in the beginning of the year. Every month he sends his tour plan for approval in advance, and works as per the plan with few exceptions based on the customer availability. The pattern of planning and working is almost similar in the companion animal team.

EXHIBIT 9

IDENTIFIED SALES DRIVERS IN DIFFERENT SEGMENTS

	POULTRY	LIVESTOCK	COMPANION ANIMALS
FREQUNECY OF VISIT BY REP	+	+++	+++
PRODUCT EFFICIACY	+++	+++	+++
COMPLIMENTS/GIFTS	+	+++	+++
PRODUCT KNOWLEDGE OF REP	+++	+	++
UNIQUE BRAND REMINDERS	+	+++	++
PRICE TO CUSTOMER	+	+++	++
CHANNEL PARTNER'S MARGIN	++	++	+++
ROI TO END USER	+++	++	+
ATTRACTIVE PRODUCT PACK	+	+++	+++

(Scale= + Moderate, ++ High And +++ Very High)

EXHIBIT 10

CALL AVERAGE OF SALES EMPLOYEE IN DIFFERENT SEGMENTS

COUNTS/MONTH	POULTRY	LIVESTOCK	COMPANION ANIMAL
END USER	70	20	5
RETAIL CHEMIST	6	30	30
DEALER	3	5	3
PRESCRIBERS	5	120	80

The way of prospecting by a sales representative varies based on segments, territories, buying behaviour, and purchase dynamics. In poultry, the representative comes to know about the usage of competitor products from the shop floor supervisors in feed mills, branch managers of large integrators, and also from purchase queries. Distributors are also a good source of information to understand current buying patterns, credit terms, and purchase dynamics of customers, be it large or small. With large corporate customers, mostly it is a consensus-based purchase decision involving multiple stake holders and influencers.

EXHIBIT 11

AVERAGE TIME SPENT BY A REP WITH CUSTOMER IN A CALL		
POULTRY	LIVESTOCK	COMPANION ANIMAL
5 MINUTES	15 MINUTES	2 MINUTES

In livestock and companion animals' segments, retail prescription audit plays pivotal role in prospecting right customers for right products. A representative compulsorily visits 2 or 3 retail chemist shops every day and monitors the shelf-availability of fast moving products. A quick scan of how much of dust is gathered on top of the product pack in the shelf provides a good clue of the pace of prescription of the same brand.

Even against all these diversities among the three different segments, the one common element that remains threaded across the sales force is the selling model. The basic pattern remains the same—Personal Selling. It is one-on-one direct communication, and the representatives interaction happens with an objective of uncovering needs of customers and offering suitable solution. The typical sales call mostly happens in an indoor environment.

"Different sales ecosystems need unique approach"—this was the first realization of the newly appointed General Manager of Sales and Marketing of the poultry division. The organization started as a hardcore livestock business and then diversified into poultry only a decade back. Vamso's poultry business has a respectable presence in several large corporate accounts but not in the "trade" customers channel, which caters to small and mid-sized customers. "Enhancing market penetration by increasing sales force has been a good step but to seize the untapped opportunities lying in the trade market and exploit the full potential of corporate accounts, Vamso must work on devising a need-based personal selling approach" the new GM was said to the Managing Director.

What do you think may be the best suited personal-selling approach that will work best for the new GM to be successful in his new assignment and take Vamso's poultry business to the next level?

(The author is a veterinarian with more than 15 years of experience in sales and marketing in animal nutrition and health sector. Having worked in large Indian conglomerates and MNCs, the author possesses a deep insight of the particular sector and the industry as well. Currently, he is employed as a General Manager-Sales & Marketing in Vamso Biotec Pvt Ltd, Gurugram, Haryana. For any correspondence, the author can be reached at drarindam80@gmail.com)

CASE 21 Amazon.com adapts its Retail Business in India

Founded by Jeff Bezos, Amazon is the world's largest e-commerce company which began its operations in US as an online book retailer that soon began to sell a large category of products. Amazon.com entered the Indian e-commerce market with Amit Agarwal at its helm in 2013 as an online marketplace offering two product categories, namely books, and movies and TV shows. As the Indian law did not permit 100% foreign direct investment (FDI) in retail business, the company decided to provide an online platform for buyers and sellers to come together instead of selling products directly to the consumers. This business model was different from the one being employed in US where the company sold its own goods along with those of the third-party sellers. Under this model of third-party online platform, Amazon handles customer queries, takes orders, ships goods, handles returns, and undertakes advertising and promotion activities.

Within three years, Amazon launched its "Global Store" in India and provided access to over 4 million global products, including several international brands that till hitherto were unavailable in India. Prior to its launch, consumers bought products online from Amazon's US portal and were required to pay in dollars. But, now they had the option to make online purchases of both global and local brands and pay in their local currency. The company provided the option of returning unused products within 30 days of delivery for full or partial refund depending upon the cause for such returns.

► Indian Market

India is the world's fastest growing economy. Its huge population of 1.25 billion led by technology-driven youth offers tremendous business opportunities to the e-retailers. Around 260 million English speaking middle class, 340 million smart phone users, and a rapid increase in mobile wallet users offer huge potential to the e-commerce companies. Increased penetration of the internet will continue to provide further impetus to rapid growth in e-commerce market. The revenue from e-commerce is estimated to grow four folds from \$ 30 billion in 2016 to \$ 120 billion in 2020, accounting for a whopping growth rate of 51% per annum. This exponential growth rate is expected to surpass any other predicted growth rate across the globe. So, it is no surprise that Amazon was attracted to India to pursue its dream of international expansion.

Amazon possessed the experience of operating as an online marketplace in nine other countries. To gain insight into the psyche and behaviour of Indian consumers, Amazon had launched a price comparing website, Junglee.com a year prior to its entry in the growing Indian market. The experiences of already operating market players provided additional vital information needed to make headway in this challenging Asian sub-continent. The home-grown companies, Flipart,

Myntra, and Snapdeal were gradually succeeding in persuading the sceptical Indian consumer to buy online by offering very low prices, return policy, and payment of cash upon delivery. Amazon also understood that Indians prefer to pay in cash and not through cheques or credit card. It adopted the policies being pursued by indigenous online retailers.

► Distribution Model

There are more than 14 million traditional retail stores in India with majority measuring less than 600 square feet. These convenience stores play an important role in making products available in cities, towns and over 6 lakh villages, where 67% of the population resides. Yet, both big and small retailers perceived e-commerce to be very complicated and had been apprehensive about online orders on various accounts. Some of these concerns included problem of handling rejected products, incorrect or arcane addresses given by the customers, inadequate infrastructure, including poor delivery logistics, buyers' habit of doing transactions in cash, and so on. Amazon's entry was perceived as a great threat to the survival of these traditional retail stores. To allay their fears, Amazon introduced *Amazon Chai Cart* which involved mobile tea carts that moved through several cities offering tea along with advice on the advantages of e-commerce to small business owners. Subsequently, *Amazon Tatkal*, "studio on wheels" was launched to provide a range of services, including cataloguing, registration, and sales training. This resulted in large number of businesses getting associated with Amazon as they felt that this partnership would provide access to bigger markets. Entry of Amazon provided great business opportunities to retailers in India who had been previously very uneasy about its entry. It engaged more than 13,000 stores across 65 cities as delivery partners in its logistic network. It also involved the mom-and-pop stores in small towns and villages in its delivery platform where internet connectivity was limited. Villagers are able to access the online products at Amazon through the store owner's internet and place their orders through him. The store owner alerts consumers upon arrival of products, delivers them, collects money, and passes it to the company. He gets paid a certain amount of handling fee in return for his services. This system is reported to have helped the stores increase their personal sales as well. Linguistic diversity in the country has prompted Amazon India to introduce staff support system to its sellers in local languages such as Tamil, Kannada, and Telugu in addition to English and Hindi.

The number of sellers on its platform rose to a phenomenal figure of 140,000 in 2016, an increase of nearly 160%. Almost thousands of products were reported to be getting added daily on its market place. To help the sellers on its platform meet their short-term financial requirements to cope with increased seasonal demands, Amazon partnered with a digital lending company called Capital Float. This initiative has helped its e-sellers who deal in fashion items, consumer durables, and electronic products procure a loan of Rs 2 lacs and above without pledging any collateral. This facility assists them in making payment to their suppliers within 24 hours. Within a span of four years Amazon has become equipped to sell over 100 million products ranging from movies, books, grocery, fashion, electronics to lifestyle categories. Its sales orders are not confined to any specific group of customers or geographical limits of metropolitan or big cities. It claims that 50% of its demand is from Tier II and Tier III cities of India. Pursuing its global strategy, the company strives to supply everything to everyone at every location within the country, and make it its second largest market after US. It has left its closest Indian rivals, Flipkart and Snapdeal, far behind with respect to business investment, numbers of products offered as well the geographical coverage of its market. Flipkart, run by former employees of Amazon, has been forced by the latter to seek foreign investments while Snapdeal is grappling with its survival.

▶ Strengthening Delivery Logistics

To improve its delivery logistics, Amazon "Global Stores" engaged the services of India Post, a government-operated postal system, and logistics companies such as Blue Dart, Aramex India, and DHL Express to deliver products to its customers. It also utilized the services of bicycle and motorcycle couriers to reach its rural and sometimes even its urban customers. Around 27 fulfilment centres were set up across ten different states in the country in direct contrast to a centralized fulfilment centre in US. Order tracking, which plays a crucial role in winning over the trust of customers, is taken care of by these fulfilment centres. Sellers drop their products to these fulfilment centres at a fee before any order is placed. Amazon provides studio facility to the suppliers for taking photographs of their wares for online posting. These goods are checked for quality, stored, packed, and shipped to the customers from these centres when the orders are received. Generally, Amazon holds back a part of the sales for about seven days as a buffer against possible returns. The accounts with sellers are settled on monthly or weekly basis depending upon their terms of agreement with the company. Decisions with respect to returned goods lie solely with the company. More than 100 delivery stations and about 15 sorting centres have been also opened up by the company.

To access its customers spread across a large geographical area, Amazon Transport Services was started as the logistics company in 2015 to accelerate the pace of delivery and provide direct delivery from the sellers to the consumers. This was expected to make the company more competitive in the Indian market which lacked the logistics facility to deliver within 24 hours of ordering, a norm followed in the US. Its closest rival, Flipkart, was forced to follow suit by promising same-day delivery facility but its charges were higher in comparison to that of Amazon. To speed up the delivery process, Amazon launched additional shipping platforms called EasyShip and Seller Flex, which helped the small vendors choose their courier partners at their own convenience. Under Easyship, Amazon couriers picked up packaged goods from seller's store for delivery to the consumer. The sellers had the option to store products for sale on Amazon portal in their own warehouse under the Seller Flex approach, and Amazon takes care of delivery from their warehouses to consumers. However, in case of stock-outs, Amazon imposes penalty on the sellers.

▶ Sellers' Displeasure with Amazon

Some reports have emerged with respect to sellers' displeasure with Amazon concerning its policy on return products, payments to them, and closure of their accounts. Sellers feel that the company maintains very tight control over the commitments it expects from them—starting from the number of products they are expected to hold, time of delivery, time of receiving payment, and also the amount of withholding of their cash. When any issue of dispute arises between consumers and sellers, Amazon is strongly biased towards the former. In case of product return through its courier service, the company is likely to deduct anything between 50–100 % of the total amount. It imposes a fine on the sellers when a dispute arises between consumers and them on the products delivered through external courier services without seeking their opinions. Sellers have to struggle to get their money refunded. Blocking of their accounts is another problem that some of them are facing. It may take several days before the account becomes functional. This poses cash problems for the sellers. Interestingly, Amazon had already faced similar accusations of high-handedness in the form of lawsuits in US.

The company, on its part, has denied accusations levied by some of the Indian sellers, and expressed that returns have been classified into four different classes under its transparent policy: damage of product by Amazon, consumer's decision not to buy, wrong product, and mismatch between actual product and its description on site. In case of damage caused by Amazon, the company takes the responsibility to fully compensate the seller. But, in case the sellers commit mistakes repeatedly and underperforms, then the company is compelled to take action against them and block their accounts. It gives seven days' time to its sellers to resolve issues when complaints arise in their use of external logistics. Contrary to the statements made by sellers, the company claims that it charges penalties only after seeking their permission. Amazon asserts that it has always helped the sellers increase their monthly sales. It is quite likely that some of them may find it difficult to match up to the expectations of the company, which is known to please its customers by providing a huge range of product choice at very low price and fast delivery.

► WAY AHEAD

In its bid to overtake Flipkart, the company had invested heavily in infrastructure, technology, and innovation which caused its losses to rise up from Rs. 1,723 crores in 2014-15 to Rs. 3,572 crores during 2015–16. It has launched Prime Video services towards the end of 2016 at an extremely low price of Rs. 499 per annum, with Rs. 250 as cash back in comparison to the existing players, Netflix and Hotstar who charges around Rs 200–500 per month. Its strategy was to provide latest movies, US TV shows, and children's programs in high quality at a low rate of data usage on 4G network so that the customers get addicted to its OTT (over-the-top) services. It was estimated that the company had invested around Rs. 2000 crores in this new venture. It has also made huge investments in providing cloud infrastructure through its web services to the business customers.

The company has continued to maintain its aggressive approach to become the market leader despite a slowdown in the expansion of online business in 2016 after a rapid growth surge in the previous two years. A sum of Rs. 2,010 crores was infused into the operations of Amazon Seller Services, its Indian flagship company which reported a turnover of Rs. 2,217 crores in 2015–16. Though advertisements, commissions, and shipping fees charged from sellers continue to be the main sources of its revenues, yet its losses swelled up to nearly Rs. 1,000 crores in the month of October 2016. However, that has not deterred the company. During a time span of March 2016–2017, Amazon has invested Rs 7000 crore in its Indian business. It intends to further invest $5 billion in the years to come. A unique characteristic of an average Indian consumer is to browse through various brick-and-mortar stores, pick up products to feel and smell them, compare them across stores, and bargain mover prices before making the final purchase decision. So, Amazon is also planning to launch its physical grocery stores to cater to this consumer segment and has named it "Project Everest". Looking at its aggressive approach of investment, critics wonder when will the company be able to breakeven. A recent development in the Indian legislation poses another challenge before this multinational company. The Indian government has introduced a new regulation that prohibits any single vendor from contributing towards more than a quarter of the total sales to its marketplace platform. It was reported that Amazon's largest seller accounted for over 40 % of its sales on its Indian website, leading to violation of the newly incorporated law. Listing of Amazon Exports Sales LLC owned by Amazon as a seller has been protested by All India Online Vendors' Association, a community of 1,000 online sellers. The association considered it as violation of the Indian laws and felt that this would impact the pricing policy of the company.

CASE 22

E-Marketing Models: Retailers Perspectives A Case of Groupon

▶ Context

Mr Mark, the Vice-President of Marketing is addressing his team of regional officers across the country in the context of improving the customer base for the firm through enabling the customers base for the use of Groupon coupons. The primary objective of the meeting is to:

1. Create an umbrella for more retailers to use Groupon deal processes
2. Generate revenue for the firm and create customers for the retailers as well
3. Enable the retailers to decide on the discount and quantum of sales for their product using the Groupon models
4. Expand customer base of the Groupon (retailers) and the users of the model
5. Create win-win situation for customers, retailers, and the firm.

The regional heads of all the regions (south, west, north, and east) are advised to submit a marketing plan and strategic proposal to attain the above objectives.

▶ Background

Consumer cooperatives (groups acting on behalf of the members to purchase and sell the required goods) are established to gain bargaining power by the individuals in the developing countries like India. The concept of bringing together the buyers to have the bargaining power by creating and inducing bulk demand for the products (refer the case given below) in an organized form are called cooperatives. The cooperative movement in India started in the early 20th century and the governments in India extend support to such cooperatives. The cooperatives can be started with and without the support of the governments and take the lead in the interest of the group and for the cause of the group (for example, agricultural cooperatives, cooperative banks, etc.). In a cooperative, the members will contribute to the cooperative and work in the interest of the members of the group, and in case of any surplus share, among the members on a pro-rata basis.

The Apex Federation (NCCF) was established in the year 1965 and is managed under the separate Multi State Cooperative Societies Act 2002 with 136 members encompassing Primary Co-op. Stores, Wholesale Societies, State-level Consumer Cooperative Federations, National Cooperative Development Corporation, and the Government of India. Headquartered at New Delhi. the business process of the federation is handled through 34 branches from across the country. The primary objective of the federation is to deliver support to the consumer cooperatives and other distributing agencies for distribution of consumer goods at reasonable and affordable prices like Groupon, with coupons of high discount, enabling customers to buy the products at a very low price.[1]

The objectives of any business determine the financing, set-up, revenue model, and major resources required for the business. The operational and supportive activities will be commensurately planned and investments will be made accordingly. One of the key elements of the supportive activities, the marketing also will be organized at a scale that will effectively garner the required demand for the products/services of the organization. In all, the scale of capacity utilization or the production or service preparedness will be organized as per the business plans and expectations. An important aspect that deserves to be particularly mentioned here is that the success of the business, its profitability, and sustainability depends upon the achievement of the projections for which sufficient demand for products/services are required.

Generally, because of optimistic plans or unexpected business changes, it may so happen that the demand may not take off as expected, resulting in shortfall of the sales and excessive stocks or idle servicing time. Organizations can explore the possibility of liquidating their excess stocks or idle servicing time by undertaking additional promotional activities. Large organizations and those with excess financial resources will expand their resources for additional promotional activities for increasing their business. Such excess spending may reduce the profit margin but will help avoiding the possible loss associated with the lower business activity.

The promotional activities should not only endeavor to liquidate the excess stocks or idle service time but should also aim at effective promotion of the business, the product, or service, and thereby create a customer base. In fact, if a tail-end promotional activity has to be planned, organizations realize that it is a second phase activity and should be effective enough to compensate for the shortfall in the first phase of promotional activity. Therefore, such an effective promotional activity may require more funding than usual spend. Medium and small-scale organizations may not be able to afford to spend additional amounts for this essential promotional activity. At the same time, such organizations also cannot afford to incur the resultant loss because of the excess stocks and idle service time. Therefore, such organizations keep trying to explore newer options and possibilities that are fruitful yet cost effective. This may also be because they may not have the expertise and strategic strength to design, coordinate, and implement the promotional plans nor do they have the time to take off from their regular business to exclusively focus on additional promotional activities. Therefore, these organizations may not mind to share some of the revenues that they could additionally achieve because of any promotional activity that any external promotional/selling partner undertakes for these organizations.

▶ Buying Process and Buying Centre (Annexure – III)

The function of buying a product or a service depends upon various aspects, including the need, availability, complementing options, and price. Usually, if a product or service is available at a lower price, it increases the affordability of the consumers. Further, the desire of consuming a product or service, to an extent, depends upon the price of the same.

Given a price of a product or service, and particularly if it is of premium category and complementary to the other kinds of products or services, consumers usually have the inquisitiveness to experience the utility on an experimental basis. However, among others, one reason that may limit the consumers from testing such premium products or services is the higher price that they may have to shell out. If there is an opportunity of consuming such products or services at a lower price, consumers will be eager to consume the same. Correspondingly, sellers resort to various practices to attract and induct new consumers and thereby expand consumer base. Such practices include free distribution of samples for consumption, combo-packed and combo-pricing of fast moving regular items, heavy discounted offers, etc. However, some of these offers cost the organizations heavily, and may cause serious financial strain on the business.

The trend of consumers experimenting premium products when are available at a discount to their tagged price is well observed across the developed and developing economies where premium consumer products are jumbo-packed and sold at lower rates which are a huge success among the consumers. Such a practice of selling at a lower price has been possible because the organizations plan and achieve a higher scale of operations, including the additional sales made at discounts.

Effectively, it is about achieving a higher scale business involved with encouraging more purchases either individual or a group of consumers. It may not be possible for a consumer to continue purchasing greater quantities of any product or service than they usually require. Resultantly, the seller also may not experience the increased volume of business continuously in this model. However, if the increased sales are because of group buying, then the seller may be able to experience the increased volume of business and the consumers will be able to get the products and services at relatively lower rates. Thus, the essence is in group buying.

▶ Modus Operandi and Metrics of Groupon

The Groupon owner combined the first and third strategies mentioned by Jack Welch, namely scaling up of production and sales and e-commerce (e-sell, e-buy and e-make). In simple words, the business model of Groupon involves online posting of unsold stocks or idle service time of various businesses registered with Groupon. These products and services are offered locally with a huge discount, usually ranging between 50% to 90% discount. Since the organizations would have written off the possibility of earning anything on such unsold or excess stocks and idle time services, whatever earned is a bonus, and hence. the discount does 'not matter for them. For consumers, it is a bonanza because they get to experience the products and services at a much lower price than they would have to otherwise pay for them.

The offers posted on Goupon are generally time-sensitive, and therefore, will help generate demand within the time, and thereby beget earnings to the organizations. Otherwise the organizations will have to wait for a longer time to liquidate the stocks and manage to avoid such idle time services, which will anyway not guarantee the liquidation and realization of earnings.

The beauty of a Groupon transaction is that offers are time sensitive and that the offers are available only if certain minimum quantity is essentially purchased by all the consumers put together. Hence, by design and default, organizations stand on a trade-off and will not be put to unexpected losses or go beyond the expense they were prepared for in exchange for liquidating their excess stocks and idle servicing times.

In return for availing the service of Groupon, the organizations earning such additional opportunity earnings will have to share about 50% of their earnings with Groupon which made the earnings possible.

The daily deals are posted on Groupon only to their registered contacts and, therefore, confidentiality is assured to the organizations. Further, to these registered contacts, online or offline vouchers are issued which can be redeemed at the organizations offering the products and services at a discount through Groupon. While redeeming the discount vouchers, the consumers pay up the price, excluding discount. As the transaction gets routed online, the Groupon gets to know the status of the transactions on a real time and debits the organization for the amounts receivable from the organizations by Groupon.

The process, seemingly, benefits everyone. The organizations that could not sell their excess stocks and the consumers who could not have otherwise afforded the products or services, and Groupon which earns its revenues from the transactions, all are, thus, benefited from the transaction.

► MODEL

A unique feature of grouping all the buyers together along with huge discounts on the products and services is the concept of Groupon. In the process of grouping the buyers together, the firm (Groupon Limited) has bargained with the manufacturer or seller to reduce the price for the products sizably i.e. if a product is available in the market for $100 it is offered through Groupon at $50 only. This reduction in the price is given to the customers as a coupon to induce the customer to buy the product. This type of group-buying models for organizations and individuals are presented by Lilien, Kotler, and Moorthy (2003) for both industrial units and individual customers.[2] Accordingly, any of the proposed models of group buying can be classified into one of three categories: non-quota schemes, where there is no pre-specified minimum number of group members who must favour an alternative for it to be related; agreement quota schemes, where the group liberates until a pre-specified number (or proportion) of the group selects a given choice; and an individual decision scheme, where one group member chooses for the group.

The models like weighted probability model, equi-probability model, the voting model and preference perturbation model fall into non-quota models. The majority rule model and the unanimity model fall into the category of quota models and the autocracy model falls into the category of individual decision model.

Primarily the weighted probability model says that the choice of a product is done by a person in charge for selection and assumes that the group members will follow and accept the same. In the case of equi-probability model, all the members in the group probably select the same. In the voting model, the product is selected by a largest number of decision participants. And the preference perturbation model assumes if the group does-not reach unanimous agreement, it is most likely to choose the alternative that least 'perturbs' individual preference structures. The majority rule model is a special case of the voting model when there is a quota (say 50% or more) that is required to agree for an alternative to be chosen. As operationalized by Choffray and Lilien (1980), the majority-rule model differs from the voting model only in how the group resolves ties (their voting model) randomizes the vote while the majority rule model must reject. In groups larger than three, the two models can generate significantly different results.

As the merchants and Groupon together decide the price to be offered to the customer, we can conclude that it is a weighted-probability model in the non-quota scheme. And the numbers are also decided by the two together which is not reflected on the website, excepting the number of people who had opted at a specified time and how much time is left for utilising the same.

► Target Group

Initially, people learned from their friends or family members about Groupon and the coupons on the website. Later, the firm to encourage word of mouth publicity gave $10 towards a future purchase for each referral that the customer brought. In January 2010, Facebook and Twitter were Groupon's top referring sites, accounting for 44% and 8% of traffic respectively. Groupon soon began supplementing these efforts with heavy spending on paid search engine advertising and other online marketing. The company launched its TV campaign beginning with an advertisement aired during the Super Bowl. The ads featured celebrities who first appeared to be speaking on behalf of some social or political cause, but then segued into a Groupon endorsement, as in one spot with actor Timothy Hutton: "The people of Tibet are in trouble. Their very culture is in jeopardy. But they still whip an amazing fish curry. And since 200 of us bought at Groupon.com, we are getting $30 off on Himalayan food for just $15 at a Himalayan restaurant in Chicago. Consumers, too, responded and availed the Groupon's services and it has become popular among the young, well educated, unmarried, and relatively affluent. Over three-fourths of subscribers were women and consumers were not only enthused about the money that they saved but also about its convenience, variety, and other benefits.[3]

► History and Evolution of Groupon

The grouping of people interested or persuaded to buy a product is the business where the website Groupon has taken up and leveraged the technology, like that of a cooperative."Andrew Mason and his team launched Groupon in November 2008 in Chicago to focus on collective buying power".[4] Groupon could help citizens find reasonably priced commodities and services devoid of irresistible choices by starting to offer one deal a day. During 2009 and 2010, Groupon experienced rapid growth and was soon serving over 150 markets domestically and over 100 additional markets internationally. In the years 2009 and 2010, the success of the Groupon deals attracted attention from many industries and those who wanted a pie in the daily discount deals market. During the same period of 2009–2010, several competitors and copycat firms entered the market like LivingSocial, BuyWithMe, and the new "Deals" section on Facebook.[5]

Groupon was launched by Mr. Andrew Mason along with his team in November 2008 in Chicago. The initiation of starting Groupon was derived from Andrew's own experience of launching, attempting, and closing a similar group-concept online entity, "'The Point'". The Point demonstrated that group activity can achieve better results, although it itself could not achieve great advertising on its site which was the key source of revenues for such an online-entity.

With its initial success of achieving promising response to its one deal per day, Groupon moved on to offering multi-products and services simultaneously to several consumers. In a short span of about two years, by 2010, Groupon started catering to about 250 markets, including 150 domestic markets and about 100 international markets.

The mission for the company was very simple—bring the customer and vendor together for an economic price and enable the customer to do, see, buy, and eat at a very low price. The vision for the firm is to help come out of the stress of many and offer one new thing a day and treat the customer in the way that they like to be treated.[6] The three vital elements that kept the business of Groupon going was:

The firm sells the products or services that its employees would be interested in. The cautious selection of new vendors meant that users should feel cosy venturing out and trying something with confidence that it is featured on Groupon. The idea of no hidden terms or conditions to avoid sour experience to the users of Groupon brings the true love to the company and improves the brand. Finally, the last tenet is unbelievable customer service, which the company defines clearly, "If you contact us, we'll do what it takes to make things right – and we'll do it fast."[7]

Andrew Mason took the lead and attracted experienced group of senior management who shared his vision, ambition, and jovial corporate culture.[8] The management has shared the drive and willingness to take risks and bring innovations in the firm. Groupon is an innovative company, not through development of a "me-too" product, but by forming an entire new market space. The company won a Chicago innovation award in the year 2009 when they were less than a year old.[9] Further, Fast Company has called them "a savior for small businesses" and "the most exciting thing to happen to retail since eBay.[10] In addition to the above, Groupon went ahead and leveraged technology in terms of improving the access to the deals through mobiles and real-time technology which offers ultra-localized services based on your GPS. The huge success of Groupon and its model has been easily duplicated by many other similar online daily deal providers. Similar organizations include LivingSocial, Buywithme, Deals, etc. Interestingly, each of them has done quite well even by merely duplicating the business model of Groupon. It shows the strength of the model Groupon has pioneered to implement and also how vulnerable the players are towards rapid and intense competition.

Groupon has been of financial interest to many investors. This is demonstrated in the ability of Groupon to mobilize substantial amounts in its initial years itself. Groupon had associated with Digital Sky Technologies and under a common program has mobilized about USD 135 million under a common program for its business expansion purposes. To expand its reach and presence in international markets, Groupon used its mobilized funds and acquired CityDeal, which has good presence and business operations in Germany. CityDeal has almost the similar business model like that of Groupon and provided an instant opportunity to Groupon to grow bigger. Groupon is understood to be among the fastest companies to achieve USD 1 billion sales. Not to exaggerate, Groupon may be the company to achieve the same with relatively less capital. No wonder Groupon is confident of its business model and its prospects that it is understood to have rejected an acquisition offer from Google Inc. for USD 6 billion.

Groupon first came to public in the capital markets in February 2011 and raised about USD 700 million and became the second largest IPO of US internet companies. The IPO was a huge success and post IPO its valuation was about US $13 billion, more than double that was offered by Google Inc. However, for various reasons, later the valuation swindled later and Gropon stock has been trading at a considerable discount to its listed price.

► Alternatives and Approaches for The Business Model

Groupon business model:

In the meeting, some of the alternatives that the regional marketing officers have listed the pros and cons for the organizations and consumers as follows:

► Advantages to Organizations

(i) Can liquidate their excess/unsold stocks or idle service time

(ii) Fixed costs can be absorbed by the additional sales through Groupon API

(iii) Customer base can be created within a short span

(iv) Products or services can be promoted effectively within a short span and with less cost

(v) Instead of reducing the operating capacity, the demand can be increased

(vi) Awareness of the product and service in the exact locality where the organization is operating and the advertisement is a concentrated one

(vii) Can provide comparison of prices of similar products and services to consumers to enable them to make the right choice.

(viii) Can focus on main business without concern about the excess unsold stocks or idle- time service.

(ix) With the promotion through Groupon and with the concurrent increase in the overall demand, the organization can achieve scale of economies and in the process can make its product or service more price-competitive.

(x) Enables the organization to assess exact demand from time to time and in various localities

► Advantages to The Consumers

(i) Get to know new products and services within their own locality

(ii) Get an opportunity to test/experiment new products and services within their own budget

(iii) Get to know about all the daily deal offers at one place viz., Groupon website

(iv) Can compare the quality and price of complementary and supplementary products or services

(v) Benefit with the discounted price which is not otherwise possible for any given individual consumer to avail by forming a group on his own and make a group purchase

(vi) A readymade bargain deal for the consumers

(vii) Secured platform with real-time delivery mechanism supported by Groupon

(viii) Have an opportunity to offer their feedback, which plays a very vital role for Groupon to decide about the future deals of the same organization and for other consumers to get to know about the feedback and make their choice

(ix) Ease in transacting i.e., choosing a product or service, obtaining vouchers through Groupon mechanism, redeem the same and get the delivery.

(x) Can change their preferences and choices very frequently without any disturbance

► LIMITATIONS OF GROUPON MODEL OF BUSINESS

(i) May not be a sustainable way of increasing sales for the organizations because it is not sure what quantum of excess unsold stock will be available on a given day, and such uncertain quantities may fail to build a loyal customer base.

(ii) Consumer expects the same discount or further more discounts every time s/he intends to purchase through Groupon mechanism.

(iii) This mechanism may act as a repellent to the existing loyal consumers who may shift to another product which they perceive is rightly priced against the one which has varying discount offers from time to time. This may result in losing out of business in the medium to long term.

(iv) Other organizations in the particular locality where Groupon discount deals are happening will be under pressure to reduce their price lest they may lose their business. This may result in reduction of quality along with the reduction in the price.

(v) Sharing the revenues with Groupon is justifies but the share, as understood to be up to 50%, is quite high and the organizations will factor in the same, and thereby again loading it on to the consumers. This may bring back the whole mechanism to square one in terms of price competitiveness, and thereby adding no value but creating another parallel intermediary.

► CHALLENGES AND DILEMMA

In the globally competitive environment, the firms are continuously looking for smarter ways of marketing and improving their sales. This is because the logic of economies of scale with low margins has become the general buzz of the business world. In that context, marketing of products and services has become a great challenge to the firms' regardless of their size, location, and the nature of business. Firms' envisage revenue at least above a minimum scale that would absorb its fixed costs and any excess over and above being profit. Particularly when the firms' are operating at less than the capacity, each increase in unit sold can make a good amount of marginal profit and contribute to value creation to the firm and the shareholder of the firm. Accordingly, their planned production or servicing capacities need to be growing over the period. Obviously, the fixed costs will commensurate with the established capacities and demand revenue levels that would at least absorb variable costs and fixed costs. Having enlisted few of the numerous advantages and shortfalls of the Groupon model, it appears that the advantages have an edge over the shortfalls, at least at this stage of the lifecycle of Groupon business model.

In the present day, with nuclear families and individualized lives world, real group-buying is hardly possible and Groupon model of group buying, which is actually several independent buys but grouped online to become an aggregate group buy of large quantities, is sufficient enough for the seller to offer convincing discounts to the mutual benefit of the consumers, organizations, and to the economy as well. In all, the two strategies of scaling up the capacity utilization and leveraging technology with intelligent marketing is enabled through Groupon and its empowered consumers.

However, the demand for the products and services may not meet the projected levels resulting in an increase in stock levels and loss of revenues. For medium and small organizations, it is very stressful and their very existence may be under threat. For such start-up organizations and also for already existing organizations, the Groupon model of group buying is a boon that their business can sustain with their required minimum volumes and the consumers can get their required products and services at affordable prices.

ANNEXURE – I

CUSTOMERS

Gupta, S., Weaver, R. & Rood, D. (2012) "the firm in the initial stages depended on a sales team that called merchants around the country, as the time passed by Groupon built sales force of account executives based in local markets.[11] A variety of businesses were brought under the umbrella of Groupon, and the services predominated in the entire sales, though deals for products were also there and more of baked goods and other foods. The mix of merchant category is as follows:

Category[12]	Percent of Deals Run	Percent of Vouchers Sold
Dining	23%	36%
Salons and Spa	18%	14%
Lessons	13%	7%
Entertainment and Culture	12%	13%
Recreation and Travel	10%	9%
Perishables	9%	8%
Apparel	4%	7%
Other	11%	7%

It is also learnt that most the companies approaching Groupon were firms with tight budget and according to a survey conducted by Marketing Services firm MerchantCircle it is found that the businesses spent less than $2500 a year on marketing without much expertise to adopt new technologies and media. The lure of an outsourced online promotion with no up-front expenses has compelled the firms to choose Groupon.

When the firm entered an agreement for promotion with the merchants, the basic standard that they had was that the merchant will supply the product or service at a 50% discount on the listed price. The deal was activated only if the number of buyers achieved a minimum number set by the merchant and with other terms like voucher's expiration date and in some cases limits on individual or total purchases.

The Groupon would put the deals only for a day and the alerts go by email, alerts, etc. The website would have the deals on the page with details like "Sandy's Sandwiches - Multiple Locations" Four $5 Groupons or Three $10 Groupons, Good for Sandwiches and Drinks at Sandy's Sandwiches (Half Off), Value $20 Discount 50% You Save $10 - Limited Time Only 6 days 00:08:32 - this means only 8 minutes 32 seconds are left and as I am writing this document the time has gone to 7 minutes and 57 seconds - also followed by the number of people bought over 630 bought Limited quantity available is also presented.[13]

ANNEXURE – II

GUIDELINES FOR MERCHANTS

Gross margin: Daily deals are most profitable for merchants who sell high gross margin products and services. Merchants, such as spas and helicopter rides, who have high fixed costs and low variable costs can benefit from daily deals by attracting new customers that cover their fixed costs.

1. Capacity Utilization: Daily deals can also be useful for merchants if they plan these deals to fulfil their unused capacity or sell perishable inventory, such as food that spoils, clothing that goes out of fashion, a seat at a live concert performance or a masseuse's 30-minute time slot. Restaurants that are at full capacity for dinner but have limited traffic at launch may offer deals for lunch to fill unused capacity and also induce trial for new customers.
2. Customer Acquisition: Our analysis shows that daily deals can be profitable if they attract new customers who have not used a merchant's service before and use deals as a means to try a new product or service. this suggests that merchants should not offer deals too frequently and find mechanism to limit redemption by prior customers. For example, in 2011 Zoots dry cleaning service offered Groupon with the condition that customers who redeemed a Groupon in the last 90 days were not eligible for this deal.
3. Repeat Visits: Daily deals especially profitable if new customers become repeat customers in the future. This has two implications. First, novelty products such as helicopter rides are less likely to have repeat customers. While these businesses may still benefit from daily deals due to high gross margin, they should assess the value of such deals from current voucher redemption only. Second, merchants should actively manage to convert new customers into regular customers. for example, anecdotal evidence shows that many merchants treat their deal customers poorly as they consider them "cheap stakes". however, this may lead to a self-fulfilling prophecy where new deal customers may see no reason to come back to the merchant in the future.
4. Merchants should also set up processes to capture new customers' information during redemption process, such as by requiring online registration to attend a class or by offering inducements to sign up for a loyalty program. this will allow merchants to market directly to these new customers.

5. Up-spend: Merchants can encourage up-spend by offering additional goods at redemption, such as concessions at a sporting event. Alternatively, they may offer vouchers with a low face value compared to the average ticket, such as $20 towards dinner at a nice restaurant.

Source: Gupta, S et al (2012) "Are Daily Deals Good for Merchants?" Harvard Business School Case No. 9-513-059, December 10, 2012.

ANNEXURE – III

API: THE TELLING TOOL OF GROUPON

Application programming interface (API) is the key tool through which Groupon is successfully implementing its business model. Organizations need to register with Groupon by signing the API Agreement which determines the way organizations should offer their products and services. Upon registering with Groupon, the organizations are given permitted access to the Groupon API and through this interface, the organizations advertise their products and services and the prices of the same.

Here are several variants in the API that are designed to ensure effective group-buying pattern of the daily deals of various organizations posted by Groupon. For instance, for disseminating the information about daily deals and to promote the products and services offered by organizations. Groupon has released a publicly available API. Groupon APIs supports two different sources. The first source is Division API. Division API provides information to the public and to the organizations about the locations where Groupon has its network and where it offers deals. This will help third-party developers and affiliate members get the required information. Organizations can plan and choose whether, how, and how much quantity and price should they advertise through Groupon for public daily-deal offers in a particular locality. Organizations also factor in the localized purchase trends in the particular locality so that it would not lose out in a locality it already has good sales. The second resource of Groupon is Deals API. This provides information about current daily deals in a particular location. This helps the consumers in knowing about the deals, and chose and avail them. This also helps the organizations to compare their product or service with that of similar other organizations, complementary product or service, and supplementary product or service. Thus, the market forces are respected by the consumers and the organizations.

The software-based online websites, webpages, webtools, and communication channels of Groupon are highly secured, encrypted and are capable of thwarting any possible cyber-attacks. They detail all the things for merchants in terms of what to do and what not to do and make them sign an agreement to adhere to the same.

ANNEXURE – IV

KEY INDICATORS TO DAILY DEALS AND PROFITABILITY

The merchants have to be careful and understand whether the daily-deals model through Groupon is profitable for them or not and what price that they can offer the product or service to the customers through the website. According to Gupta, S et al (2012) Groupon has achieved great success in a very short time on the daily deals—services that encourage businesses by selling intensely discounted vouchers paid in advance to a group of people meeting online.[14] And, by all accounts, their experiences have been amazing. On the contrary, the criticism emerged over a period was that on the value creation for the merchants whose goods and services are promoted. What will be the factors one has to take into consideration while evaluating the value creation for merchant? Obviously, the number of vouchers sold, the actual proportion of vouchers redeemed, and the willingness of the consumer to spend extra at the time of cashing of vouchers. The basic principle of value creation should be that after approaching Groupon the customer base has increased and the merchant is able to sell more units than that of the sales prior to Groupon. Secondly, lesser time and effort is required to generate the same revenue as compared to what the merchant is generating from marginal increase in the sales after Groupon. Gupta, S et al (2012) have given the model and discussed as follows:

Long Term merchant Profit[15]	= Voucher Purchase and redemption	- cannibalization from prior customers	+ future profit from new customers	
Voucher Purchase and Redemption	= (merchant share of Voucher Revenue)	+ (up-spend at redemption - Cost of goods)		(Redemption rate)
Cannibalization from Prior Customers	= (forgone profit)(% prior Customers)(Redemption Rate)(Cannibalization Rate)			
Future Profit from New Customers	= (profit per visit) (% new customers) (redemption rate) (future visits per year)			

The important points the merchants have to understand is that there could be cannibalization of the existing customers, or the shift from normal mode of payment to discount option using Groupon. Therefore, the merchants have to have a clear idea of as to how much percentage of customers are shifting from the normal mode of payment to discount vouchers.

Secondly, the merchant also has to take care of the terms and conditions of redemption of vouchers and the time to use them. The merchant will be offering the products or services with price discrimination to the customers. The coupon holder would pay just 50% of what the customer who does not hold the coupon—is it going to harm the long-term interest of the merchant or not? The research in that area argues that the discount vouchers prepare the customer to pay higher price in future. On the other hand, others argue that the discount vouchers make the customer expect such discounts in future.

The third important thing that the merchant needs to understand from data whether the customer is spending more than what he was spending. If not, and it has shifted from the normal payment to discount voucher, is it not going to effect his business sustainability.

Another vital aspect is that how many new customers are attracted to the business and the product or service after Groupon vouchers—is it enabling the business to grow and increase the turnover substantially or at least more revenue is being generated than the additional cost that the business is incurring.

Is the customer, post using the vouchers given over Groupon, visiting and purchasing the product? If yes, what is the percentage and if no, what could be the reasons and what has to be done to attract the customer and retain him/her?

► QUESTIONS

1. How to identify potential consumers, here the retailers who want to buy the Groupon products and differentiate these retailers as per "Retails Formats".
   (Hint: Refer Annexure I in TN given (i.e., Table 22.1, p688; Table 22.2, p690 and Table 22.3, p691, Kotler, 15th edition) 20 minutes.
   Learning outcome is about understanding different retail formats and how it varies.
2. What are the business factors the target groups retailers consider to evaluate and use the Groupon business deals or offers? (Hint: Refer Annexure III in the case study) 20 minutes.
   Learning outcome is about the retailers' understanding of the business deals, coupons offers, and analyzing the rationale of choice.
3. What should be the offer mix given to the retailers by the sales team of Groupon for different retails formats. (Hint: Refer Annexure I in case study) 15 minutes.
   Learning outcome: Buying criterion of different products retailers when they choose different deals.
4. What are the various factors that retailers should consider to generate profits with respect to doing business in different product category or assortments? (Hint: Refer Annexure IV Key indicators to Daily Deals and Profitability) 20 minutes.
   Learning outcome: The dynamics of learning the product assortment and profit generating alternatives objectives with respect to different retailers.

CASE 23

Unilever: Working Beyond the Horizon

In Asia, Unilever has championed a number of holistic marketing initiatives that has been replicated in other parts of the world. The company has undertaken a lot of rural marketing initiatives, which have led to sales getting tripled or quadrupled.

► Pool Women to Power Sales

With its Shakti initiative, Hindustan Unilever Limited (HUL), its Indian subsidiary, pioneered the concept of training local women as sales agents of its products for door-to-door selling in rural areas of India. As of 2016, the initiative had grown to 74,000 sales agents serving 167,000 Indian villages, and HUL had provided them smartphone apps for the sake of managing inventory and other facets of business. The company has tweaked this model for Bangladesh, Vietnam, Sri Lanka, Egypt, and other countries.

In Pakistan, Unilever took the concept to a new height by training hundreds of village women as beauticians. During a three-month program, the women, called *Guddi Bajis*, or "good sisters," learn and assimilate ways of applying makeup, shampoo to hair, and provide a bevy of beauty services, in addition to selling Unilever products to their customers. They price their services and earn commissions on those sales. Points are also awarded for incentives such as salon tables or mirrors.

What underlies is the fact that rural women have a high interest in beauty but little access to advice or products. The *Guddi Bajis* provide that access and help turn out to be brand ambassadors for Unilever products. This kind of social marketing also furnishes income streams for women. The market potential is a huge mass-powerful 4.5 million women in 5,000 villages.

► Undertake Grassroots Distribution

Philippines is another nation of small retailers. About 95% of the 1 million retail locations are small variety shops called sari-sari stores. Even with their small size, some stores sell as many as 200 different products, thus accounting for 36% of the country's fast-moving consumer goods sales.

Unilever recruited some of the larger stores to do double duty as sub-distributors. Owners of the superstores get discounts on Unilever products; the sari-sari stores get better access to prestigious Unilever brands. The superstores also act as venues for fiestas that organizes product demonstrations combined with giveaways with games and entertainment. Unilever organizes about 500 fiestas a year, and the said sales of highlighted brands typically fork up 30-80% during the "fiesta" weeks.

This has reduced distribution costs. They use other direct-distribution channels in Pakistan, Bangladesh, and India to intensify the rural reach of its brands.

▸ Offer Services for Rural Customers

Unilever Thailand launched "Platinum store" campaign to churn out an urban shopping experience to rural customers—an alternative to typical rural stores with limited product or brand offerings. Unilever assists the layouts, develops promotions, and brings in partner companies for services such as ATMs. The stores must meet certain requirements, including assuring high-visibility displays for Unilever products. The Platinum stores get more customer footfalls and consequent revenue.

This initiative has helped Unilever manage competitors like 7-Eleven, which has been registering briskly in urban regions. Sales at Platinum stores were booming at triple the rate of the channel overall, as per reports.

▸ Create New Channels for Advertising

One challenge in tapping the rural market is how to reach consumers in remote areas with limited electricity and little access to mass media.

In India, Hindustan Unilever has used mobile technology to create audio entertainment for rural areas by adapting a common practice among frugal cellphone users—the missed call. In 2011, HUL used the tactic in a pilot promotion for its Active Wheel detergent in a few of India's poorest rural areas. Customers were asked to call a number that cut off after two rings so it cost them nothing. An automatic free callback provided some comic dialogue from Bollywood star Salman Khan and ads for Wheel. In four months, HUL got 17 million calls and Wheel sales went up by 300% in the region.

▸ Design Products (and Set Prices) for Rural Consumers

Years ago, HUL pioneered the use of low-cost, single-use packets to make its products affordable for low-income groups who are at the bottom of the pyramid. Now these packets are ubiquitous in both developed and developing countries. HUL itself sells 28 billion sachets a year.

In the Philippines, it turned out to be the answer to increasing rural sales of the company's Rexona deodorant. Unilever faced a tough challenge—only half of Filipinos buy deodorant, and standard package sizes were expensive for rural consumers. To gain market share, Unilever developed a cream version in a single-use-sized packet that costed much less.

▸ Train Managers to Adopt a Rural Mindset

Underlying HUL's success in rural India is a project that necessitates managers to compulsorily spend a month of their first year of work living in a village. Ten countries in Asia and Africa are inhabited by about 2.3 billion rural people. Rural markets have presented a huge marketing opportunity due to government projects, remittances coming from rural migrants, and extensive participation of NGOs and social organizations in cultivating better farming and sustainable living skills. Increasing penetration of mobile phones, internet, and satellite TV is making these rural consumers demand aspirational products and services. Urban markets are witnessing a hot bed of competition with little scope of growth. Holistic companies like Unilever are adapting their inclusive growth strategies for rural consumers as part of their future plans for growth and expansion.

In India, Lifebuoy's "Swasthya Chetna" (LSC) has been a five-year health and hygiene education program launched by HUL. The program was formally launched in 2002, in eight states across India.

The objective of this program was to impart knowledge to 200 million people across rural and urban areas of India. Adopting good "health and hygiene" practices was the credo. It was ostensibly to spread awareness about germs and their adverse effects on health. Basic mantra was bathing and washing hands with soap that can prevent diseases like diarrhea.

According to HUL, these are not a social activity, but a marketing strategy with a tinge of social benefit. HUL sought to grow the Lifebuoy brand in India by attracting those consumers who never used soap. Through this campaign, the company wanted to evoke a behavioral change by stating that people to use soaps more often, thus creating more users (customers)for its brand. This activity was also a prelude to successful public–private partnership.

These initiatives, called "Pledge Programmes", have now fanned out in many countries and regions across the globe.

► Promoting Healthy Body Images

Unilever has own standards for healthy body images. Since 2007, the company is bent on preventing the use of "size zero" models or actors in their advertising. This is to ensure that product advertisements do not promote "unhealthy" body types. All brand directors and agencies are expected to use models and actors with a Body Mass Index (BMI) of between 18.5 and 25 as a standard watchword. This is in consonant with the World Health Organization's benchmarks on what level of BMI can be considered healthy.

The company's charter says:

- Committed to building trust through responsible practices and total transparent communication—both directly to consumers and indirectly through other key stakeholders and thought-leaders
- Committed to ensure that our products are safe and that we provide clear information on their use and any risks thereof with use
- Committed to support a consumer's right to know what is in our products and will be transparent in terms of ingredients, nutrition values, and the health and beauty properties of our products
- Committed to leverage a combination of channel that includes product labels, websites, careline phone numbers, and/or consumer leaflets to communicate openly with global consumers

► Responsible Marketing and Advertising

The company, in retrospect, is committed to responsible marketing and advertising. As a leading global consumer goods company, they promote the benefits of products and product innovations using many different channels of brand communication. For example:

- Dove's campaign for Real Beauty challenges current stereotype concepts about beauty.
- Omo/Persil's "Dirt is good" campaign pitches getting dirt as a natural and positive part of the learning and development process for children.

- With less saturated fat than butter, Flora/Becel helps people look after themselves by offering healthy, nutritious, and tempting tasting products that can be enjoyed at any meal time.
- Comfort One Rinse's campaign points out to consumers that they only need one bucket of water for rinsing their clothes rather than three, thus helping them to conserve water.

At the same time, the company ensures that the baseline test of being "legal, decent, honest, and truthful" is followed for all its ads.

Brand and Marketing Investment (2005 - 2015)

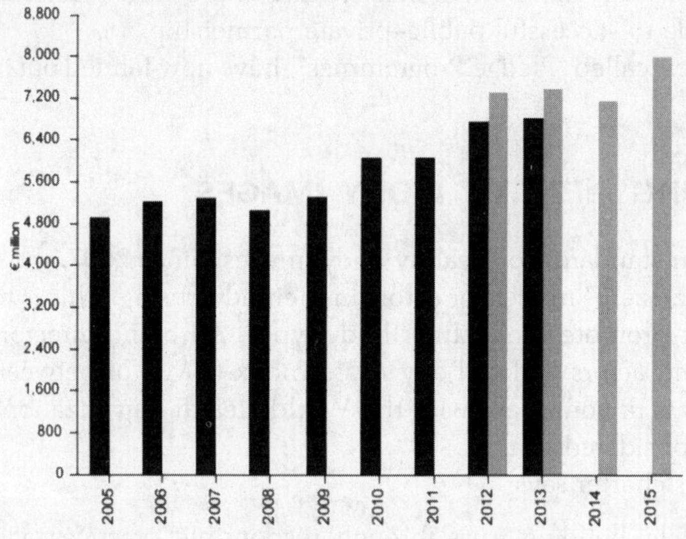

Source: Unilever website.

► Discussion Questions

1. What are the factors that were considered by Unilever to launch social marketing projects-India and elsewhere?
   a. A customer focus: A genuine curiosity, even hunger, to know what the potential customer thinks and feels
   b. Planning process. Deep understanding of target audience, nurture their needs, to know current and specific knowledge, beliefs, attitudes, and practices towards products and needs
   c. Barriers to reach target audience: What they have to give up in order to perform desired behavior? What concerns they have regarding behavior? Can they change, and do it? Why have not they done in the past? These factors can be thought of as the "costs" the target audience perceives.

d. Benefits that can accrue: What will they get if they perform the desired behavior? How likely do they think it is that they will get this? What exactly do they want to get? These are potential "motivators" for the target audience.
e. Competition exists: What type of behavior are they doing instead? Why it is so? What benefits do they perceive in competing offers? How much does this cost? How does it compare with other offers?
f. Influential others. Relative to the company's desired behavior, who does your target audience listen to most? Are influential others engage in this desired behavior? What are they saying, or likely to say, to your target audience about this behavior?

2. Does this socially oriented marketing have to use all 4 Ps in order to usher a change in the behavior of target consumers?
   a. No, but this is best practice. Efforts will be more successful when the company does so. All the 4Ps are necessary to surpass audience barriers, increase benefits, and upstage the competition.
   b. A winning strategy requires an integrated approach. It demands all tools relevant. It is not just relying on advertising and other persuasive communication. Strategies must be tailored to unique needs, wants, resources, and current behavior of differing market segments.

3. Does there have to be a narrowly defined and targeted audience segment?
   a. No. But again, this is also a best practice, based on few homogeneous segmental behavior. Different segments within a particular population have different barriers and benefits sought. It requires different interventions.
   b. The target segment must perceive benefits that equal or exceed the perceived costs they associate with performing the desired behavior.
   c. It benefits the target segment as well as the society. It is an exchange deal (Lee and Kotler, 2011).

4. Is communication-only campaign a social marketing campaign?
   a. It may be.
   b. A campaign that uses only words meets the criteria for a social marketing effort. However, it is more likely to be successful if other influence tools are used as well (demonstration).

5. Should there be a plan for social diffusion?
   a. Social diffusion is a model that describes the diffusion or spread of an idea or behaviour through a population.
   b. This is a "natural" force and requires diffusion of the desired behavior.
   c. Successful campaigns establish ways to measure progress and make adjustments to support current or planned objectives and resultant strategies.

6. What approach should be chosen?
   a. Segments need to be set in a priority order.

b. A disproportionate amount of resources should be allocated to most effective segments.
c. Target audience (markets of greatest opportunity) emerge as those with greatest need for action.
d. Targets should be the best match for the organization.

7. How to assess measures for target audience reach and performance?
   a. Utmost need: size, incidence, severity, and helplessness.
   b. Most ready to receive: ready, willing, and able to respond
   c. Easiest to reach: identifiable, venues for distribution channels, and communicate.
   d. Best match: In terms of organizational mission, expertise, and resources.
   e. Additional segments can be reached over time.

Endnotes and References

Case 01

i Needs wants & Demands Kotler 15e. P 9

ii USP: the **unique selling proposition** (**USP**) or **unique selling point** is a marketing concept first proposed as a theory to explain a pattern in successful advertising campaigns of the early 1940s. The USP states that such campaigns made unique propositions to customers that convinced them to switch brands. The term was developed by television advertising pioneer Rosser Reeves of Ted Bates & Company. Theodore Levitt, a professor at Harvard Business School, suggested that, "Differentiation is one of the most important strategic and tactical activities in which companies must constantly engage."[1] The term has been used to describe one's "personal brand" in the marketplace.[2] Today, the term is used in other fields or just casually to refer to any aspect of an object that differentiates it from similar objects.

iii Marketing Mix known as Product, Price, Place, Promotion defined by McCarthy as base marketing operational tools. https://en.wikipedia.org/wiki/Marketing_mix#McCarthy.27s_4_Ps

iv https://www.ibef.org/industry/indian-food-industry.aspx

v *Ministry of Food Processing Industries (MoFPI), Agricultural and Processed Food Products Export Development Authority (APEDA), Media reports and Press Releases, Department of Industrial Policy and Promotion (DIPP), Press Information Bureau (PIB), Confederation of Indian Industries (CII),Union Budget 2016-17, Union Budget 2017–18*Note: ! - A joint report by IIM-Calcutta and Academic Foundation, @- India Food Report 2016, # – Venture Intelligence report, ## - According to a joint study by the Associated Chambers of Commerce and Industry of India (ASSOCHAM) and TechSci Research

vi https://en.wikipedia.org/wiki/Mavalli_Tiffin_Room

vii Marketing Mix known as Product, Price Place Promotion defined by McCarthy as base marketing operational tools. https://en.wikipedia.org/wiki/Marketing_mix#McCarthy.27s_4_Ps

viii The Food Safety and Standards Authority of India (FSSAI) plans to invest around Rs 482 crore (US$ 72.3 million) to strengthen the food testing infrastructure in India, by upgrading 59 existing food testing laboratories and setting up 62 new mobile testing labs across the country.

ix https://www.mtrfoods.com/products/mtr-snackup

x http://www.marketing91.com/marketing-mix-mtr-foods/

xi http://www.marketing91.com/marketing-mix-mtr-foods/

Case 02

1. http://brandequity.economictimes.indiatimes.com/news/business-of-brands/fashion-superpower-the-forces-of-flipkart-myntra-and-jabong-are-about-to-combine/53552375
2. http://brandequity.economictimes.indiatimes.com/news/business-of-brands/flipkart-prepares-for-war-as-amazon-pledges-to-invest-3-billion-more-in-india/53279116
3. http://brandequity.economictimes.indiatimes.com/news/business-of-brands/offline-stores-for-private-brands-to-be-the-new-mantra-for-myntra/53821109
4. http://brandequity.economictimes.indiatimes.com/news/business-of-brands/myntra-jabong-will-play-by-same-logistics-now/57682036
5. http://brandequity.economictimes.indiatimes.com/news/business-of-brands/flipkart-slashes-myntras-budget-to-focus-on-battle-with-amazon/56433829
6. http://www.thehindubusinessline.com/info-tech/flipkart-to-consolidate-logistics-supply-chain/article9535216.ece
7. http://brandequity.economictimes.indiatimes.com/news/business-of-brands/myntra-jabong-to-combine-private-labels/56076749
8. http://brandequity.economictimes.indiatimes.com/news/business-of-brands/etail-wars-flipkart-reinvents-itself-aiming-to-beat-amazon-to-the-top-spot/54597482
9. http://brandequity.economictimes.indiatimes.com/news/business-of-brands/now-e-commerce-giants-move-their-focus-to-in-house-brands/57982543
10. http://brandequity.economictimes.indiatimes.com/news/business-of-brands/myntra-goes-low-on-discount-and-high-on-exclusive-brands-for-its-latest-sales/58076724
11. http://brandequity.economictimes.indiatimes.com/news/digital/flipkart-remodels-its-core-fashion-category-to-lure-a-larger-market/56213001
12. http://brandequity.economictimes.indiatimes.com/news/business-of-brands/myntra-launches-its-first-retail-store-for-online-brand-roadster/57700078
13. http://brandequity.economictimes.indiatimes.com/news/marketing/heres-what-online-and-multi-brand-retailers-can-learn-from-each-other/58415704
14. http://brandequity.economictimes.indiatimes.com/news/digital/amazon-rolls-out-chatbot-tools-in-race-to-dominate-voice-powered-tech/58272056
15. http://brandequity.economictimes.indiatimes.com/news/business-of-brands/flipkart-to-change-online-buying-experiences-heres-how/58058081
16. http://brandequity.economictimes.indiatimes.com/news/business-of-brands/amazon-to-double-investment-on-seller-infrastructure-in-india/58233149
17. http://brandequity.economictimes.indiatimes.com/news/business-of-brands/flipkart-says-it-is-now-sellers-favourite-marketplace-but-guess-who-disagrees/58271959
18. http://brandequity.economictimes.indiatimes.com/news/business-of-brands/amazon-launches-prime-in-india/53391627
19. http://brandequity.economictimes.indiatimes.com/news/business-of-brands/alibaba-and-amazon-watch-out-now-flipkart-has-a-new-business-plan/58139924
20. http://brandequity.economictimes.indiatimes.com/news/business-of-brands/paytm-mall-to-outdo-competition-by-offering-same-day-delivery-installation-of-appliances/58353840
21. http://brandequity.economictimes.indiatimes.com/news/business-of-brands/heres-what-amazon-is-doing-to-project-itself-as-an-indian-company/58157794

Case 03

1. http://brandequity.economictimes.indiatimes.com/news/business-of-brands/heres-how-amazon-is-quietly-making-indian-buyers-its-repeat-customers/58587968
2. http://www.livemint.com/Opinion/BL1QdKXjeyY3LKEclAxccJ/Of-free-trials-and-conversions.html
3. http://brandequity.economictimes.indiatimes.com/news/marketing/heres-what-online-and-multi-brand-retailers-can-learn-from-each-other/58415704
4. http://brandequity.economictimes.indiatimes.com/news/business-of-brands/consumer-loyalty-is-our-boosting-organic-growth-oneplus-co-founder-carl-pei/53462309
5. http://www.adweek.com/sponsored/conversational-commerce-improves-the-retail-customer-experience/
6. http://www.adweek.com/brand-marketing/infographic-multicultural-millennials-take-brand-loyalty-seriously-174416/
7. http://brandequity.economictimes.indiatimes.com/news/business-of-brands/now-future-group-eyes-ration-shop-tie-ups-in-chhattisgarh-and-madhya-pradesh/54357054
8. http://brandequity.economictimes.indiatimes.com/news/business-of-brands/easyday-launches-har-mahine-bonus-its-first-ever-loyalty-program/54207513
9. http://brandequity.economictimes.indiatimes.com/news/business-of-brands/future-group-to-setup-loyalty-driven-convenience-stores-soon/58001437
10. http://brandequity.economictimes.indiatimes.com/news/digital/future-group-introduces-digital-loyalty-wallet-futurepay/54709100
11. http://brandequity.economictimes.indiatimes.com/news/digital/infographic-how-an-unsatisfactory-digital-experience-can-jeopardize-customer-loyalty/58222191
12. http://brandequity.economictimes.indiatimes.com/news/business-of-brands/breakfast-revolution-hits-india-expect-masala-dosa-burgers-and-more-at-mcdonalds/56468588
13. http://brandequity.economictimes.indiatimes.com/news/marketing/mcdonalds-undergoes-brand-revamp-launches-experience-store/57554714
14. http://brandequity.economictimes.indiatimes.com/news/business-of-brands/nestle-to-deploy-new-technology-that-reduces-sugar-in-chocolate/55723179
15. http://brandequity.economictimes.indiatimes.com/news/marketing/loyalty-programs-should-consumers-be-wary-of-the-catch/58038710
16. Iglesias,O. , Singh,J. and Batista-Foguet, M.(2010). "Role of Brand Experience and Affective Commitment in Determining Brand Loyalty by Brand Management", *www.palgrave-journals.com/bm/* Vol. 18, 8, 570-582.

Case 04

Adkins, A. (2015). *Starbucks & Its Use of Technology*. *Smallbusiness.chron.com*. Retrieved 19 April 2017, from http://smallbusiness.chron.com/starbucks-its-use-technology-28272.html

Anand, A. (2017). *Meet Manmeet Vohra, the brain behind Starbucks' massive growth in India : Featurephilia*. *Indiatoday.intoday.in*. Retrieved 19 April 2017, from http://indiatoday.intoday.in/education/story/meet-starbucks-marketing-brain-growth-india/1/893957.html

Bamb, N. (2016). *Starbucks, roasting data and brewing analytics!*. *www.linkedin.com*. Retrieved 19 April 2017, from https://www.linkedin.com/pulse/starbucks-roasting-data-brewing-analytics-nigrah-bamb

Boulton, C. (2016). *Starbucks' CTO brews personalized experiences*. *CIO*. Retrieved 19 April 2017, from http://www.cio.com/article/3050920/analytics/starbucks-cto-brews-personalized-experiences.html

Business Ethics and Compliance | Starbucks Coffee Company. (2017). *Starbucks Coffee Company*. Retrieved 19 April 2017, from http://www.starbucks.in/about-us/company-information/business-ethics-and-compliance

MIS- Starbucks. (2015). *UKEssays*. Retrieved 19 April 2017, from https://www.ukessays.com/essays/management/management-information-system-at-starbucks-management-essay.php

Privacy Statement | Starbucks Coffee Company. (2017). *Starbucks Coffee Company*. Retrieved 19 April 2017, from https://www.starbucks.co.uk/about-us/company-information/online-policies/privacy-statement

Starbucks. (2014). *Starbucksinformationsystem.blogspot.in*. Retrieved 19 April 2017, from http://starbucksinformationsystem.blogspot.in/2014/11/starbucks_10.html

Starbucks. (2017). *www.statista.com*. Retrieved 19 April 2017, from https://www.statista.com/topics/1246/starbucks/

Starbucks Coffee Company. (2017). *Starbucks Coffee Company*. Retrieved 19 April 2017, from http://www.starbucks.in/about-us

Case 05

Bhasin, H. (2017). *Marketing strategy of Amazon - Amazon marketing strategy*. *Marketing91*. Retrieved 24 April 2017, from http://www.marketing91.com/marketing-strategy-of-amazon/

Introducing RACE: a practical framework to improve your digital marketing - Smart Insights Digital Marketing Advice. (2016). *Smart Insights*. Retrieved 24 April 2017, from http://www.smartinsights.com/digital-marketing-strategy/race-a-practical-framework-to-improve-your-digital-marketing/

Madden, S. (2012). *How Companies Like Amazon Use Big Data To Make You Love Them*. *Co.Design*. Retrieved 24 April 2017, from https://www.fastcodesign.com/1669551/how-companies-like-amazon-use-big-data-to-make-you-love-them

Relationship Marketing for amazon.com - O2I. (2017). *Outsource2india.com*. Retrieved 24 April 2017, from https://www.outsource2india.com/kpo/samples/amazon-web-research.asp

Sen, S. (2014). *Amazon India's approach is to focus on long term: Amit Agarwal*. *Businesstoday.in*. Retrieved 24 April 2017, from http://www.businesstoday.in/opinion/interviews/amazon-amit-agarwal-on-business-in-india/story/202791.html

Sen, S. (2016). *How it made itself Indian: The amazing rise of Amazon in the country*. *http://www.hindustantimes.com/*. Retrieved 24 April 2017, from http://www.hindustantimes.com/business-news/how-it-made-itself-indian-the-amazing-rise-of-amazon-in-the-country/story-YfyzGUuNVTAHEHHenNmxvO.html

Shah, S. (2016). *What's So Amazing About Amazon In India?*. *Seeking Alpha*. Retrieved 24 April 2017, from https://seekingalpha.com/article/3959953-amazing-amazon-india

Ray, R., Litsa, T., DiSilvestro, A., Elliott, N., & Singer, A. (2013). *3 Things Amazon.com Can Teach Us About Marketing Automation | ClickZ*. *Clickz.com*. Retrieved 24 April 2017, from https://www.clickz.com/3-things-amazon-com-can-teach-us-about-marketing-automation/35100/

Warrillow, J. (2015). *The Surprising Way Companies Like Netflix and Amazon Do Market Research. Inc.com*. Retrieved 24 April 2017, from https://www.inc.com/john-warrillow/the-surprising-way-companies-like-netflix-and-amazon-do-market-research.html

Youderian, A. (2017). *How to Do Successful Amazon Market Research | eCommerceFuel. eCommerceFuel*. Retrieved 24 April 2017, from http://www.ecommercefuel.com/amazon-market-research/

Case 06

1. https://www.warc.com/Topics/consumer-research/consumer-attitudes
2. http://brandequity.economictimes.indiatimes.com/news/digital/80-3-indians-dont-want-to-share-their-personal-details-while-shopping-online-study/53646234
3. http://brandequity.economictimes.indiatimes.com/news/digital/indians-most-savvy-about-using-customer-support-tech-survey/57765542
4. http://brandequity.economictimes.indiatimes.com/news/marketing/contemporary-middle-class-families-no-longer-wait-for-diwali-to-shop-max-fashions/55107091
5. http://brandequity.economictimes.indiatimes.com/news/digital/ipg-medias-laboutlook-2017-taps-into-the-important-tech-trends-of-consumer-behaviour/58338999
6. http://brandequity.economictimes.indiatimes.com/news/business-of-brands/the-secret-behind-global-brands-swelling-popularity-social-media-influencers/57644897
7. http://economictimes.indiatimes.com/magazines/brand-equity/is-google-and-tata-trusts-internet-saathi-program-working-lets-find-out/articleshow/57511909.cms
8. http://brandequity.economictimes.indiatimes.com/news/business-of-brands/the-new-power-consumer-group-women-in-rural-india/51229058
9. http://economictimes.indiatimes.com/magazines/brand-equity/women-are-more-active-and-engaged-on-tinder-than-men/articleshow/57511620.cms
10. http://brandequity.economictimes.indiatimes.com/news/business-of-brands/one-in-every-four-scooter-buyer-is-a-woman-survey/58427189
11. http://brandequity.economictimes.indiatimes.com/news/business-of-brands/survey-says-women-shoppers-go-for-luxury-products-because-of-their-social-circle/58452667
12. http://brandequity.economictimes.indiatimes.com/news/business-of-brands/indians-prefer-natural-and-organic-in-personal-care/54597594
13. http://www.livemint.com/Opinion/5tJsAdzFa5TXZQRk1WGvcI/Why-advertising-is-getting-more-socially-inclusive.html
14. http://brandequity.economictimes.indiatimes.com/news/advertising/tata-tea-jaago-res-latest-ad-campaign-sensitively-tackles-student-depression-suicide/58531455
15. http://brandequity.economictimes.indiatimes.com/news/business-of-brands/the-scientific-link-between-diapers-fueling-lingerie-and-beer-sales-on-amazon/57662376
16. http://brandequity.economictimes.indiatimes.com/news/digital/match-degrees-not-kundalis-is-matchmaking-based-on-academic-qualification-lucrative/57400482
17. https://www.statista.com/statistics/255146/number-of-internet-users-in-india/
18. Ind, N., and Riondino, M. C. (2001). Branding on the web: A real revolution? Journal of Brand Management, 9(1), 8–19.
19. Yamaoka, T. (2004). The elements of customer advocacy marketing. Available at http://hdl.handle. net/1721.1/17877
20. http://brandequity.economictimes.indiatimes.com/news/business-of-brands/the-new-indian-consumption-in-india-is-set-to-triple-to-4-trillion-by-2025/57753463

Case 07

1. http://zicom.com/page/company-profile
2. http://zicom.com/pramoudrao/
3. http://in.reuters.com/finance/stocks/companyProfile?symbol=ZICO.BO
4. http://www.indiainfoline.com/article/news-top-story/zicom-to-touch-new-horizons-with-its-security-solutions-116010400274_1.html
5. http://www.governmentbids.com/cgi/en/bidding.advice.articles/Article/federal-contract-opportunities-for-your-business
6. http://www.business-standard.com/article/opinion/is-the-l1-tender-system-the-best-105110901019_1.html

Case 08

Abutaleb, Y. (2015). *Modi trip gives Facebook, Google chance to press on Indian expansion. Reuters*. Retrieved 24 April 2017, from http://www.reuters.com/article/us-usa-india-tech-idUSKCN0RN26D20150923

Challenges to Facebook International Strategy - The India Case. (2017). *Internet Globalization News*. Retrieved 24 April 2017, from http://blogalize.typepad.com/micro/2016/07/facebook-international-challenges.html

Chu, J. (2014). *For Facebook, As India Goes, So Goes the World?. Fast Company*. Retrieved 24 April 2017, from https://www.fastcompany.com/3031261/for-facebook-as-india-goes-so-goes-the-world

Forbes. (2016). *Forbes.com*. Retrieved 24 April 2017, from https://www.forbes.com/sites/greatspeculations/2016/04/14/why-is-facebook-entering-the-hyperlocal-services-market-in-india/#7a63e0391f71

Horwitz, J. (2015). *The only way Facebook enters China is as a tool of the government. Quartz*. Retrieved 24 April 2017, from https://qz.com/644588/the-only-way-facebook-enters-china-is-as-a-tool-of-the-government/

Isaac, M. (2016). *Facebook said to create censorship tool to get back Into China. CNBC*. Retrieved 24 April 2017, from http://www.cnbc.com/2016/11/23/facebook-said-to-create-censorship-tool-to-get-back-into-china.html

IANS. (2016). *Facebook grants $40,000 to this Indian startup - Times of India. The Times of India*. Retrieved 6 May 2017, from http://timesofindia.indiatimes.com/trend-tracking/Facebook-grants-40000-to-this-Indian-startup/articleshow/55724629.cms

Joishy, M. (2012). *CASE STUDY: Successes and Challenges for Facebook in India. United States - India Monitor*. Retrieved 24 April 2017, from https://usindiamonitor.com/2012/06/21/case-study-successes-and-challenges-for-facebook-in-india/

Mathur, N. (2016). *73% of Indian SMBs are bullish about future: Facebook survey. http://www.livemint.com/*. Retrieved 24 April 2017, from http://www.livemint.com/Consumer/K37MV9C8tpU4qgi7I0HRiP/Facebook-survey-shows-Indias-best-days-are-ahead.html

Nair, A., & Kashyap, S. (2016). *How global technology businesses are breaking into the India market*. *YourStory.com*. Retrieved 24 April 2017, from https://yourstory.com/2016/06/global-technology-businesses-india/

Thomas, T. (2016). *Facebook nears 150 million users in India: Dan Neary*. *The Hindu Business Line*. Retrieved 6 May 2017, from http://www.thehindubusinessline.com/info-tech/social-media/facebook-nears-150-million-users-in-india-dan-neary/article8673625.ece

CASE 09

1 http://www.mahindra.com/Who-We-Are/How-We-Got-Here

2 http://www.mahindra.com/news-room/press-release/1308288714

3 http://www.icra.in/Files/ticker/PV-Industry-201103.pdf

4 https://en.wikipedia.org/wiki/Utility_vehicle

5 http://www.icra.in/Files/ticker/PV-Industry-201103.pdf

6 http://www.thehindubusinessline.com/todays-paper/mahindra-unveils-multi-purpose-vehicle-xylo/article1039685.ece

7 http://economictimes.indiatimes.com/articleshow/3986327.cms?utm_source=contentofinterest&utm_medium=text&utm_campaign=cppst

8 http://business.mapsofindia.com/automobile/car-manufacturers/sport-utility-vehicle-market.html#sthash.1kjsVCgK.dpuf

9 http://www.icra.in/Files/Articles/2010-January-PV-Note.pdf

CASE 10

1 Euro Monitor International Report on Breakfast Cereals in India (April 2015). Retrieved from http://www.euromonitor.com/breakfast-cereals-in-india/report. Accessed in November 2015.

2 Shukla, R, Sharma, V, TechnoPak Report on India Food Services Trends (2014) Retrieved from http://www.technopak.com/Files/breakfast-cereals-market-in-india.pdf. Accessed in November 2015.

4 Rogrigues, M (2012, June 9), Kellogg's: From cornflakes to munchies, Economic Times. Retrived from http://articles.economictimes.indiatimes.com/2002-06-19/news/27331748_1_kellogg-india-cornflakes-breakfast-cereal , Accessed in November 2015

5 Kumar, R. (2012, April 5), Kellogg's Nashta Is A Family Matter. Retrieved from http://pitchonnet.com/blog/2012/04/05/kelloggs-nashta-is-a-family-matter . Accessed in November 2015.

6 Iyer, L., Kumar, N.(2014, June), A Study Of Breakfast Habits Of Urban Indian Consumers, Research Journal of Economics and Business Studies, Vol. 3, No. 8. Retrieved from http://www.theinternationaljournal.org/ojs/index.php?journal=rjebs&page=article&op=view&path%5B%5D=3013

7 Haig, M, 2005. Brand Failures: The Truth about the 100 Biggest Branding Mistakes of All Time. 1st ed.: Kogan Page. Retrieved from http://citeseerx.ist.psu.edu/viewdoc/download?doi=10.1.1.424.468&rep=rep1&type=pdf

8 Bolton, R.(2012, May 08) , Are You Targeting a Phantom Market, Harvard Business Review, Retrieved from https://hbr.org/2012/05/are-you-targeting-a-phantom-in . Accessed in November 2015.

9 Kellogg's Indian Experience: A Failed Launch, (2001). Retrieved from http://www.icmrindia.org/free%20resources/casestudies/Marketing%20freecasestudyp1.htm, Accessed in November 2015.

10 Sangameshwaran, P. (2004, June 7), Second Thoughts on the Indian consumer, Business Standard. Retrieved from http://www.business-standard.com/article/management/second-thoughts-on-the-indian-consumer-104060701131_1.html , Accessed in November 2015

11 Taneja, G., Girdhar, R., Gupta, N. (2012, July), Journal of Arts, Science and Commerce, Volume 3, Issue 3 Marketing Strategies of Global Brands In Indian Markets.

12 Gupta, V., Retrieved from https://vaibhavgnnugupta.files.wordpress.com/2012/01/marketing_sem1_group11_kellogs_final1.pdf

13 Sangameshwaran, P.(2008, February 5), Beyond breakfast, Business Standard. Retrieved from http://www.business-standard.com/article/management/beyond-breakfast-108020501018_1.html. Accessed in November 2015.

CASE 11

1 http://www.business-standard.com/content/b2b-chemicals/personal-care-market-to-touch-20-billion-in-india-by-2025-116070800419_1.html

2 http://www.mensxp.com/buzz-on-web/lifestyle/6650-anushka-sharma-endorses-niveas-go-sleeveless-campaign.html

3 http://www.beiersdorf.com/about-us/our-profile/strategy

4 http://www.beiersdorf.com/about-us/our-profile/our-core-values

5 https://fontsinuse.com/uses/3170/nivea-redesigned-identity-and-packaging

6 http://marketingpractice.blogspot.in/2006/10/nivea-gentle-care.html

7 https://www.wisdomjobs.com/e-university/strategic-brand-management-tutorial-350/building-the-brand-through-systematic-extensions-nivea-10958.html

8 https://www.slideshare.net/nikitasanghvi/nivea-case-study-7545830

9 http://www.campaignindia.in/article/nivea-celebrates-100-years-with-an-ad-featuring-anushka-sharma/414826

10 http://epaperbeta.timesofindia.com/Article.aspx?eid=31818&articlexml=CHANGING-CONSUMER-TRENDS-Made-in-India-Nivea-Brands-17032017005020

11 http://www.afaqs.com/news/story/31209_Nivea-Centennial-celebrations-for-the-Cr232me-de-la-Cr232me

12 http://www.exchange4media.com/advertising/nivea-repositions-male-grooming-category-to-grab-larger-market-share_50983.html#sthash.USUYpX3r.dpuf

http://www.exchange4media.com/advertising/nivea-repositions-male-grooming-category-to-grab-larger-market-share_50983.html

13 http://www.campaignindia.in/article/nivea-celebrates-100-years-with-an-ad-featuring-anushka-sharma/414826

14 Euromonitor Passport 2016

15 http://www.campaignindia.in/video/nivea-salutes-moms-touch-supports-mothers-in-need/423126

CASE 12

1. http://brandequity.economictimes.indiatimes.com/news/business-of-brands/vitara-brezza-puts-maruti-ahead-of-mahindra-in-the-uv-segment/53648818

2. http://brandequity.economictimes.indiatimes.com/news/business-of-brands/mahindra-to-jazz-up-suv-variants-as-competition-hots-up/56511161

3. http://brandequity.economictimes.indiatimes.com/news/business-of-brands/when-going-gets-tough-fmcg-leaders-get-going/58102125
4. http://brandequity.economictimes.indiatimes.com/news/business-of-brands/maruti-is-revamping-alto-to-strengthen-its-hold-in-the-entry-segment/54775654
5. http://brandequity.economictimes.indiatimes.com/news/business-of-brands/now-maruti-owns-one-half-of-the-auto-market/56993672
6. http://brandequity.economictimes.indiatimes.com/news/business-of-brands/maruti-suzuki-continues-to-take-the-lead-position-in-fy17/57486410
7. http://brandequity.economictimes.indiatimes.com/news/business-of-brands/maruti-suzuki-now-the-lord-of-all-surveys/58022099
8. http://www.adageindia.in/marketing/cmo-strategy/the-story-behind-designing-nexa-marutis-premium-dream-in-india/articleshow/49795243.cms

CASE 13

[1] Pidilite Industries Ltd(2017). *2016 annual report of Pidilite Industries Limited*. Retrieved from http://www.pidilite.com/company/financial_reports/pdf/annual_report_121_1.pdf

[2] Narayanan A. (2014).*Pidilite*. Origins, 58–63

[3] Ken Research (2015). *Ken Research: India Adhesives Market is Expected to Reach INR 88.2 Billion by FY'2020*.Retrieved from http://www.newsvoir.com/release/ken-research-india-adhesives-market-is-expected-to-reach-inr-882-billion-by-fy2020-5784.html

[4] Jubilant Industries (n.d.).*In wood-working adhesives*. Retrieved from http://www.jubilantindustries.com/woodworking-adhesives.html

[5] Chatterjee, P.(2016, March 30). Asian Paints in distribution tie up with Henkel . *The Hindu Business line*. Retrieved from http://www.thehindubusinessline.com.

[6] TechSci Research (2014, June). *India furniture market forecast and opportunities*. Retrieved from https://www.techsciresearch.com.

CASE 15

Endnotes

[1] 'Food processing' is mainly defined as *a process of value addition to the agricultural or horticultural produce by various methods like grading, sorting and packaging. In other words, it is a technique of manufacturing and preserving food substances in an effective manner with a view to enhance their shelf life; improve quality as well as make them functionally more useful. Source: Ministry of Food Processing Industries, Government of India.*

[2] www.ibef.org

[3] Ministry of Food Processing Industries (MofPI), Technical Report, December 2015.

[4] Source: CII

[5] www.foodsafetyhelpline.com

[6] Aachi in Tamil means Grandma

[7] www.aachigroup.com

[8] The company website: www.aachigroup.com

[9] *Masala* in India denote a blend of ground spices that can be readily used for cooking.

[10] Travelling sales people, who transport products in smaller vehicles to retailers / consumers in small quantities

[11] www.infobharti.com

[12] www.mtrfoods.com

[13] www.sakthi*masala*.com

References

1. https://www.ibef.org/industry/indian-food-industry.aspx
2. www.mofpi.nic.in
3. http://foodsafetyhelpline.com/2016/02/food-processing-industry-in-india-is-the-largest-and-expected-to-grow-further/
4. http://www.aachigroup.com
5. http://infobharti.com/tag/top-10-masala-brands-of-india
6. www.mtrfoods.com
7. http://www.sakthi*masala*.com

CASE 16

Endnotes

[1] Heat, Light, Power (HLPW) and Salaries, Welfare, Benefits (SWB) expenses are not considered while computing this variable cost.

[2] Average Room Revenue

[3] Variously called Fully or Flexible Independent Traveller

[4] Company Volume Guaranteed Rate (CVGR) Letter is offered by the hotel to a client to use the hotel services at a special discounted rate for the high volume bookings agreed by the client]

References

1. http://www.frotels.com/info/no-need-use-public-washrooms/
2. http://www.frotels.com/info/hourly-hotel-booking/
3. http://www.economist.com/blogs/gulliver/2012/10/micro-stays
4. https://www.quora.com/What-is-a-micro-stay

CASE 17

India 'Twists, Licks, Dunks' with Oreo

1. https://www.warc.com/content/article/India_Twists,_Licks,_Dunks_with_Oreo/97608
2. http://m.businesstoday.in/story/how-kraft-foods-won-over-customers-in-china-and-india/1/193162.html

Oreo fact sheet

1. http://in.mondelezinternational.com/brand-family

CASE 18

1. http://stories.wondercement.com/
2. http://www.wondercement.com/aboutus
3. https://www.socialsamosa.com/2017/04/best-social-media-brands-winners/

4. http://www.socialmediaexaminer.com/facebook-page-metrics/
5. http://www.rajasthankhabre.com/category/blog/1
6. http://www.samacharjagat.com/category/wonder-cement/1
7. http://www.campaignasia.com/article/you-can-learn-a-lot-from-these-10-brands-that-excel-on-social-media/427803
8. http://www.indianmirror.com/indian-industries/cement.html
9. http://www.outlookindia.com/outlookmoney/invest/cementing-its-pLakhe-399
10. http://www.afaqs.com/advertising/creative_showcase/index.html?id=59573andmedia=Digital
11. https://www.kulzy.com/work/151672/wonder-cement/brand-film/-storiesofwonder-wonder-cement/

Case 19

Endnotes

[1] It Is a small gift given to the guests at a wedding / party as a gesture of thanks for their attendance, a memento of the occasion. Also referred to as Wedding / Party Favor in Western culture

[2] "The flourishing Indian Wedding Industry", www.retail.franchiseindia.com

[3] Marriage Market is used synonymously with Wedding Market

[4] "The Big Fat Wedding Industry in India: Recap of 2015 and outlook for 2016", The Business Insider

[5] Only Hindu wedding practices are discussed in the case for better focus.

[6] For more on Indian wedding, refer to www.indianholiday.com

[7] http://www.thenational.ae/business/economy/india-weddings-a-billion-dollar-industry

[8] "The Big Fat Wedding Industry in India: Recap of 2015 and outlook for 2016", The Business Insider

[9] "The flourishing Indian Wedding Industry", www.retail.franchiseindia.com

[10] Consists of betel leaves and nuts, haldi (turmeric), kumkum, coconut along with a gift, generally put together in a personalized pack

[11] Referring geographical location of the regions. Generally the northern and western regions, including parts of east are commonly referred to as North India and the four states in the southernmost tip of the country constitute the South India

[12] The capital city of Tamil Nadu, a southern state in India

[13] A set of sweets and savories given as a part of *Seer* – includes apparels, jewelry, utensils, grocery, to the brides as a part of Indian custom

[14] Boxes of chocolates / nuts etc., given along with the invitations or given to the family of the bride groom as soon as they come to the wedding venue

[15] Used for packing bridal goods. Here for packing the Seer items

[16] Given to the guests with Tambulya items and small packs of seer backshanam inside

[17] Minakari or Enamelling is the art of painting, colouring and ornamenting the surface of metals by fusing over it brilliant colours that are decorated in an intricate design. www.iranreview.org

[18] A type of traditional ear rings worn by Indian women on special occasions and festivals

[19] Sweets and Savory set given as Seer (Ref: Footnote 13) that includes sweets like Ladoo, Mysorepak, Adirasam and snacks like Murukku. Thenkuzhal, Mixture

[20] For this case it is predominantly traditions and customs of Tamil Nadu

[21] www.prashanti.co

References

1. https://retail.franchiseindia.com/article/whats-hot/trends/The-Flourishing-Indian-Wedding-Industry.a247/
2. http://www.business-standard.com/article/companies/start-ups-target-the-big-fat-indian-wedding-industry-116050600818_1.html
3. http://www.businessinsider.in/The-Big-Fat-Wedding-Industry-in-India-Recap-of-2015-and-outlook-for-2016/articleshow/51008952.cms
4. http://www.thenational.ae/business/economy/india-weddings-a-billion-dollar-industry
5. www.iranreview.org/content/Documents/The_Art_of_Minakari_2.htm
6. https://www.indianholiday.com/wedding-tourism-india/reception-ceremony.html
7. www. Wedtree.com
8. www.prashanti.co

Case 20

1. http://www.animalhealthindia.com/blog/tag/Animal%20Feed%20Market
2. http://www.infah.org/
3. http://www.vamsobiotec.com/
4. https://dir.indiamart.com/impcat/poultry-feed-supplements.html
5. http://www.clfmaofindia.org/

Case 21

Amazon India biased towards customers, claim unhappy seller. (2017). Retrieved 24 April 2017, from http://www.livemint.com/Industry/PKKkPfUdzqjmSuEqjECtDM/Amazon-India-biased-towards-customers-say-unhappy-sellers.html

Bailay, R. (2017). *Amazon's India strategy: Focus on every geography to become 'everything for everyone'*. Retrieved 24 April 2017, from http://economictimes.indiatimes.com/small-biz/startups/amazons-india-strategy-focus-on-every-geography-to-become-everything-for-everyone/articleshow/57761644.cms

Balakrishnan, R. (2017).*How Amazon dreams of being the new prime-time for India*. Retrieved 26 April 2017, from http://economictimes.indiatimes.com/magazines/brand-equity/how-amazon-dreams-of-being-the-new-prime-time-for-india/articleshow/57144720.cms

Capital Float partners with Amazon India to disburse loans to e-sellers. (2017). Retrieved 24 April 2017, from http://economictimes.indiatimes.com/small-biz/startups/capital-float-partners-with-amazon-india-to-disburse-loans-to-e-sellers/articleshow/57731086.cms

Chanchani, M. (2016). *Aggression's on, Amazon to scale up investments in India*. Retrieved 24 April 2017, from http://economictimes.indiatimes.com/small-biz/money/aggressions-on-amazon-to-scale-up-investments-in-india/articleshow/56112787.cms

Ganguly, P. (2017). *Amazon India head Amit Agarwal elevated to SVP*. Retrieved 26 April 2017, from http://economictimes.indiatimes.com/industry/services/retail/amazon-india-head-amit-agarwal-elevated-to-svp/articleshow/57672959.cms

Govindrajan, V. and Warren, A. (2016). *How Amazon adapted its Business Model to India*. Retrieved 26 April 2017, from https://hbr.org/2016/07/how-amazon-adapted-its-business-model-to-india

Piper, D. (2014). *Amazon chases Indian dollars but faces big challenges*. Retrieved 24 April 2017, from http://www.foxnews.com/tech/2014/08/07/amazon-sees-potential-in-india-but-faces-big-challenges.html

Case 22

1 http://nccf-india.com/aboutus.asp

2 Lilien, G L, Kotler, P & Moorthy, K S (2003), "Marketing Models", Prentice Hall of India

3 Gupta, S., Weaver, R. & Rood, D. (2012) "Groupon" Case from Harvard Business School

4 Groupon. (2011). About us. Retrieved June 29, 2011, from http://www.groupon.com/about

5 The Week. (2010, December 3). The Groupon phenomenon: A Timeline. Retrieved July 8, 2011, from http://theweek.com/article/index/209996/the-groupon- phenomenon-a-timeline

6 Groupon. (2011). About us. Retrieved June 29, 2011, from http://www.groupon.com/about

7 Groupon. (2011). About us. Retrieved June 29, 2011, from http://www.groupon.com/about

8 Reuters. (2010). Groupon buys 3 discount sites, expands into Asia. Retrieved July 6, 2011, from http://uk.reuters.com/article/2010/12/01/groupon-asia-idUKTOE6B005N20101201

9 Shames, A. (2011, February 17). The Groupon Phenomenon. In Innovation on my mind. Retrieved July 7, 2011, from http://innovationonmymind.blogspot.com/2011/02/groupon- phenomenon.html

10 Fast Company. (2011). The World's Fifty Most Innovative Companies. Retrieved July 8, 2011 from http://www.fastcompany.com/most-innovative-companies/2011/

11 Gupta, Sunil, Ray Weaver, and Dharmishta Rood. "Groupon." Harvard Business School Case 511-094, March 2011. (Revised August 2012.)

12 Ibid.

13 www.groupon.com/deals/sandy-s-sandwiches accessed on 17th October, 2013

14 Gupta, S, Keiningham, T., Weaver, R & Williams, L (2012), "Are Daily Deals Good for Merchants?", Case No. 9 - 513 - 059, December 10, 2012.

15 Ibid.

Case 23

Andreasen , A. R. 2006 . Social Marketing in the 21st Century. Newbury Park, CA : Sage .

Belz , F-M. and Peattie , K. 2009 . Sustainability Marketing: A Global Perspective. Chichester : Wiley .

Cheng, H., Kotler P., and Lee,N.(2003), Principles and practice of social marketing, Victoria, Cambridge Univ.Press.

Cohen , D. A. , Scribner , R. A. and Farley , T. A. 2000 . A Structural Model of Health Behaviour: A Pragmatic Approach to Explain and Infl uence Health Behaviours at the Population Level, Preventive Medicine 30 : 146 –54.

Dawson , N. (ed.) 2009 . Advertising Works 17: Proving the Payback on Marketing Investment . Oxfordshire : World Advertising Research Centre .

Doane , D. 2005 . The Myth of CSR: The Problem with Assuming that Companies can do Well While Also Doing Good is that Markets don't Really Work that Way, Stanford Social Innovation Review, Stanford Graduate School of Business, Stanford University .

Donovan , R. J. and Vlais , R. 2005 . Review of Communication Components of Social Marketing/Public Education Campaigns Focusing on Violence Against Women, Report to VicHealth, Melbourne , Australia . 2006 .

Evans , W. D. and Hastings , G. (eds.) 2008 . Public Health Branding: Applying Marketing for Social Change . Oxford University Press .

Green , L. W. and Kreuter , M. W. 2005 . Health Promotion Planning: An Educational and Ecological Approach, 4th edn. New York : McGraw-Hill

Kotler, P.,and Lee, N, (2009), Up and out of poverty, PA: Wharton School.

Maibach , E. W. , Abroms , L. C.and Marosits , M. 2007 . Communication and Marketing as Tools to Cultivate the Public's Health: A Proposed 'People and Places'model,www.usatoday.com/news/science

Siegel M, and Lotenburg, L.D., (2007), Marketing public health: strategies to promote social change, 2nd edn, Boston, MA.

Waitzkin , H. , Iriart , C. , Estrada , A. and Lamadrad , S. (2001), Social Medicine Then and Now: Lessons from Latin America, American Journal of Public Health 91 :10,

Weinreich, N.K. (2010), Hands-on social marketing. Thousand Oaks, Sage.